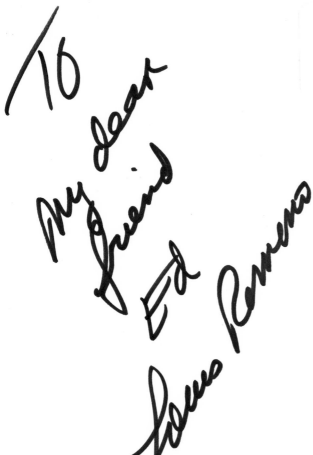

To
My dear
friend
Ed

Louis Romero

JUSTIFIED

LOUIS ROMANO

Also by Louis Romano

Detective Vic Gonnella Series

INTERCESSION
YOU THINK I'M DEAD
JUSTIFIED

Gino Ranno Series

FISH FARM
BESA
GAME OF PAWNS

Zip Code Series

ZIP CODE

Poetry Series

Anxiety's Nest
Anxiety's Cure

ACKNOWLEDGMENTS

Thanks to Kathleen Collins for her daily advice on this book

The pre-readers are becoming a small army of advisors: Al Maurice Esq., Frank Cali, he demolishes me, Linda Longo, Mary Romano, and Debbie Craig

Gracias and Merci to Lucia Natal and Elsa Mauro for their language translations.

Thanks to my pals Colin Lively and Joshua Plant for allowing me to consult them as needed

To Centurion Associates Marketing and Publicity for all they do, and to my publisher, Vecchia Publishing

Always thanks to Bob Hoatson at Road to Recovery for his tireless advocacy of survivors of clergy sexual abuse.

Rocco Romano, my Jack Russell has been at my feet or in my lap through all nine books so far. Hope I can get another few with him around

To all those who have hope
for a better world

A powerhouse sequel!

— Garrard Hayes, author of Bourbon & Blood

CHAPTER 1

It had been a short five years since John Deegan had been the most hunted man on the planet.

John and his wife Gjuliana have enjoyed their time and anonymity at their expansive Villa on Lake Lugano in the Ticino region of Switzerland. The Deegans named their home *Villa Cielo* because to them it was truly heavenly. John wanted a classic, Italian home while Gjuliana favored more of a modern look and feel. They both got what they wanted in *Villa Cielo*. Three stories high with a red-slated roof and a pastel pink and tan exterior, Gjuliana often wondered why they were living in a home with six bedrooms and six baths. The gardens were lavish with sub-tropical exotic plants, purple rocket, lavender Angelina, and sensational Rose Salvia plants were complimented by yellow and white elephant ears and fragrant, honeysuckle bushes. Two splendid fountains, one in the front of the villa and one in the rear were illuminated in the evenings. The property was dotted with dwarfed palm trees so as not to detract from the breathtaking view of the deep blue-green Lake Lugano and surrounding mountains. A speedboat stood at the ready on a small dock adjacent to a lakefront beach.

The interior of *Villa Cielo* was totally renovated with the latest in Italian designed furniture. A large sectional sofa in the living room and black leather and chrome chairs and sofa in the den led to a dramatic ceiling to floor window with a magnificent view of the lake. Glass and marble tables, with white and black marble accenting the earth tones of the brown, beige and pink walls, flowed from room to room on the first floor. Jackson Pollack, Pablo Picasso, Willem de Koonig, and Mark Rothko original paintings were strategically placed and illuminated to add dramatic effect. An enormous, ultra-modern kitchen with the very latest appliances was orphaned by Gjuliana's lack of cooking skills.

An elevator rose to each floor from the first floor to a tower that John used as his study, complete with sophisticated telescopes to expand John's knowledge and imagination of the universe.

Gjuliana had an extensive library with direct access to the master suite on the second floor. The Deegan's sleeping quarters, with brown and white bedding and draperies were finished with teakwood and inlaid marble walls. The room was complete with his and her gold appointed bathrooms, a sauna, a king and a half-sized custom bed, and a sound system which could be heard anywhere in the Villa.

All this and more for two people who, other than a full time staff, would likely never have a visitor.

Because of his past, John had a new identity. John, now Giovanni De Luca, and his vast wealth allowed John and Gjuliana to live out the rest of their lives together in total opulence and peace.

It wasn't that long ago John broke his exile and traveled back to the United States to assist the very man who had hunted him down after his own murderous spree, to help solve a many years old case of a little boy trafficked for sex, murdered, and basically forgotten by the inept Philadelphia Police Department, the infamous boy-in-the-box case.

Gjuliana had also returned once to New York for a few days to attend the funeral of her father, an Albanian Muslim refugee who raised his family in the old tradition, fashioned after the Kanun of Lekë Dukagjini. Gjuliana had not seen her family since fleeing to Switzerland and marrying Deegan, the love of her life. The loving couple was now in their mid-sixties.

Both John and Gjuliana vowed never to leave each other or Lugano again after they returned from the states. They worked side-by-side in the gardens surrounding *Villa Cielo* and perfecting the Lombardese Italian dialect of Lugano.

Little did John know he would again have to break his promise to Gjuliana. He had once before abandoned his solemn first vows as a novice of the Roman Catholic Church.

This particular morning Gjuliana rested her head on John's chest and said, "Honey, I am so glad everything is behind us now."

John nodded his head pulled the sheets back and excused himself to the den to go listen to American music from the 1960s. Deegan needed to strengthen himself with a shot of homemade *grappa* before approaching his wife.

He poked his head back into the bedroom and said, "My love, I have something to tell you that is not so pleasant. Please join me on the veranda so we may share the lake together."

Deegan opened the double wooden doors to the veranda; the white sheer draperies billowed from the breeze. Lago Lugano is one of the most spectacular places on earth. Deegan stood for a moment waiting for Gjuliana to join him. He took a deep breath of air from the magnificent glacial lake that is surrounded by the Lugano Prealps Mountains. Lugano frames a picture of beauty and tranquility that can soothe even the most tortured soul. "The Monte Carlo of Switzerland" is Lugano's well-deserved nickname.

John had already buzzed his houseman to serve coffee and biscotti and requested he then leave he and Gjuliana alone.

John held Gjuliana's soft hands in his, gazing into her large, brown eyes.

"My love. My love. Fate has once again played its tricks on us. I often think of how you had waited for me to come back to you after so many years when we were younger, long past your child bearing years. That is my biggest disappointment for you. For us," John said somberly.

"Tell me what you need to say, John. I know the news is not good. I am not without eyes and ears."

"The doctors have confirmed I have a fatal disease. I do not have much time. Perhaps a year at best. Likely a lot less. Only God knows when he will call me for judgment."

"Your pancreas?" Gjuliana's words trembled from her lips.

"Yes. They tell me there are some new treatments, but I will need to go to Zürich if I choose to go that route."

"Well, do I get a say in that matter?" Gjuliana asked. She was bravely fighting back tears.

"How selfish of me. Of course, my love."

"Honey, don't worry. We will face this demon together, and I will be with you every step of the way. You are my husband and every moment together is precious. We will fight for every day you have."

"I'm told the treatments are no picnic. They will not be able to tell me the magnitude of the cancer I have until more tests and surgery are completed. Part of me wants to just let go and be done with it."

Gjuliana gasped. "You will not rob me of one day, John. Not one hour." Gjuliana's throat tightened at the thought of her life without her one and only, true love.

John laughed. "I will do whatever you want. After all, I was the one who left you when we were young to pursue that rotten, failed priesthood calling and the rest of my inglorious life."

"Call Zürich today and set the appointment at the hospital. We will take a residence there for the time you need. I will attend to details."

"I will do as you say, my love." Deegan said.

"I insist."

"After I call the doctors, I need to go into town to pick up some medicines. I also have some business to attend to. Tonight we will have dinner right here and enjoy one another. I now realize how every moment is precious," John said.

"We always knew that. And we have lived the past few years to the fullest. I have no regrets, nor should you. I will pray for the miracle that you deserve. And so should you."

"Pray? Me? After what I did in my life? I'm positive God would laugh his ass off." John laughed at that imagery. Gjuliana pursed her full lips to prevent a laugh so as not to be sacrilegious.

The business that Deegan mentioned to his wife was unknown even to him. A week before, he had received an encrypted message coded in the way Deegan had used when he was a government or Army military assassin in Nicaragua. The urgent message came from a shrouded, third party, communicated through Deegan's private banker in Zürich.

"MUST MEET WITH YOU URGENTLY... IN LUGANO ON 22. NO DANGER TO YOU. 3 P.M. BLUE UMBRELLA PARCO CIVICO, ON LAKE. CONFIRM VIA THIS CHANNEL."

Deegan was curious yet naturally suspicious, but his one word answer was relayed immediately.

"YES."

Across the pond as they say, in the great city of New York, the handsome and former New York City police Detective Vic Gonnella was preparing to leave his office for the day. Vic couldn't wait to get back to his apartment to spend time with his business partner Raquel Ruiz, also a former member of the NYPD, and their baby daughter.

Vic and Raquel's company had now become an international investigative agency for high-end clients. Centurion Associates LLC with Global Headquarters at 56th Street and Park Avenue was arguably the largest and most effective criminal investigative operation in the United States and Europe.

Every single day of his life Vic thought about the John Deegan case and how it catapulted him into worldwide fame. The fortune followed.

And every single day of his life Vic was also haunted about how the case of the international serial killer, John Deegan had ended. He often dreamt of being back in the detective squad in the 41st Precinct in the South Bronx, the body of Father Edward O'Gorman, emasculated in the confessional at St. Martin of Tours church, and the other victims who were murdered by a pointed, wooden crucifix.

On Gonnella's office wall, along with mementos of his NYPD days and a myriad of photographs with powerful notables of himself and Raquel, hung a framed poster of the Giuseppe Verdi Opera, *La Forza del Destino, the power of destiny.*

After a brief encounter three years ago with the genius murderer in Philadelphia, Vic never imagined that Deegan and he would cross paths again.

Although at times Vic was tempted to discover if Deegan was still alive, he preferred to let dead dogs lay.

CHAPTER 2

It isn't often that a bishop is forced to resign his post from the Catholic Church, but canon law stipulates, should a bishop "who has become less able to fulfill his office because of ill health or some other grave cause is earnestly requested to present his resignation from office."

High on the Vatican totem pole was Bishop Franco Di Siena of the Pontifical University of the Holy Cross, overseen by The Prelature of the Holy Cross and Opus Dei, was forced to resign due to illness two years ago.

Truth be told, Bishop Di Siena, a short man who wore clear-rimmed eyeglasses, and longish gray hair was in perfect health.

The real cause of his resignation was that the Most Reverend Di Siena had a penchant for young boys. A pedophile since his days as a seminarian, the bishop escaped the eyes of church officials as none of his victims came forward. Ultimately three grown men, in their mid-thirties filed complaints with the Vatican.

The victim's claims were deemed credible and the church settled the matter quietly with a sum of money and promises of psychological assistance. The victims took the money thinking they would feel a sense of justice. The money would run out quickly, but the emotional scars of being raped as a child would raise its ugly head with a vengeance.

Rather than deal with an additional sexual abuse scandal, Di Siena was not defrocked and allowed to remain in Rome at a private residence in the *Piazza Navona*.

The piazza is a lively and eclectic place with mimes, artists, street hawkers and a mass of tourists.

Di Siena lived in baroque *palazzo* in a scarcely furnished second floor one-bedroom apartment, across from the Bernini fountain of Neptune.

One pleasant evening after a double scoop of chocolate ice cream from the famed *Tre Scalini Gelateria,* a pair of men followed the bishop to his flat. One of the men was tall and wore a suit, a fedora hat, and large sunglasses. The other, short and stocky, dressed in jeans and a tank top shirt with a Sicilian sailors cap.

The bishop, unaware and feeling safe and protected the church's best attorneys, used his key to open the front door of the *palazzo,* when the shorter of the two men grabbed him with a vice grip on the back of his neck, pushing him further into the building, causing him to almost stumble and fall. The taller man draped a wet towel over Di Siena's mouth and nose rendering him unconscious. Chloroform did its job.

The two men carried the bishop to his apartment door using his key to enter. Once inside the men sat the insentient bishop in his chair, using duct tape to secure his arms and legs and gag him. The shorter man left immediately, but not before he spit upon the bishop calling him a "*cacasodo.*"

"Wake up, Your Excellency. It's time we met," the tall man said. A few well-placed smacks to the bishop's face made him aware of his condition. His eyes bulging with fear, Di Siena grunted an inaudible response.
"So all those years, how many little boys do you think you raped? Dozens? Hundreds? Did you keep track of your handiwork?"

Di Siena attempted to wiggle free from his bondage.

"No matter, Excellency. In my book one is too many. So now it is time that you are brought to justice. The Lord knows that Holy Mother Church is more worried about reputation than righteousness. This is why I am sent as a messenger of Jesus Christ Himself."

Bishop Di Siena could taste the chocolate ice cream mixed with bile coming up from his stomach.

"I will be fair to you although you don't deserve any kindness. I will allow you to say a good act of contrition. I suspect that you believe in that, Bishop Di Siena, yes?"

The tied bishop's eyes squeezed tightly, tears running down his cheeks, his heart pounding near its maximum, a vein in his forehead seeming as if it would burst, the prelate knew he was about to meet his doom. The last fucking thing on the bishop's mind was prayer.

After a minute, the tall man exposed his weapon for his prisoner to see. Di Siena gasped air through his nose while the smell of adrenaline and intestinal gas filled the room.

"That aroma is very nasty, Excellency. No matter if you soil yourself, the undertaker has seen that before. I suggest you let loose."

The killer raised his weapon over his head and plunged it deep into the bishop's throat. As it penetrated, the bishop and the justifier both let out a scream, drowning out each other's anguish. The blood from the wound, first pumping black before it turned to a crimson red, shot almost to the ceiling. In less than thirty seconds Bishop Franco Di Siena was dead.

The next evening, when the bishop was found, bound and gagged in his chair, the blood soaked body, walls, and carpet were not nearly as shocking as what was protruding from his neck.

One of the *carabinieri*, a veteran captain who was among the first to arrive on the crime scene called his commander from his cell phone.

"Sir, the murder in the *Piazza Navona* is not an ordinary killing. It is the work of the monster John Deegan."

A shaved to a point wooden crucifix was the tall man's weapon of choice.

CHAPTER 3

At *La Farmacia San Salvatore e Attiva a Lugano-Paradiso* at *2 Via Geretta*, a small store, crowded with aisles of cold remedies and vitamins, an eighty something year-old farmer, dressed in gabardine work pants, a faded blue, checkered, button down shirt, and a sweat stained black cap, approached the pharmacist's counter

"Can I be of assistance, sir?" the pharmacist asked.

The old man looking confused and intimidated, his hands trembling, handed the pharmacist a crumpled piece of paper. The man's hands were rough and dirty from the soil of his farm.

"I need this, please," the farmer said in a barely audible voice.

The pharmacist quickly scanned the script.

"Can you wait a few minutes? I must make this compound."

"Certainly. I need to return to my stand. My daughter is there alone, and today is a busy day for us," the farmer said. The old man's eyes scanned the store as if it were the first time he was in a pharmacy.

The pharmacist smiled broadly. "Ah, yes. Wednesday in Lugano! Every Wednesday in Lugano center, there is a festival of open farmer's markets, live music, street food vendors, mimes, jugglers, and artists. What do you sell, my friend?"
"Some fruits, kiwi, peaches. Some vegetables, escarole, string beans a little asparagus. Some beans and few mushrooms."

"This will make a delicious meal I think."

The farmer put his hands together in true Italian fashion for emphasis. "True, if prepared correctly."

"I will rush. Just a moment please. Have a seat or walk around the store if you wish."

Not long after the farmer took in the shelves of the store the pharmacist handed the bottle of blue liquid to the farmer. "Here you go, Mr. De Luca, good health to you."

John Deegan now had his oral steroids quickly paid for with Swiss Francs and stashed the bottle into his front pants pocket. He mumbled to himself about what a pain in the ass cancer was and wondered how he would adhere to his macrobiotic diet which was supposed to help keep him wanting to eat and keep his strength up, but he promised Gjuliana he would abide by his lead physician, Dr. Jon Baumer's instructions who was a world renowned oncologist. With a nod and a smile to the pharmacist, he straightened his cap and exited the store.

A master of disguise, Deegan had chosen his farmer wardrobe to meet with his mystery suitor.

Now the "farmer" was on his way to his second stop. A fifteen-minute walk to the *Parco Civico*. The old man walked along the *Piazza della Riforma* passing the old vibrant pastel colored two and three story buildings. The Neoclassical *piazza* is as serene as it is stunning. For a moment the elderly *contadino* thought of paying a visit, perhaps lighting a candle at the *Cattedriale di San Lorenzo* but thought better. He wanted to make sure he made his appointment on time.

The old man passed the three-story, light pink, town hall adorned with a green, copper dome with a dagger-like spike on its top which was directly across from the Swiss Bank buildings. The farmer thought for a second about which took more advantage of the people.

The church or perhaps the bank? He put the thought out of his head, focusing on his meeting.

Walking slowly into the grand park, along the *Piazza Indipendenza* the farmer headed toward the shore of *Lago* Lugano. A slightly hunched back and a noticeable limp betrayed a man who had long labored at his duty.

A handsome man, obviously a German tourist was sitting under a blue umbrella at the lake's shore. He wore sunglasses, a floppy brown hat, a thick belt that held up a pair of khaki shorts past his knees, black sandals with black socks that went above his ankles and a t-shirt that advertised Heineken beer. A Canon camera hung around his neck. The man was perusing a tourist's map of the area.

The old farmer passed the table where the tourist was sitting a few times. The man noticed that the farmer's limp had changed. The limp at first favored the old man's right leg. On the third pass, the limp was now on his left leg.

The tourist knew his appointment had arrived. It was now exactly three o'clock.

"Would you like to rest yourself, my friend? Please join me," the tourist offered.

"Why, thank you. My leg is hurting as you can see," the farmer said.

"Which one bothers you more?"

Deegan knew only a practiced eye would notice this detail. He sat across from the tourist, his back to the lake.

"How did you find me?" Deegan asked.

"I have a long reach into things here in Switzerland. My occupation allows me to open many doors."

The man removed his sunglasses. Deegan recognized him immediately and was taken aback by the presence of this man although he showed no sign of surprise.

"Are you here to arrest me, Colonel?" Deegan asked.

The one and only commander of the Pontifical Swiss Guard of the Holy See, supreme protector of the pope, Colonel Adrien Zellweger, persuasively had Deegan, the notorious priest killer, within his grasp.

"On the contrary, Mr. Deegan. I am here only for a chat."

John Deegan recalled Zellweger's face from newspaper and magazine articles when Pope Francis appointed the colonel in 2014. Zellweger's predecessor was removed because the Holy Father thought him to be too "Teutonic". Simply too strict with the rank and file among the Swiss Guard. Francis was pushing his Franciscan man-of-the people image. There was no better place to start than in his house.

"A simple chat? You could have easily called me on the telephone, Colonel," Deegan countered.

"What I have to say to you is private. Simply between two men who may have a common goal," Colonel Zellweger said.

"My goal at the moment is to stay alive and to spend my last days with my wife," Deegan said.

"I'm also aware of your illness, Mr. Deegan or should I say, Mr. De Luca. As I said, I have a long reach."

"Clearly you do, Colonel. I feel as if you know my fate as well."

"That, sir, is in the hands of the Lord, our God. I am hoping you live a long life, as I am hoping you will help me with my plan," Colonel Zellweger said. The Colonel studied Deegan's face for any tell that he would show a true intent. There was none.

"A plan? May I be so bold as to ask about the plan and why you have selected me?"

Zellweger's eyes grew wide as he leaned forward in his chair placing his forearms on the table, hands into fists to make his point without shouting. He enunciated clearly and spoke slowly in just above a whisper. "What you did to awaken the world during your murderous spree only worked for a short time." Zellweger sat back in his chair calming down realizing he might otherwise be giving up their incognito appearance. He continued, "I'm afraid that since Francis has taken the seat, the church has not gotten better; on the contrary, things have gotten far worse."

"A blind man can see that, Colonel," Deegan replied. His manner was aloof and matter-of-fact.

"His Holiness is doing nothing to remove the cardinals, bishops, and priests who have turned the church into a veritable, pedophile's playground. What is worse is how the Catholic clergy, in their arrogance, are all but laughing at the world, continuing their evil and degenerate ways with total abandon."

"Do you expect me to sharpen more crucifixes and start slaughtering some priests again?" Deegan asked without emotion.

"Not at all, sir. Please hear what I have to say. Not only are these so-called priests continuing to commit these atrocious acts on a global basis, it is clear for anyone behind the Vatican walls to see that they have no intention of changing their ways. The church does not even acknowledge that raping little boys and little girls is the slight bit wrong. Sure, they will throw money at the problem, but the Curia does not think their priests should be held accountable for what they are doing. The cardinals and in effect the pope use the Vatican bank as a cash machine to silence their victims. Something must change. The church must be cleaned of these evil men if it is to survive."

"The Roman Catholic Church has been controlling this world for centuries. Their vast wealth makes it nearly impossible to make changes. One pope lies and the next one swears to his lies. Nothing will ever change. You of all people must realize this, Colonel," Deegan postulated.

The head of the Swiss Guard was getting giddy as he continued to speak. "My plan... with the right people in place? It can be carried out, and will force the church and all of the entire faithful... nearly a billion and a half human souls, to eradicate the evil and build the church anew. Wipe the slate clean. Start over again," The Colonel said. His piercing blue eyes were studying Deegan closely. Still no tell, no emotion, no reaction from Deegan.

"A neutron bomb over Vatican City would not be enough to make the appropriate changes to Holy Mother Church. You know this as well as I do, Colonel."

"I know one thing. It will take more than posting ninety-five theses as Martin Luther did on some silly, church door, for them to navigate themselves out of the sea of shit they have created," Colonel Zellweger said.

"So you call me for advice, Colonel? A rich, retired, almost forgotten serial killer, who has a fatal disease, who couldn't care less about the direction the church is heading? There is nothing I can do."

"If I told you that you would be able to change the course of history. To perhaps right the wrongs of the Roman Church forever, would you tell me then, you are not interested?" the Colonel asked.

"I will listen with interest. But I will make no promises," Deegan said.

CHAPTER 4

Deegan noticed Colonel Zellweger's Glock 19 handgun, under his t-shirt. The letters AG *Ausrusting der Garge, Equipment of the Guard,* he was sure, was embossed on the handle of the pistol.

"Mr. Deegan, let me tell you a few things about myself which may make sense to you later."

"I began my service to the Swiss Guard when I was twenty-four years old. To be a member of the guard is an honor to which I devoted my youth. I am from a prominent family in this country so some doors were of course opened to me, but I had to meet all of the Guards' strict qualifications. Education, height, I was well above the five foot eight and a half inch minimum, I was single, Swiss born, and Catholic. I excelled in combat training in the Swiss army, and was accepted as a *Halberdier* a private in the Pontifical Swiss Guard."

Zellweger continued, "I even remember my solemn oath as if it were yesterday. I swore my allegiance in front of Pope John Paul II on the sixth of May, 1985. That day is in remembrance of the one hundred forty- seven Guards who gave their life when soldiers of Charles attacked the Vatican the sixth of May, a long time ago. One of my ancestors, a Guard member accompanied Pope Clement the Seventh as he attempted to escape through the secret *Passetto di Borgo* to the safety of *Castel Sant Angelo.* With over five hundred years of loyalty to the pope, my family was overjoyed when I was accepted.

I can still recite the pledge I took in the Saint Damaso courtyard."

"I swear I will faithfully, loyally, and honorably serve the Supreme Pontiff Francis and his legitimate successors, and also dedicate myself to them with all my strength, sacrificing if necessary also my life to defend them. I assume this same commitment with regard to the

Sacred College of Cardinals whenever the See is vacant.

Furthermore, I promise to the Commanding Captain and my other superiors, respect, fidelity, and obedience. This I swear! May God and our Holy Patrons assist me!"

My name was called and dressed in full uniform of the guard, I, with my left hand, I held the Guards' standard, and with my right hand with three fingers open, symbolizing the Most Holy Trinity, Father, Son and Holy Spirit, I confirmed my oath to the Holy Father.

"I, Adrien Zellweger, swear I will observe faithfully, loyally and honorably all that has now been read out to me! May God and his saints assist me!"

Zellweger sat back down but began speaking faster and faster, barely taking a breath, his irritation with the church blaring.

"I was devoted to the Pope, Saint Martin, Saint Sebastian and Saint Nicholas von Flüe.

"Working my way up through the ranks was my life's work. I worked hard, never married, studied and got my advanced degrees, and stayed a devout Catholic. I became a non-commissioned officer, then first sergeant, then after nearly ten years I became one of the two Lieutenant Colonels, the Vice Commandant, and now Colonel.

"In 1998 I was on duty when our Commander Alois Estermann and his wife were killed by Cedric Tornay, before he killed himself. I was the first to discover the carnage. It is true that Estermann and Tornay were involved in a homosexual affair. From that day forward I was slowly becoming jaded by what was going on behind the walls of Vatican City. I asked myself many times, *Is this what I devoted my life to? An organization steeped in sexual deprivation and degeneracy?*' "

"Very interesting history and the life of your dedication and service, Colonel. I'm still waiting to hear why you contacted me," Deegan said cooly.

Zellweger scooted to the edge of his seat, his eyes squinting at Deegan, finger wagging at him, clearly irritated at John's lack of interest in his plan.

"Listen, when you went on your killing spree, Mr. Deegan, we followed your activity from your first murder in New York City. As you moved toward Europe we were concerned for the safety of the Holy Father and took every conceivable precaution. For one, I was convinced that you were on a mission to kill the pope, and knowing your background I knew nothing would stop you."

"I accomplished my task, Colonel. Pope Francis, and for that matter anyone in the church, is no longer in danger from me," Deegan stated.

Coyly challenging Deegan's ability, and only to ruffle Deegan's feathers, Zellweger spoke this low blow, "Have you *really* fulfilled you mission, Mr. Deegan? In the years since you escaped, the church has not changed from the human cesspool that it has become." Deegan noticed that Zellweger's eyes were now full of fury.

"The Vatican bank is nothing more than a corrupt institution that is bankrolling a pedophile playground. Behind closed doors, the priests and bishops mock the entire world. They laugh at the attempts of the laity to make changes. Molesting children and vulnerable adults continues on a global basis. True, some sacrificial lambs are defrocked and laicized, but it is all purely theatre," Zellweger said.

The colonel continued. Deegan's cold, blue eyes were intent on the colonel's hazel glaze.

"Homosexuality is rampant in the Vatican. For that matter, gay men somehow lead nearly every parish in the world. The priests, bishops, and cardinals preach against such a lifestyle from the pulpit yet continue those so called immoral acts among themselves. Aside from the blatant homosexuality, the entire clergy all turn a blind eye to the pedophiles. Many of them do not even accept the fact that raping children is even wrong. Mr. Deegan, this must stop. That is why I want to see if you are in a place in your life where you can help me to cleanse the church of these vermin once and for all."

"Listen, I have nothing but contempt for the leaders of this religion. And please don't misinterpret what I am saying. My issues with the church have never been with faith. That has never been my dispute with Catholicism. I feel much like you do, Colonel. But I have other problems to deal with at the moment. I don't see how I can be part of your undertaking, whatever it may be," Deegan said.

"You may not have long on this earth, Mr. Deegan. Wouldn't you want to leave knowing you have changed the world for the better?" Colonel Zellweger said.

"So what is your plan?"

"Here is where I have difficulty exposing my plot you, Mr. Deegan. If you are not willing to commit your skills to me, if you are not willing to put your life on the line as I will, to free the world from the yoke of these madmen, then we part never to see one another again," Colonel Zellweger said.

"So, in effect you do not trust me. You believe my curiosity will entice me to hear your plan, but perhaps then I may disclose you to the powers that be."

"That is correct."

"And what will stop you from pulling that pistol out and shooting me dead where I sit? The world will applaud that you had killed a serial killer. The infamous John Deegan, a man you and many others have been trying to apprehend for several years. Frankly, you may be doing me a bit of a favor."

"Only God himself will take you when he is ready Mr. Deegan. Remember that He is all forgiving and paradise will be yours if you atone for your sins," Colonel Zellweger preached.

"There was a time when I truly believed that. Now I find everything I was ever told, everything I ever had faith in, is nothing but myths and lies," Deegan said.

Colonel Zellweger reached into his pocket and pulled out a pack of English Oval cigarettes. He lit the smoke with a match, cupping his hands as soldiers do, guarding the flame away from the slight breeze from the lake.

"Excuse my indiscretion. I never smoke in the Vatican or around my men. Now let me tell you my plan."

CHAPTER 5

The ceremonial, Swiss Guard *halberd*, the two-handed, long, pole weapon that carries an axe blade topped with a spike is not only for the amusement of tourists. The men are all trained to dispatch a potential threat within seconds. In the hands of a Swiss Guard, the halberd is nearly as deadly as a Sig SG 550 assault rifle, the Steyr TMP machine pistol, or the Heckler and Koch MP7 personal defense weapons with armor piercing ammunition which are carried by the Guard.

Within the walls of the one-hundred and nine acre Vatican City State, Colonel Zellweger is the commander of Papal security and controls all aspects of the pope's safety. He is the one the pope relies on to be his personal bodyguard whenever and wherever Francis travels.

He had been appointed *Oberst*, or Colonel, by the two hundred and sixty-sixth leader of the Holy Roman Catholic Church, Jorge Mario Bergoglio, a Jesuit Cardinal from Argentina who became Pope Francis.

He dresses sharply in a specially tailored, black business suit with a thin, black tie, striking an imposing figure, and is the first and final defense against any attempt on His Holiness' life. Zellweger commands one hundred and ten Swiss Guard members, all who have taken the exact same oath he did to protect and defend the Papacy.

Along with the *Corpo della Gendarmeria dello Stato della Citta Vaticano*, the one hundred and thirty member police force of the Vatican led by Inspector General Claudio Festa, the pope and the Vatican are well protected. The *Gendarmeria* have special counter assault teams, anti-sabotage units, and explosive ordinance disposal units, called EODs to use if necessary.
The modern firepower of the Swiss Guard and the *Gendarmeria* make them one of the most effective security forces on the planet.

In other words, the pope is well-protected, until now.

The responsibility to guard the entrances to Vatican City is with the Swiss Guard. The Gendarmeria, along with the most modern day technology available assists them.

CHAPTER 6

Back under the blue umbrella on beautiful sun lit Lake Lugano, Colonel Zellweger continued his pitch.

"Francis and that scumbag Benedict before him could not...did not want to... make the sweeping changes needed to be done within the church, and sadly, the clergy are too far gone. The Cardinals protect the bishops, the bishops protect the priests. Stealing parish funds, pedophilia, murder, homosexuality, whatever the "sin", there is only ever prayer and penitence advised as punishment with no justice for the victim. Every member of the clergy, including the pope himself, is guilty by association. They all know what is going on with their charges and they are complicit in the crimes these men have committed, and will continue to commit unabated unless they are stopped," Colonel Zellweger said.

Now, fear is not in John Deegan's vocabulary. In fact, the only fear he could remember in his life was when the priest came to his classroom in the second grade to select him for "special assignment". He was fearless when he killed the enemy for his country in Nicaragua, and courageous when he slaughtered his victims who were known child molesters. However, the venom in Zellweger's eyes began to concern Deegan. *Was this man insane? How could he turn on nearly five hundred years of family tradition, to renounce his vow to protect the pope, turn on his faith, and forfeit his freedom? Was he, too, abused?*

"Colonel, forgive me please. It sounds to me that you want to rebuild the entire Roman Catholic Church. An organization that has been in existence for over two thousand years. I don't have to remind you of their vast wealth, the enormity of their followers, and their sheer power politically and economically. My god, you would have to drop a nuclear bomb on the Vatican, killing millions of people to destroy the church. I would have no part in that, sir," Deegan said.

Zellweger sat back in his chair, crossed his left leg over his right in European fashion and lit another English Oval with the nearly finished first one.

"Ahhh, you underestimate me. Innocent people will not suffer under my plan. These are the very people I will be saving from this… this cabal of human waste. My plan is fairly simple. Let me continue please.. It is your genius that I am after…your genius is what I need to fulfill my destiny as a savior of Catholicism. You will be heralded along with me forever. Certainly not now, but history will mark us as the heroes of our time! We will be immortal by our reputations for going about the Lord's work." Zellweger took a long drag on his cigarette, never taking his eyes off Deegan's.

Zellweger continued, "My friend, you may not know this because you are engrossed in other things in your life right now, but Francis is not well. He certainly looks vibrant, and his face never shows his true disdain for the Curia. At least not in public. But behind the closed doors, Francis is terrified for the Church. The position of pope has been nothing but a silly child's game since John Paul II. John Paul II was made a saint not because of his miracles but due to his compliance. Ratzinger sincerely wanted to affect change. He was met with a stone wall of red capes and hats with the Curia. Ratzinger was virtually forced to resign, and lives a life of misery for his fears and failure."

Zellweger continued, "Francis is planning to resign as well due to his health. His death may come sooner, but the plan is to be announced within a month. Then he will step down, as his predecessor did, and a Conclave will be called. Every one of the two-hundred and thirteen Cardinals from around the world will be summoned," Zellweger said. He hesitated and glared at Deegan.

"Go on, Colonel. I have a feeling I see where this is going. Perhaps you would feel better if I finished your thought?" Deegan asked.

"Please allow me, Mr. Deegan. While they are assembled in the General Congregation and just before the election of the new pope, in the Sistine Chapel, every Cardinal will be killed," Zellweger said. He dropped his cigarette to the ground and twisted his foot upon it, for a bit too long. Deegan noticed the dramatic move and paused before he spoke.

"Sending the One, Holy, Catholic, and Apostolic Church into a tailspin. The church may never fully recover from this sort of terrorism," Deegan said.

"I don't consider saving generations of followers of Jesus Christ from the evils of a church gone mad an act of terrorism, Mr. Deegan. On the contrary, we are about to embark on an act of contrition. Wiping away our sins at the altar of our Lord and Savior and embarking on a new and everlasting covenant."

Zellweger went on, "I'm sure you've read the end of the church as we know it has been predicted by St. Malachy, the first Irishman to be canonized. St. Malachy said that from his time there would be only one hundred and twelve popes. Pope Francis is that very pope."

The colonel reached into the back pocket of his short pants and took out a folded sheet of paper. He handed the note to Deegan.
"This is what the Archbishop of Armagh wrote in the year 1139 while he was summoned to see Pope Innocent II. St. Malachy had a miraculous vision of the future. His predictions are interpreted for the last one hundred and eleven popes prior to Francis, with some degree of accuracy, I might add," Zellweger offered.

Deegan took the note, but never took his eyes off Zellweger as he opened it. Glancing down he read what the note said:
In the final persecution of the Holy Roman Church, there will sit as bishop, Peter the Roman, who will pasture his sheep in many tribulations, and when these things are finished, the city of seven hills will be destroyed, and the dreadful judge will judge his people. The End.

Zellweger allowed Deegan to absorb his note, and then continued to speak. "There is also Quatrain II. 46, from Michel di Nostredame that states...

Deegan interrupted the colonel.

"I fail to see the difference in your plan and the global issue we have with fundamentalist Muslims. You propose immortality, but the only thing you haven't offered so far are seventy-seven virgins,"Deegan said.

"Please don't insult my intelligence by bringing nonsensical spewing from the dark ages of the Catholic Church and their sordid past into our discussion. I have studied the rants of Malachi, or as I prefer to call him, "malarkey". According to his prediction, Peter the Roman is Pope Francis. He is the Roman because Francis was born of an Italian father and Peter because St. Francis' father was named Pietro and Pope Francis, a Jesuit, is a follower of St. Francis. Just a bit if a stretch, Colonel? And Nostradamus was a druggist that they called a philosopher because he wrote these very cryptic *Quatrains*. And I quote; 'the great star for seven days shall burn. So nakedly clear like two suns appearing. The large dog all night howling. While the great Pontiff shall change his territory.' Now I ask you, with all due respect, Colonel Zellweger, shall we also discuss Santa Claus and the Tooth Fairy?"

"Putting these predictions aside for the moment, know that I will attempt this coup d'etat with or without you, Mr. Deegan. I know your disdain for the hypocrisy of the church is at least as strong as mine, so I have no fear that you may expose me. So you are not interested, John?" He took his "documentation" back from Deegan and shoved it in his pocket.

"I haven't said that, Adrien. I need time to think."

"Think? You need time to think? I am preparing to give up my life for the Lord. The question is...are you going to help me? There will be absolutely no danger to you."

"Colonel, what you are asking is an involved, interesting question.

Seemingly barring a miracle, my life is near its end. You are still relatively young. I see your zeal and I understand it well, but there is business in Zürich I must attend to. Promises have been made between my wife and me to treat this disease which has taken hold of me. I will think, while I am there, of the best way to fulfill your plan. If for some reason I cannot join you, I will certainly share my thinking with you. That is the best I can offer at the moment," Deegan said.

"I am returning to Rome this afternoon, Mr. Deegan. Here is my personal cell number. It is secure and untraceable. I will await word from you. May God's will be done," Colonel Zellweger declared.

Both men walked from the park in separate directions.

Deegan's final stop that afternoon was to a small, stone fronted church on the *Piazza Cioccaro* in Lugano. The stones are a mix of very old gray and brown square and rectangular boxes surrounding an old pair of wooden entrance doors. The exterior of the church gives no indication of the artistic treasures within.

Chiesa di Santa Maria degli Angeli was originally a Franciscan monastery which was built in 1499. Deegan would often visit this church to marvel at the Renaissance fresco that covered the entire wall of the nave and enjoy the quiet serenity.

This time, however, Bernardino Luini's 'Passion and Crucifixion' a magnificent rendition, second only to Michelangelo's work at the Sistine chapel, which normally captures the imagination from fervent believers to avowed atheists, gave Deegan pause. The destruction of victims' lives seemed equal to if not worse than what Christ Himself had to endure. Deegan wasn't sure if he believed any of that story anyhow, which only made the decision of what he was being asked to do even worse.

John Deegan, the serial killer, now who would perhaps be one of the destroyers of the modern Catholic Church sat in a small pew for an hour, surrounded by the colorful painting of the scourging by Roman soldiers and Christ on the cross, with only his thoughts and his calculating imagination.

CHAPTER 7

Two days later, John and Gjuliana were resting comfortably in a rented villa on Lake Zürich. Their domestic help would arrive later that day to see to the Deegans' every need.

"Tomorrow we will be at the *Klinik Hirslanden* to see Dr. Baumer. John, you will not be angry and grumpy. You will not try to outsmart his team as you do with everything else. I know you have been fervently studying your disease online. Please remember that these doctors have devoted their lives to their professions. I expect you to behave well and follow their prognosis and plan," Gjuliana lectured. It was if she were speaking to a petulant child.

"If they were so good, they would have found a cure by now. Cancer is a big business, my love," Deegan said.

"Cynicism is also not permitted, John."

And Gjuliana was right. Deegan's physicians, awaiting his visit to Zürich were among the best and most progressive in the world and had already outlined various treatment options, by stage, which would include targeted radiation therapy, aggressive chemotherapy, and surgery. A multidisciplinary group of doctors awaited Deegan's arrival at the *Klinik Hirslanden*. The *Klinik* is part of the largest private cancer group in Switzerland. On the *Witellikenstrassa*, an avenue in a zone known widely for health care, with physicians, nurses, and medical students engrossed in healing their patients rather than medicating them, the *Klinik* is in a white, three-story modern building surrounded by serene gardens and a soothing waterfall wall.

At nine o'clock sharp the next morning, the Deegans found

themselves in front of Dr. Jon Baumer and his team of six other physicians all dressed in white lab coats. They met in a brightly lit, white walled conference room with photographs of happy, smiling patients conferring with their physicians. John Deegan remained silent at first.

"Mr. De Luca, your disease is generally fatal; we will not lie to you. However, we have, in many cases, been able to prolong lives for a good many years. With, I will add, a good quality of life. The first step is to determine the real stage of your disease, and no matter what it is rest assured there are several treatments we can offer. We will perform various tests today, and depending upon the results of those tests we will then perform surgery early tomorrow morning. Mr. De Luca, you will stay with us tonight, and Mrs. De Luca can of course stay with you if she pleases," Dr. Baumer said.

"Yes, I will be staying," Gjuliana immediately answered.

"Very well. Your recuperation from surgery will be only a few days in the hospital at most, then you can return to your home here. I don't want to put the cart before the horse and discuss further treatment until we know more, but I will say that our course of treatment is very aggressive. The best way to beat an aggressive cancer is with aggressive therapy." And sternly he stated, "And that will include proper nutrition and a good mental state." Pointing with his clipboard, he introduced another member of the team and more gently said, "And our fine Dr. Thomas Eschmann here is a psychiatrist who will meet with you twice daily to assist you in any psychological difficulties which you may encounter," Dr. Baumer said.

"A shrink? I have entertained myself with plenty of Dr. Eschmanns in my lifetime. Dr. Eschmann, you look like you are sixteen years old!" Deegan laughed.

"Giovanni!" Gjuliana scolded.

"I am twenty-nine, Mr. De Luca. Graduated top in my class at Harvard Medical and at the Sigmund Freud University in Vienna. I'm afraid my baby face is inherited from my Irish mother." Dr. Eschmann spoke perfect English and smiled broadly at Deegan.

"I had one of those as well. An Irish mother that is. A wise writer once said, 'whatever else is unsure in this stinking dunghill of a world, a mother's love is not'," Deegan said.

"James Joyce, I believe," Dr. Eschmann said.

"Indeed it was! We will get along famously, Eschmann," Deegan said smiling. He sat back in his chair studying the young doctor's features.

"So now, do either of you have any questions?" Dr. Baumer asked.

John and Gjuliana looked at one another. John tucked his shoulders into his neck.

"Not at the moment," Gjuliana stated.

"Alright then. Onto a CAT Scan and then lots of poking and prodding," Dr. Bauman said.

CHAPTER 8

Back in Vatican City...

"You seem distracted today, Colonel," Inspector General Festa said. He was addressing Colonel Adrien Zellweger during their daily inspection walk inside Vatican City.

"Ah… yes perhaps I am, Inspector. I am thinking ahead to the conclave. So much to do to prepare my men," Zellweger replied.

Statues of the Apostles and Jesus Christ which surround the perimeter of St Peter's Square seemed to be gazing down upon the two men as they walked from their offices behind the great basilica to the papal audience hall.

"There are many young and new guards since Benedict left. I can understand your concern."

"I sometimes wish our requirement for service was a bit more than two years. Training new men is becoming a full time task for us. Our responsibility, both mine and yours, at time seems daunting. Especially with the crazed Muslims doing what they do."

"It keeps me awake most nights, believe me. I also have similar training issues. As men retire, or are removed, we must replace them with the most qualified young men. There is always something unnerving on our minds Colonel," Festa said.

"I have not heard of a definitive date for the conclave to begin. Have you?" Zellweger looked sideways at the Inspector, trying to glean information from his counterpart.

"We should know in a few days, I suspect. You know as well as I that information coming from the Holy See is like pulling teeth. It never changes. Secrecy seems to be the way the Holy See flourishes. Well, shall I say secrecy with leaks?" Festa asked rhetorically.

"This place will once again be a mass of humanity once the voting begins. Everyone awaits the *habemus papam* declaration so that the faithful can tell their grandchildren that they were in St. Peter's Square when such-and-such Pope was announced," Zellweger said.

"Indeed. 'We have a Pope.' This will be my forth pope. Sorry, my fifth. Lest I forget the thirty-three days of John Paul I. He was such a wonderful man. The smiling pope was swallowed up quickly, if you get my meaning," Festa said.

"I understand, fully. I think I was still in secondary school when he was elected. I spoke to a few of my colleagues about his death. No one is willing to go beyond the official cause of death, but I have studied the case carefully. I am convinced that he died of natural causes. The assassination is purely conjecture and myth in my opinion."

"And you conclude that because... ?" Festa asked.

"Simply put, the man had a bad heart. I have spoken to nuns who served him. They are elderly now, but they recall that His Holiness complained of chest pains quite often. Even as a cardinal he had health issues that were kept quiet. The nuns told me they were constantly calling for his doctor. As a matter of fact, the night before he died, he complained about severe chest pains to his priest secretary. Then the pain left and he attributed the pain to gas. No doctor was summoned."

"Well, I for sure do not know. All I know is that without an autopsy there will always be the shadow of assassination connected with him," Festa said.

"In the Holy See, rules are rules, as you know. And an autopsy on the pope is not permitted."

"At any rate, I sometimes enjoy the gossip of the Vatican. It keeps one's imagination going. Like an opera," Festa offered.

"Okay, give me something to imagine then."

"Well, I am a lot older than you. I was a rookie when Paul VI reigned. You know, the flamboyant *sedia gestatoria* and all."

"Yes, the portable throne the popes were carried upon. Come to think of it, John Paul I did away with all that comedy. He also didn't use the tiara when he was coroneted. Paul was a bit flamboyant, wasn't he?"

"In more ways than you can imagine," Festa said as he looked behind the two walking men to see if anyone was within earshot.

"Please, are those rumors actually true?"

"Here we are like two college kids whispering about who is gay. Yes, Paul VI was indeed homosexual. He was caught in Milan when he was Cardinal Montini with some unsavory characters. There were other allegations as well. But the most compelling was his assigning gay priests to high positions in the apostolic palace. It was an open secret. Much like today, I might add. Then there was the first-hand accounts by Paul's Chamberlain of the Cape and the Sword, Franco Bellegrandi who was an eyewitness to the debauchery in the papal apartments," Festa spoke rapidly, covering his mouth as though his information was being listened to.

"My God in heaven," Colonel Zellweger said.

"Then I was told about a movie actor, I've forgotten his name, who was as gay as they come. He was allowed total access by the Swiss Guard. Especially in the evenings after dinner. I'm told they even saluted him."

"No way! Impossible!" These priests preach against homosexuality. They denounce sodomy, yet even the pope lived the lie of his celibacy? I find this to be unforgivable. Beyond rational comprehension."

"Look, every man has his demons. Paul had his. The fact that he was pope was meaningless. He was still just a man," Festa said.

"And look what we have today. This place has become a virtual sewer. It's almost difficult to watch at times. I only hope something can be done one day," Colonel Zellweger said. He studied Inspector Festa closely for any sign of collaboration. There was none.

The inspector took in a long breath and exhaled slowly before speaking.

"To survive in the Vatican, you must close one eye. And sometimes you need to close both, my friend."

CHAPTER 9

Deegan's surgery went off without any problems. Dr. Baumer stopped by for a visit to Deegan's private suite on the third floor of the *Klinik* early that same afternoon. His patient was comfortably sitting in a luxurious, high-backed chair.

"So, how is my star patient? Mrs. De Luca, is he behaving himself?" Dr. Baumer inquired.

"Behaving is a relative term, doctor," Gjuliana said.

"Giovanni, any pain or discomfort? How are you feeling?"

"I have a pain in my ass. My lunch was a piece of tree bark and some grass. How about some nice homemade Shepard's Pie or a Mulligan's stew, or a pizza?" Deegan asked.

"That is all history for you. I'm afraid you will have to get used to this diet for quite some time," Baumer said, while looking at his patient's chart.

"So by the time I can eat a cheeseburger I will be near death so it won't matter what I eat, and I will not even feel like eating anyway," Deegan said to his fingers.

"Giovanni, now stop it. Answer the doctor's questions," Gjuliana scolded.

"I actually have pain way up in my shoulders. It's not unbearable, just uncomfortable."

"That is air. A large part of the surgery was done laparoscopically. We pump air into your belly so we can work around in your abdomen. It will pass in a few days. How about in your lower abdomen?

Any pain?"

"None, as a matter of fact these nurses had me walking while I was still groggy. Tomorrow I suppose they will have me doing a 5K around the lake," Deegan said. He was grumpy.

"I will ask them to push you so that you move around as much as possible. We need to get your blood circulating into your extremities. Ah…I see we have company."

Young Dr. Eschmann arrived wearing his white lab coat and an orange bow tie.

Dr. Baumer said, "I will be back later. I will have all of the pathology reports in the morning and we will then discuss a protocol. For now Mrs. De Luca, I suggest you leave your charming husband in the hands of his Irish buddy with the expressive tie. We have a beautiful organic garden you can walk through. Come along, I will point you in the right direction."

Gjuliana kissed her husband on his forehead and left the room with Dr. Baumer. John didn't react to the gentle kiss.

"How are you, Giovanni?" Dr. Eschmann asked.

"Truthfully, if you really care to know, I am very angry."

"How so?"

"How am I here, in Zürich, in a cancer clinic, when my wife and I were planning to spend our golden years together? It really pisses me off. More for Gjuliana than myself."

"That feeling is natural and very normal. So let's discuss why you are felling this way, all right with you?"

"Look, I get it. I'm in the second stage of the classic cancer patients psychology. I've already blown by denial and refusal to accept the diagnosis. That lasted a few days, maybe a week. It can't be me, and all that crap. The diagnosis must be a mistake; the doctors are all idiots and assholes, present company excluded. Now this god damned raging anger. I can't wait until the other three stages arrive. Why don't I just skip the next two and go right for the gusto, right to acceptance that I am dying," Deegan said sarcastically.

"I see that you have been studying. As far as you dying? I don't believe you are. There are fantastic things we are doing here. A guarantee? Not at all. But I also can't guarantee that you will not drop dead of an unknown, cerebral aneurysm tomorrow. Having a fatalistic mindset is like worrying about the outcome. Do you really want to waste time and energy on that?"

"I like your mind, young Eschmann. So how do I get past this time of anger?" Deegan asked.

"By facing it, like any enemy. Talk it out. Laugh at the maneuvers your anger is playing against you."

"And I have had many enemies that were as ferocious, even more so," Deegan laughed.

"Good. So now you have at least laughed."

"Mind you I am not at all afraid to die. I have had many brushes with the grim reaper. More than I will admit to you. I just hate being robbed."
"The disease will rob you if you allow it, Giovanni. So, very simple… do not permit it to steal your time."

"Again, I am impressed. I thought our talks would be a terrible waste of time. After this little tete-a-tete, I feel the shadow of depression beginning to leave."

"Keep your mind busy. On your business, on a project perhaps?

Do you have something that you are involved with at the moment? A challenge?" Eschmann asked.

"As a matter of fact, I do. Something has recently come to me that may be more of a contest than anything I have ever encountered. I haven't decided if I will even participate at the moment."

"And your timeline?"

"Probably within the next several months I suspect.

"Is the thought of your illness holding you back?"

"Somewhat… but there are other concerns that I have. Taking the time from my wife for one."

Deegan reached out to Doctor Eschmann to take his hand as he attempted to stand. Eschmann complied.

"How about a nice walk, young Eschmann?" Deegan asked.

"Where to?"

"Down the hall. That would be a good first attempt at moving my fat ass out of this damn room."

"Brilliant," Eschmann agreed.

After their stroll twice around the third floor wing, Deegan began to tire. Doctor Eschmann and Deegan returned to the suite. The doctor saw to it that Deegan was comfortable in his bed and summoned the nurses to do what nurses do.

Across from Deegan's bed, on a carved, antique, mahogany table was a very large, elaborate floral display along with a basket of fresh fruits and vintage wines. There was no card attached, but Deegan knew from whom the thoughtful gift came. The vase was filled with large petal, white lilies surrounded by full fragrant, star gold azaleas. A red bow was interlaced between the flowers.

The gold and white flowers, and the red bow, the colors of the Vatican flag gave away the sender.

CHAPTER 10

Rumors abound within the walls of Vatican City. There are always mundane stories and gossip among the clergy as to what the next papal encyclical may or may not say, which cardinal will be removed and which one will be assigned to head the Vatican Bank, and of course, what position of faith His Holiness will declare.

Stories of the resignation, health, or impending death of a Pontiff spread like wildfire. Once the news is leaked to the media and, somehow it always does, the world becomes a very small place.

Reports of an impending announcement regarding the papacy of Francis had been circulating for months. Perhaps a brain tumor, maybe some other illness or affliction would force Francis to follow in the nearly unprecedented resignation of his predecessor Pope Benedict XVI.

Francis wasted little time with his announcement:

DECLARATIO

Dear Brothers,
I have called you to this consistory to announce to you all, a decision of great importance for Holy Mother Church. After much prayer and a full examination of my conscience before God, I have decided that my strength, due in large part to my age, can no longer continue with the demands of the Petrine ministry. I hereby declare, with full freedom, that I am compelled to recognize my incapacity to fulfill the ministry of Bishop of Rome, Successor of Saint Peter the Apostle that was given to me by the Cardinals on 13 March 2013. Therefore, as of 12 July 2016, at 20:00 hours, the See of Rome, the See of Saint Peter will be vacant. Therefore, a conclave to elect the new Supreme Pontiff must be

convoked by the proper authorities in place.

 My Dear Brothers, I thank you for all of your hard work and love, and the manner in which you have so ardently supported me in my short time as Supreme Pontiff. Now we must entrust the Holy Church to the care of Our Supreme Pastor, Our Lord Jesus Christ, and implore, through her intercession, his Holy Mother Mary, that she may guide the Cardinal Fathers with her maternal love, in electing the next Supreme Pontiff. With regard to myself, I will dedicate my days to prayer. May Jesus Christ forgive me of my inadequacies, and I beg Him to understand my human defects.

From the Vatican, 28 June 2016

Franciscus PP

The world was in shock by the resignation of Francis. Was there more to it than the pope's health? After all, he seemed jovial and robust for a man his age. Did the prolonged scandals of clergy sexual abuse; the difficulties at the Vatican bank, or some other unknown element play a role in forcing the pontiff's hand?

One person in particular was not at all surprised. He had seen Francis in his quarters, who no longer wanted to use the papal apartments born out of his Franciscan desire for less opulence, and witnessed the pontiff often too tired to remove his own shoes. He saw firsthand Francis' exhaustion from the many meetings required of the man who is the spiritual heartbeat of well over a billion people and how he was frustrated by the Curia who stood in his way when he tried to affect change as Benedict had.

This individual was privy to the political positioning by cardinals behind Francis' back, their tongues wagging with less respect than he thought should be granted the Supreme Pontiff. The rumors had started by some cardinals in high places that the pope was becoming increasingly angry and frustrated by the Vatican political machine.

Colonel Adrien Zellweger was prepared for this moment in time. Zellweger's own twisted and murderous agenda to destroy the church, with the hope that a forced Catholic revival would wash away the sins of the past and begin anew was, in his sick mind, fulfilling the prophesy of St. Malachy. A metamorphosis that Zellweger himself realized he would not live long enough to see, he truly believed that his plan to murder nearly every cardinal of the church was his destiny.

Zellweger had the best access to the Vatican of anyone. He commanded the Swiss Guard and intimately knew the working of the *Gendarmeria* and their special task forces.

The Colonel also knew that with the calculating genius mind of John Deegan it would guarantee a successful outcome to his mission. Now time was of the essence. Would Deegan accept his plot? Was he even well enough? Several of Zellweger's men saw that he was mumbling to himself, pacing back and forth near the Apostolic Palace and going outside the Vatican walls to chain smoke.

The evening of the Papal *Declaratio,* after Francis was tucked safely away in his room, Zellweger met with Inspector General Claudio Festa. They walked around the perimeter of St. Peter's square under the statues of Jesus and his apostles.

"We haven't much time, Inspector. The Conclave will be upon us in a few short weeks. I recommend that we outline our plan and prepare the men immediately, Zellweger said.

"I wholeheartedly agree. I've already called the Rome police and the Italian reserves to determine how many extra men will be available to us. An additional show of strength is needed. Especially with ISIS, Al Qaeda, and Boko Haram and whatever the newest terrorist group is calling themselves these days who are, I'm sure, licking their chops," Festa added. Festa is a man that thinks of every possible contingency.

"Excellent thinking. I was going to mention that very thing to you. My concerns are aligned with yours."

"A daily sweep of the *Domus Marthae Sanctae* will be done until the new Pope is elected. I plan to have everyone of those one hundred and thirty-one rooms in that building checked for any devices that might may put those cardinals in danger while they are here." Festa said, his mind already racing.

"And snipers on the roof tops of the *Domus* I suspect?"

"Naturally, and every rooftop including the Basilica. We will leave nothing to chance."

"Do we know how many Cardinals will be staying at the *Domus* and for how long?"

"Approximately one hundred thirteen, perhaps a few more. I'm hoping the election doesn't take more than a day or two. The more time they spend in the Sistine, the greater our risk becomes."

"True. My position and my oath demand that the Guard protect these cardinals on their way to the Chapel. I will see that my men are stationed along the route and even in the kitchen where their meals are prepared as was done for the last Conclave," Zellweger assured.

The colonel continued, "Communications are vital. You and I must be joined at the hip, Inspector. The world has changed for the worse since 2013. The dangers are enormous."

"Indeed they are. I recommend a meeting tomorrow of our senior men. Depending of course upon the Holy Father's schedule. Are you available in the morning?" Festa asked.

"Late afternoon is better. Francis has a full schedule still."

"Say 4 P.M., then?"

"Yes. Perhaps at the Sistine? We will need blueprints and schematics of the Vatican Museum as well as the Chapel," Zellweger offered.

"Of course. You know what ran through my mind when the announcement was made?"

"Tell me."

"Francis is the one hundred and thirteenth Pope since St. Malachy's prediction. The last Pope."

"A fairytale. It entered my mind as well if I am to be totally honest. We both know that it was medieval witchcraft at best. I for one have more important fish to fry."

CHAPTER 11

The day after the announcement of Pope Francis' resignation, Vic Gonnella was in his New York City office, drinking a double espresso and reading the commentary from both the Italian and
American press with great interest. High up in a steel and glass office
building on 56th Street and Park Avenue, an office space that rivaled
any white shoe law firm or international conglomerate, Vic's personal
corner office was designed to be impressive with rich, mahogany furniture and the latest in communication technology.

Knowing some of the players at the Vatican, Vic had a clear
visual of what was really going on behind those "holy" walls. Gonnella
was getting flashbacks of his time in Rome when he and Raquel were
pursuing John Deegan. He recalled when they saw Deegan outside
the Hotel Bernini Bristol, next to Bernini's Triton fountain in midtown Rome and took chase after him. Vic recalled with word for word
clarity his conversation with Deegan that evening. The entire case was
etched in Vic's mind forever, and was now pouring into his consciousness. Vic sat for a few minutes, his hands covering his face, in total
disbelief of the day's latest events.

Vic buzzed his wife on the office intercom.

"Baby, got a minute?" Vic asked.

"Be right there," Raquel answered abruptly.

A few minutes later Raquel entered Vic's office. Her figure
looked amazing in a tapered, St. John studded knit and matching
pleated skirt. The beige and brown colors complimented her hair and
olive-toned skin nicely. There was no evidence of a baby pouch as Raquel worked hard at the gym to keep herself trim and sexy.

"Vic, I had a few people meeting in my office just now. I love when you call me baby, but how many times do I have to tell you to call me Raquel here? It's a little embarrassing and not professional," Raquel admonished. "But what do you need, honey?"

"Sure, okay. Here look at this. Wait, I'll put it on the big screen."

Vic was behind his massive desk looking at his desktop computer. He punched a button and in a split second the recessed, eighty-inch remote screen, on a wall across the room flicked on.

"I was reading about Pope Francis and then switched to Interpol's I-24/7 as I do everyday. Look what the fuck I found."

I-24/7 is a secure, global police network Interpol shares with law enforcement officers globally allowing better communication between their members.

Raquel read the report aloud.

"Wednesday 21 June 2016…yada yada…Poschiavo, Switzerland, district of Bernina Canton of Graubünden Homicide… Fr. Gustav Miner, 88. Found dead at Augustinian Cloister of Santa Maria. C.O.D. multiple stab wounds, evisceration. Investigation underway. Local police matter."

"Holy shit, Vic. Could it be him? Could it possibly be Deegan?" Raquel asked.
"I'm certainly going to find out. I have a call into an inspector friend at Interpol. I'm sick over this." Vic said.

"Would Deegan dare?"

"Anything is possible. I'm sure Deegan remembers what I said to him in Rome. I told him if he did another murder, I would find him and kill him myself," Vic said.

Vic's secretary interrupted the conversation on the telephone intercom.

"Mr. Gonnella, Inspector Frank of Interpol on line one."

Vic pressed line one and put the call on his speaker.

"Tony, how are you? It's been way too long. I have you on speaker. Raquel is in the room with me," Vic stated.

"How are my dear friends?" Tony Frank said.

"We are all fine. We hope you and your family are all well," Raquel said.

"Thank you. My children are all grown. My wife and I are enjoying our freedom," Frank said laughing.

"Congratulations, Tony. The last time we spoke you weren't Deputy Commissioner," Vic said.

Thank you. I'm still mostly in the Specialized Investigations Unit. I just have another star on my lapel and a few extra Euros per month."

"You are too modest!" Raquel stated.
"Tony, can you shed any light on the latest homicide in Switzerland?" Vic asked.

"I was expecting to speak with you about this homicide. I was getting ready to contact you when your call came in. The deceased priest had been accused of sexually abusing children. The Archdiocese of Lausanne in Geneva sent him to the Cloister in Poschiavo a number of years ago. He was exiled to the nuns because they found the allegations to be credible. Several children were interviewed and all had a similar story to tell about Father Miner. He was ordered by the Archdiocese to spend his life in prayer and penitence. Evidently, the

Archdiocese settled the cases with the families, and details were never announced."

"That always seems to be the church's M.O. Sweep the crime under the rug and throw money at the problem. No different in the States," Vic noted.

"It certainly seems like their pattern, doesn't it?" Tony said.

"Can you give us any details of the homicide?"

"Of course. Miner was tortured before he was eviscerated. His bowels were all over the crime scene, as if the perpetrator pulled them out manually, and strewn them around his small room. I'm sure you have speculated as to the weapon used," Inspector Frank said.

"A shaved, wooden crucifix?" Raquel asked.

"Of course. It looks like your John Deegan may have come out of retirement. Do you have any idea where he might be?" Frank asked.

Raquel noticed that Vic began tapping his chin with a closed fist, an unconscious habit he had acquired as a boy when he was under stress.

" The last we knew he was somewhere in Switzerland. That's why I called you. That's what leads us to believe he is a suspect," Vic said. "If that mother-f.."

Raquel interrupted, "Vic!"

"Interpol has not been asked to get involved at this point, but we are sending our local investigators to look over the shoulders of the local law enforcement authorities. They should be there by now."

"Would you mind keeping us in the loop, Tony?" Vic asked.

"By all means, and if it is indeed Deegan, you know better than anyone he will not stop here," Frank said.

"Right. Thank you. Be in touch, my friend," Vic ended the call.

"It's him, Vic. It has to be Deegan," Raquel said.

"That clearly is an assumption. I guess in a way I'm hoping it is so I can end this thing once and for all."

"So what, you will go and fulfill your promise and kill him in a foreign country? Have you really lost your mind?"

"Absolutely, to both questions."

"So I guess we are going to Switzerland?" Raquel asked.

"Call your mom. Ask her to come to the apartment tonight to watch the baby. We are going on the first plane tomorrow."

"Calm down, will you? Don't you have Deegan's phone number from our discussions with him on the Boy in the Box case in Philly? Why not just call him?"

"And say what? 'Hi, John. Did you kill another priest?' C'mon Raquel, let's be real. Chances are that number is long disconnected," Vic said.

"So, what do we have to lose?"

"The element of surprise for one."

"Just try the number, Vic."

Vic fumbled through his contact information and found Deegan's cell number. He paused for a moment, staring at the screen.

"Here goes nuttin'," Vic said.

Vic pressed the green call button on his cell phone under the name DEEGAN, again using the speaker for Raquel to hear what he was suspecting to be a message in Swiss that the number was no longer in use. The phone rang with that European beeping sound that sounded like two, quick, muffled beeps.

"Well, to what do I owe this honor? The great international, celebrity policeman of truth, justice, and the American way," It was Deegan. He sounded older, his voice weaker.

"How are you, John?" Vic said.

"I've been better. I suspect that lovely Raquel is on the line as well. How is the baby?"

Raquel looked at Vic with astonishment.

"Hello, John, we are all very well," Raquel added.

"Good to hear. Although I'm happy to hear your voices, I am waiting for the reason for this call," Deegan said.

"Okay, I will cut to the chase. I guess with that masterful brain of yours, you have already figured out my motive for calling," Vic said.

"Haven't a clue. Unless you are thinking I should throw my name in to be the next Supreme Pontiff," John laughed.

"An elderly priest was murdered in Poschiavo, Switzerland. Your M.O. is all over this one," Vic said.

"Really? I wasn't aware of this. Perhaps this priest required killing," Deegan said. There was sarcasm dripping from his words.

"That doesn't bring us too much comfort," Raquel said.

"Well, just so you know, I'm retired at the moment."

"Can you account for your whereabouts, John?" Vic asked.

"Depending on when this cleric was killed I may be able to. However, you should know that I've been in the hospital. I'm now resting in the safety and bosom of my darling wife," Deegan said.

"So if we check out this hospital they will verify that you were there?" Raquel asked.

"No, they will not. And I have not mentioned where I am, have I? I haven't used my real name in years, for good reason as you can imagine. My doctors have no idea who I am. My conjecture is that a crucifix was the weapon of choice and it was left at the scene?"

"You still play the game well, John," Vic said.

"No game this time. Why don't you ask me why I am hospitalized? That would be a good and empathetic place to start, don't you think?"

"Okay, we will bite. Why are you there?" Raquel asked.

"I have pancreatic cancer. I've undergone extensive tests and some surgery. I think what you have on your hands is a copycat, my dears," Deegan said.

Raquel looked at Vic and mouthed, *"What the fuck?"*

"If it's true and not another one of your chess games, we are both sorry to hear this news," Vic said.

"No game now. Perhaps you should point your attention to the Holy See. I hear they are pretty good at killing off people who get in their way. They have had plenty of time to perfect the art, don't you know? Anyway, have to go, it's time for my medication." Deegan ended the call as he always had. Abruptly and leaving his listeners hanging.

"What do you think?" Vic asked Raquel.

"He never really lied to us before," Raquel noted.

"But now he may have reason to. He knows his life may be on the line."

"Let's go to Switzerland," Raquel said.

CHAPTER 12

The morning after Deegan's surgery, Dr. Baumer and his staff of oncologists met with both John and Gjuliana to report on the pathology and John's overall condition.

Gjuliana was naturally anxious. John seemed distracted and stoic.

Dr. Baumer was clinical in his approach and did not partake in any greeting or small talk. Deegan looked closely at his mannerism and even more closely to Dr. Eschmann, the psychiatrist for any facial tells they might display. John sat in the winged back chair with Gjuliana sitting in a small chair to his right. Dressed in a white cotton hospital gown, John had a red, wool blanket over his legs for modesty. Gjuliana, in a smart, blue pantsuit held her hands in front of her almost like she was in prayer.

"You seemed to have tolerated the surgery well. The cancer was partially resectable, that is, I was able to remove a good portion of the tumor. Fortunately, we saw no growth into the large blood vessels. Pathology indicates the margins to be clear, and there seems to be no metastasis. That is excellent news for at least a reasonable chance at being completely cured. Any questions so far?" Baumer asked.

"But you didn't remove all of the cancer?" Deegan asked.

"To fully answer your question, Giovanni, I will need to become somewhat technical. Your cancer began in the head of your pancreas. Because you are otherwise healthy, we performed a pancreaticoduodenectomy. This is commonly known as a Whipple procedure. Those many tests we took on you? They indicated you were a good candidate for this delicate surgery. When we spoke last you complained about pain in your shoulders. I explained that we did your surgery in part, laparoscopically. Only about half of the cases of pancreatic cancer we encounter can have this kind of surgery. So, thankfully in your case, much less blood loss, a faster recovery time, and fewer post-surgical complications are indicated. During the procedure it was clear we could not remove the entire tumor without putting your life in danger. The cancer has not spread to the tail of the organ, which is wonderful news. Still with me?" Baumer asked.

John was still looking for signs of the doctor sugar coating the results of the surgery. Dr. Baumer was not one to hold back anything from his patients.

"I fully understand what you are saying, Dr. Baumer," John said. There was a slight hint of sarcasm in his reply. Gjuliana looked at her husband, admonishing him with her eyes.

"Good! Our next course of action is to attempt to shrink the tumor, or remove the tumor if you will, using chemotherapy and chemoradiation. We have several drugs we will be using, which we've had excellent results within the past. Gemzar, the most prescribed for this type disease is the main drug we will be using. Questions, yet?"

"Any side effects?' Gjuliana asked. John seemed annoyed at her question. Dr. Baumer and Dr. Eschmann both took note of John's impatience.

"Very good question, Mrs. De Luca. From the surgery there may be some weight loss. We will do our best to control that with proper nutrition. We will also need to closely monitor his blood sugar levels. Diabetes is possible, but we can control that with medications if that occurs," Baumer said.

"Okay, Dr. Baumer. Let's go for the big question. How long do I have?" Deegan asked.

"I can only give you statistics, Giovanni, as only God knows that answer for sure. The success rate with pancreatic cancer is better than it was twenty or thirty years ago. Our results show that twenty-five percent of our patients in your position live five years or longer. Node-negative patients such as yourself have a higher survival rate.

"So should I take a three or a five year lease on a new Bentley Doctor?" John said jokingly.

"Giovanni, please!" Gjuliana blurted. She was just as upset but trying to hide it for John's sake. She could feel the tears welling up in her eyes.

"Honestly, we never really know. It is very possible, like with any cancer perhaps cells have already spread to other parts of your body. These cells can form new tumors in vital organs and cause death." Dr. Baumer said.

"Well that's certainly hitting between the eyes, Deegan said.

"That is the reality of this disease. Now, we will begin the therapeutic procedures in a week or so. You need to fully recover from the surgery. You can be released in a few days, and return to your home for a while or you can stay with us here."

"We are staying, Doctor Baumer," Gjuliana said.

"I guess I've been told!" Deegan said, squeezing Gjuliana's hand and forcing a smile when he looked at her.

Colonel Zellweger attempted to call Deegan at the *Klinik Hirslanden* a number of times. Zellweger was starting to be concerned that Deegan would not take on the challenge he had proposed at their meeting at Lake Lugano. Or perhaps Deegan's health condition was rapidly deteriorating. Either way, Zellweger was quickly becoming a bag of nerves. Some of his men noticed that the colonel had begun mumbling to himself, pacing back and forth near the Apostolic Palace, and smoking more than usual.

Zellweger, having access to private plane transportation and a pilot, flew to Zürich for a face-to-face with Deegan.

Again in the disguise of a German tourist, Zellweger arrived at the *Klinik* early the evening of the day Deegan received his prognosis. The Colonel, using his guile and deception worked his way past the reception desk and up to Deegan's third floor suite.

"Well, if it isn't my old friend from Bavaria! How are you, Hans?" Deegan said to cloche Zellweger from Gjuliana.

"My dear friend, Giovanni, how are you? I came for a short visit," Zellweger said in a good but put on German accent.

"May I present my wife, Gjuliana? This is Hans. We met not long ago," Deegan lied.

Pleasantries were passed all around. Gjuliana wasn't buying it for one minute.

"My love, please let Hans and me have a few minutes in private," Deegan said. Gjuliana quickly retired to the bedroom.

"I'm not surprised to see you, Colonel. Your behavior is quite compulsive, wouldn't you agree?"

"Deegan, I tried to call you to check in on your condition. I was concerned is all."

"Please colonel, some decorum. Do not use my real name. To respond to your check in, I believe you are more concerned that I have rejected your plan, I imagine." Deegan said.

"Well, of course. By now I'm certain that you have heard that

Francis, as I told you, has indeed resigned. Time is of the essence now as the conclave is nearing. Can't you just see it? The time to strike has never been better, Deegan, I mean, Giovanni. Christ. Together we can bring the See to its damn knees, to make a fresh start and eliminate the filth, and have you heard the latest?" Without even giving John a chance to answer, Zellweger continued on his grandstand. "Allow me to fill you in," Zellweger was now speaking very rapidly, and the crazed look in his eyes had escalated since Deegan had seen him last. Zellweger continued, "Pope Emeritus Benedict has come out with confirming information. Yes, he resigned due to his poor health but he now has exposed a homosexual lobby that clouded his papacy. He does not mention anyone by name but emphatically states four or five people, all homos, tried to influence decisions at the Vatican. I can tell you their names if you like…no matter. These sodomizing bastards helped each other move up in the Vatican. Within the Vatican! The Holy Church! Do you hear what I am saying? Benedict also admits he was surprised Francis was chosen as his successor. I can only imagine why. You want to know why? Because Francis is owned by a cabal of degenerate pedophiles and homosexuals that's why. There! I've said it! Every single, last, mother-fucking cardinal in this entire world is complicit in the crimes of sodomy and child rape…every one of them!" Zellweger's arms were flailing in gesture.

"Colonel, you should calm yourself. You will cloud your judgment with this kind of ranting. Take a step back and look at yourself," Deegan said.

As if the colonel didn't even hear Deegan, he continued, "Are you able to assist me, Deegan? I need your cunning intellect, your masterful, plotting mind to fulfill my obligation to so many of the misled and misguided faithful," Zellweger ranted. He made the sign of the cross and looked up toward heaven.

"Colonel, I have been very good at some things in my life. Some that I am not so proud of, but I can tell you, I do not make apologies. For example, making money, lots and lots of money was child's play for me. Killing people also came easy. I could kill a person and go have a great, big, spaghetti and meatball dinner with no remorse. I've also been excellent at planning ahead, figuring things out with little available information. And one of my best attributes is the ability to recognize a fellow survivor when I meet one," Deegan said. He sat upright in his winged chair.

"Survivor? I fail to see what you are referring to," Zellweger said, his sweaty brow now furrowed in a suspicious manner.

"Colonel, you have been a victim of clergy sexual abuse just like I have. And more likely than not, during the most critical time of your life. Seven maybe eight years of age. When your sexuality was beginning to just develop. And the abuse, by a trusted priest or other clergy member continued into your late teens or beyond." Deegan said. He watched Zellweger's hawkish face closely.

"Nonsense!" Zellweger said. The twitching of Zellweger's face and the trembling of his lips were the tell signs that Deegan was correct in his assumptions.

"You retreated into the military and then into the Swiss Guard with a single mindset to become *Oberst*. Protecting the Supreme Pontiff with your own life, was your attempt to gain favor with God, the one who let you down the most."

"You're insane, Deegan."

"I probably am, but that doesn't mean I'm not correct. You've never married, but not due to your dedication to the career or your family's legacy to the guard. You never married because you could never understand your own sexuality. It was robbed from you at a young age. Your hatred of homosexuals is not because of your faith and the fact that you were told being gay was sinful. That deep hatred is because for a long time you weren't sure if you were attracted to men."

"I have never touched another man with passion… never in my life," Zellweger said.

"But you were touched *by* men. And there were times you looked forward to it. That you may have even enjoyed the experience and enjoyed the fact you were pleasing a man of God, but I know it also left you feeling very confused," Deegan said. His clinical review of Zellweger's past was dead on point.

"Very well, then. I admit to you I was molested by a priest. By several priests if you want the bold and perverted truth. Even a bishop who later became a cardinal molested me as well. So what? Does that take away the need to destroy these evil men? Or more likely does it add credence to my design to rebuild the church with true priests?" Zellweger asked. His trembling stopped and his face now seemed relaxed.

"Colonel, why did you kill that priest at the Cloister in Poschiavo? Was he one of the men who abused you? And why did you make it seem like I did the murder?"

"What are you talking about? I would never do such a thing," Zellweger responded. The Colonel stood hovering over Deegan.

"You would never kill an elderly, lone priest, but you would kill one hundred plus Cardinals? Of course you killed Father Miner. I did my research, Colonel. The pig Miner was ordained at the Seminaire St. Charles Borromee in Fribourg, Switzerland. At the time you were in grade school in Geneva, Father Miner was a priest in your parish. Years later Miner was accused of sexual acts against children and removed to the Cloister where you ended his miserable life. You had motivation, vengeance; and you were in Switzerland the night he was killed. You likely checked into the Cloister as a visiting tourist with forged identification. You carved a wooden cross and mutilated one of your tormentors. And you feel so good, you can't wait to do it again."

"Deegan I swear, I will…"

"Under this blanket I have a 40mm Heckler and Koch semi automatic. I will blow a hole in you the size of the main gate to the

Vatican. Now, quietly turn and leave this place. If I see you again, you will die that moment. As far as your plan goes, do what you need to do. As far as I'm concerned, I don't have a dog in this fight," Deegan said.

Zellweger saw the cold killer in Deegan's eyes. He turned and briskly walked from the suite.

At that moment, Deegan knew he had a problem more dangerous than his cancer.

CHAPTER 13

The Roman Catholic Church is one of the most complex, layered, and deceitful organizations on earth.

At the heart of the church is the Roman Curia. The Curia's name derives from the Medieval Latin word *court*. Not as a court of law, but a court to the Pope which acts as the central government of the Holy See, the central government of the church.

And, as with any large, governmental organization, the church has cabinets. In the Catholic Church these are headed by cardinals, and in some cases diocesan bishops and are called Congregations.

Falling under that are several congregations, each significant, reflecting the faith-based work of the Church. Cardinals and archbishops vie to head those positions.

As an example; the Congregation for the Doctrine of the Faith, the Congregation for Divine Worship and the Discipline of the Sacraments, the Congregation for Institutes of Consecrated Life and Societies of Apostolic Life, and several others.

But, the most important and powerful position within the Roman Curia is The Secretary of State of His Holiness, The Pope. This Cardinal Secretary is appointed by the reigning pope and is responsible for political and diplomatic matters and functions of the Holy See to the rest of the world. The Secretary of State leaves upon the death or resignation of the pontiff. The next pope selects his own cardinal to fill that position. Securing their own position takes on a life of its own for these cardinals with inner politics and posturing. In what some call the highest court on this planet, no one seems to trust anyone.

During any period of *sede vacante,* the vacant seat, many important details at the Vatican are relegated to the *Camerlengo* of the

Holy Roman Church. The *Camerlengo* is responsible for the property and finances of the church. The largely ceremonial work begins with the Camerlengo declaring that a pope is officially deceased. For example, when Pope John Paul II died, the *Camerlengo* asked, *"Karol Jozef dormisme? Karol Jozef are you sleeping?"*

The Camerlengo then takes the 'Ring of the Fisherman" and cuts it with shears in the presence of cardinals signifying the end of that pope's reign and authority.

Organizing the voting for the new Supreme Pontiff falls under the ceremonial responsibility of the *Camerlengo*. The meeting between the two high officials and Zellweger and Festa unfortunately was going to bring out the arrogance in them all as the conclave drew nearer.

At the same time, while the church is in *sede vacante*, the governance of the church falls upon the College of Cardinals. The *Camerlengo* has no authority in such State matters, but the two department heads must work together for everything to run smoothly.

Cardinal Giuseppe Magnone the current Secretary of State and Cardinal Paulo Bazzini, the *Camerlengo* called Colonel Zellweger and Inspector Festa for a meeting at the Apostolic Palace two days after the announcement of the resignation of Pope Francis. Zellweger and Festa were unaware of the agenda these two prominent men had set.

Each Cardinal had two assistants with them. Magnone's two priests, one a monsignor, were both young and officious. Ready to take notes and record the meeting. Bazzini's two priests, both very young men, seemed at bit more flighty but very attentive. Zellweger thought to himself, *they are all raging homosexuals.*

"The communication of the Conclave is completed. Now we must attend to details of the election of the new Supreme Pontiff. We would like to know your plans for security of the attending Cardinals" Bazzini said. As the *Camerlengo*, Bazzini had an air of authority and a tone that was a bit condescending.

"If I may, Commander?" Inspector Festa began, "We are nearly prepared with the additional manpower required for the conclave. The exact numbers of men and their positioning is highly confidential to prevent any leaks of vital information."

One of Bazzini's priests squirmed in his chair, pursed his lips, and let out an audible sigh.

"Inspector, I am the sitting Secretary of State to his Holiness. The security of the cardinals during this conclave is of the utmost concern to The Holy See. You will divulge any and all information to us," Cardinal Magnone said, his voice getting louder.

Zellweger interjected. "Your Eminence, pardon me, and with all due respect to your position, the security of this pope and the cardinals, and whoever the future pope may be rests with the two people you have before you. We have both reviewed the security details for this conclave and are in total agreement with the overall plan. Our men are all well trained and ready for any potential breach. However, the plans we have will not be allowed to be exposed to anyone outside of our authority."

"Is this a matter of trust, Colonel?" Bazzini asked.

"I suppose it is, Eminence. All of us here are well aware of the leaks which have occurred within the walls of the Vatican. I'm telling you here and now, if you have specific concerns on security, we will listen and act accordingly. Otherwise, our plans are secret," Zellweger said.

Bazzini's two young priests looked at each other and made a point of letting everyone see them rolling their eyes. Magnone's two priests made no such physical comments and busied themselves taking copious notes.

"Do I have to pull rank and go to a higher authority? Do I need to ask the Holy Father to insist that you comply with our requests?" Magnone asked.

"Feel free to speak with His Holiness, Your Eminence. I will tell you that the Holy Father has never interfered with any of our security measures. With the exception of when he wanted to touch the faithful, spontaneously stopping his motorcade, Pope Francis has made his thoughts very clear to me. Security is strictly in our hands," Zellweger insisted.

One of Bazzini's priests leaned over and whispered into the other priest's ear, shielding his lips with his hand.

Festa cleared his throat loudly, "I've had just about enough of these two and their mocking our authority. My patience has worn thin. If you have any specific questions regarding security, now is the time to ask. We are both very busy at the moment and I for one will not sit here and be insulted."

Bazzini looked at the two priests with furiously scolding eyes.

"Gentleman it is not our purpose in any way to be confrontational. Our concern is terrorism. The cardinals of the church will all be in the same locations for the duration of the conclave. The threat of a bomb or an attack by the Muslim extremists is greater than ever. An incident at the living quarters and at the Sistine Chapel is worrisome to us. So tell us what are you doing to counter such activity?" Cardinal Bazzini asked.

"Your question has been asked and answered, Eminence," Zellweger said abruptly.

"Eminences, our counter-terrorist group has been adequately strengthened. You will notice in a few days, highly trained and vetted members of the Italian military inside and outside of Vatican City. I will not be specific about numbers. We are certainly aware of what is going on in the world today and we also are quite concerned. This is nothing new to either Colonel Zellweger or me. Our plans include various scenarios all of which we are prepared to handle, of that make no mistake. I hope you understand our need for strict confidence with all due respect, Your Eminences," Festa added.

Colonel Zellweger was now leering at both of Bazzini's priests with a look of contempt. Zellweger's cold eyes were darting from one priest to the other. The young priests kept their eyes lowered, both feeling Zellweger's hazel glare.

Cardinal Magnone paused for a moment and spoke softly and slowly. "Very well, gentleman. Let us adjourn this meeting with a prayer for the safety of all involved with the conclave."

CHAPTER 14

The morning after Colonel Zellweger was unceremoniously chased from Deegan's suite at the *Klinik*, John and Gjuliana were waiting for their breakfast to be served. They were sitting at a table on the veranda outside of their suite, overlooking lush trees that were gently swaying in a light, warm breeze. A wrought iron table with a green-speckled, white marble top was set with German made Versace by Rosenthal dinnerware imprinted with the striking head of Medusa.

John could sense that Gjuliana's mood was tense. Breakfast arrived. Gjuliana had asked for some feta cheese and a croissant, with a cappuccino. John was served a hot millet porridge that was cooked in almond milk topped with organic strawberries. Hot water with lemon was his drink.

"Lovely! This macrobiotic diet will probably kill me before the cancer does," John proclaimed.

"John, I have something to say. We were both born and raised in the Bronx, and every once in a while the Bronx comes to the surface with me. 'Hans, my new friend from Germany' my ass. I am no fool. Who was that strange man and what the hell are you up to?" Gjuliana demanded.

John took a spoonful of porridge and made a face as if it tasted like cod liver oil. He plunked the spoon back into the bowl and glared at the breakfast for a few moments.

"He is strange, and he is not a friend. I doubt that he will be returning," John said.
"That hasn't answered my questions."

"He is the thirty-fifth Commander of the Pontifical Swiss Guard," John said.

"And I'm Mary Poppins. Who was that man?"

"I'll say it in German, *Oberst der Schweizer Garde.*"

"I don't speak German. I will not ask you again, John."

"That was Commander Andrien Zellweger of the Pontifical Swiss Guard. Really and truly."

"And if I am to believe you, what was he doing here? Does it have anything to do with your past?"

"In a manner of speaking, yes. That man is a maniac. Look at me, calling the kettle black. He has a scheme to eradicate the evil men of the Vatican and has asked me to join him," John said.

"What scheme? Stop speaking in riddles and just tell me what this is all about. Don't you think I have a right to know? Especially now?"

"I've told you all I am going to tell you, my love. You don't need to know any more. Suffice it to say, I have no intention of helping this man. Now let's just eat our breakfast and enjoy this beautiful day."

"Are you certain?"

"Of course I am. Look around you. Have you ever seen such a morning?" John laughed.

"No, are you certain that whatever this commander is scheming that you will not be part of it?"

"Yes, I'm certain. Can I have a piece of cheese?"

"No, and of that, *I* am certain."

Vic Gonnella busied himself doing research on cancer hospitals in Switzerland while Raquel made travel, baby-sitter arrangements, and cleared her schedule for the next week. Raquel also made arrangements with friends of hers and Vic's at JFK airport's Transportation Security Administration to transport their personal firearms to and from Europe. Raquel carried her Beretta PX4 Storm Compact while Vic preferred his Glock 22 heavy caliber automatic.

Vic found several cancer treatment centers in Switzerland's largest city. Vic called a friend at Sloan Kettering Memorial Hospital is New York City, a well known oncologist, and asked him to recommend the best hospital with five star accommodations in Zürich. Without hesitation his friend referred the *Klinik Hirslanden.*

At 10:50 the next morning, arriving on Swiss Air flight 15 rested and well fed, Vic and Raquel took the short ride in a rented, sleek, silver AMG GT S, from the airport in Kloten to Zürich.

"I am in love with this whip," Vic said, as he punched the 503 horsepower engine.

"I think the best invention ever made was the GPS. We will be at the *Klinik* in no time. I just hope you selected the right hospital. At worst we will need a couple of days to find Deegan if he's at another place," Raquel said.

"I know how he thinks Raquel, well, maybe just a bit. He would select the place that would give him the best chance for a cure. Money certainly is not an object."

"Time will tell, won't it?"

"I'm getting one of these cars when we get back. It's perfect.

Two seats, one for me and one for my golf clubs," Vic said.

"No, Vic, one seat is reserved for your girlfriend… and that would be me, you jerk," Raquel said with a chuckle.

"Okay, you get to pick the color, just nothing Puerto Rican," Vic laughed.

Vic and Raquel approached the reception desk at *Klinik Hirslanden*. The desk is surrounded by inlaid, dark cherry wood with a light green granite counter top.

"Good afternoon. I hope you speak English," Raquel said to the pretty young woman at the desk.

"Yes, of course, and five other languages. You have an American accent, I see. Maybe from New York?" The receptionist inquired. Behind the desk, in the same marble as the counter top was an elegant K H logo.

"Yes, good for you. Have you spent any time in the states?" Raquel asked. Raquel had a marvelous way of knocking down barriers and making fast friends.

"I lived in Upper Manhattan for a few years. I studied journalism at Columbia University. And look what I'm doing now! Nothing to do with my major."

"I went to Columbia as well. Where did you live?"

"The Inwood section. My apartment was right on Broadway. I loved it there. So diverse! Are you Dominican by any chance?"

Raquel seethed for a scant second. Some Puerto Ricans and Dominicans, depending on the mood, have a problem being mistaken for one another.

"I'm a proud Puerto Rican. But you were very close. And, you?" Raquel asked.

"I was born in Sicily. In Palermo."

"What is your name?"

"Angela. Angela Quagliata. Yours?"

"I'm Raquel, and this is my boyfriend, Vic."

Vic gave a modest smile and tried very hard not to look at Angela's delightfully abundant cleavage.

"So what brings you here, if I may ask, Angela?" Raquel asked.

"What brings us anywhere? In my case, it was a man. He is long gone so evidently it was the wrong man."

"Been there, done that," Raquel replied quickly.

"Vic's father has been diagnosed with pancreatic cancer. We were told that the *Klinik* is doing great things with that particular disease. We were hoping for a tour and to spend some time with your administrator to discuss admission."

Angela moved a few files on her desk and smiled at Vic and Raquel. "Yes, you have come to the right place. I can arrange for a tour immediately. As a matter of fact, I will conduct your visit. Please give me a moment while I get someone to watch the desk," Angela said.

Vic joined in the conversation. "I have a question, if I may. My father is very particular. He will not stay in a normal hospital room. Do you have accommodations for my mother as well?"

"But, of course. Depending upon his budget we can put him in a private room for two, or alternatively, we have luxurious suites available.

"Money is not an issue. May we see the suites?" Vic asked.

"Let's take the tour. The suites are on the third floor. We will work our way there. Ah… good, here is my replacement."

Angela came from behind the reception desk. She wore a short, beige Italian knit dress that clung to a magnificent figure. Her matching beige three-inch peep-toe high heels were just the right finish for her outfit.

Raquel tugged down at her own short, brown skirt thinking Angela's skirt was way too short.

Vic took Angela in, from top to bottom. Her long, brown hair and large, chestnut color eyes with a perfect, white smile put a slight grin on Vic's face. Raquel almost laughed at Vic's reaction.

Angela led the way, walking between but just a bit ahead of Raquel and Vic.

"Let's begin by going to the first floor offices and solarium. That will lead us to the kitchen."

"Take your time," Vic said.

Raquel flipped Vic a bird, that she held close to her side and mouthed, *"Fuck you."* Vic reached over and gave Raquel's hand a squeeze and puckered his lips "throwing" her a kiss. They both smiled.

The trio soon made their way to a passenger elevator up to the third floor to inspect the suite area.

The elevator door opened and the feeling of obvious elegance hit them.

Plush carpeting and classic oil paintings adorned the rich, inlaid maple and oak, wood paneled walls. Each painting had subtle ceiling lighting that highlighted the artwork perfectly. Luxurious antique chairs and divans were in perfect harmony with the well-placed antique tables, each topped with old world reading lamps. Crystal candelabras dotted the eighteen-foot high ceilings.

"This place is something out of a book," Raquel said.

"Thank you. We've attempted to make this an elegant living experience. Our patients need all the luxury they wish to have, and of course, afford," Angela said is a low toned voice.

"How many patients are here now?" Vic asked.

"I believe only one at the moment. We have six suites. I will show you one. Right this way, please." Angela said.

Vic mouthed to Raquel, *"He's here!"*

CHAPTER 15

The same night that Vic and Raquel traveled the three thousand nine hundred miles from New York to Zürich, Switzerland, Colonel Adrien Zellweger had taken a trip himself, albeit not nearly as far.

His Holiness, Pope Francis took to his room early that evening leaving Colonel Zellweger to go about his business. Zellweger flew a small, private plane, dressed again as the German tourist, to the town of Sulmona in the Abruzzo region of Italy. It was a quick flight from Rome, barely thirty-five minutes, when Zellweger was met by a small, late model, blue Fiat Sedan. The driver, Rocco Rotigliano, a Sicilian and a local with ties to the Cosa Nostra, *mafia*, in Palermo, was of joint mind with Zellweger. Rotigliano despised homosexuals as much or more than Zellweger, and he, too, was severely sexually molested as a child by his parish priest. Rotigliano wrongly saw pedophilia and homosexuality as one in the same.

Zellweger had previously met the Sicilian mafia man through his law enforcement associates when Zellweger was second in command of the Swiss Guard. The Colonel had asked for Rotigliano's "assistance" with another delicate matter, and fifteen thousand Euros changed hands. Zellweger was happy, Rotigliano was happy, and his mob bosses were very happy.

That job was fairly straightforward. A monsignor, one Gaspare Battapaglia, who was based in Palermo was heavily involved with a child trafficking ring with ties to a group of priests in Rome. Monsignor Battapaglia was gunned down on the *Via Oreto*, in a seedy part of Palermo. The official report stated that the probable cause of the homicide was robbery.

Rotigliano knew nothing of Zellweger's grandiose plan to kill every cardinal at the upcoming conclave.

All Rotigliano knew and cared about now was that Zellwe-ger had a 'piece of work' to accomplish in the tiny town of Pacentro, a twelve minute drive by car from the small airport in Sulmona. He also knew that Zellweger would pay him handsomely for a few hours of his time.

Rotigliano, a dark, barrel chested, thick necked man with enormous forearms deposited the colonel at a restaurant in Pacentro, *Taverna de li Caldora*. It was evening, so Zellweger could not take in the sights of Pacentro, a medieval town which boasts a twelfth century ruined castle, quaint homes, and stone faced churches. Barely twelve hundred people inhabit quiet Pacentro, making it the perfect backdrop for Zellweger's current mission.

At the *Taverna*, Zellweger sat on the outside patio enjoying a glass of local, white wine as the commander only allowed himself one glass when he flew. He could scarcely see the beauty of the stone build-ing that housed the *Taverna*, or the medieval piazza that surrounded the restaurant.

An elderly man, dressed in a tan shirt with a well-worn, blue, sports jacket and a black fedora was about to enter the Taverna as well and caught Zellweger's friendly demeanor. They spoke in Italian.

"Good evening, young man. A beautiful day followed by a pleasant evening."

"And now a delicious dinner," Zellweger replied.
"This is the best place in all of Pacentro. Possibly all of *L'Aquila* for that matter."

"Maybe all of Abruzzo?" Zellweger laughed.

"I would not argue with that statement."

"Enjoy your dinner, young man. I'm meeting an old friend inside, otherwise I would impose myself upon you."

"That would have been delightful," Zellweger said.

"My name is Emilio Caserta. Look me up next time you are in town. I will show you around the place of my birth. There is much to see and more to taste. We Abruzzese are the best cooks Italy has to offer."

"Indeed I will, Signore. You can count on seeing me again," Zellweger said, smiling broadly.

CHAPTER 16

Zellweger couldn't recall having a better meal than what he had had for dinner that night at the *Taverna de li Caldora*.

A small antipasto with a variety of local salami and cheeses, a homemade pasta dish with peas and wild mushrooms, and lamb chops with Majella herbs. The herbs were named after a massif in the Central Apennine mountains that bordered the provinces of Chieti, Pescara, and L'Aquila in Abruzzo.

A double espresso and some freshly made anisette cookies and a few small cream puffs ended the meal nicely.

Colonel Zellweger paid his bill and walked across the *piazza*. He waited in the dark, hidden in a small alleyway between two, small stores, a cigarette hung from his mouth.

The old man who Zellweger had encountered earlier that evening, Emilio Caserta, left shortly after with his "friend". The two men embraced and kissed each other on both cheeks in the Italian fashion and went their separate ways.

Zellweger followed Caserta inconspicuously at a good distance. The Colonel started to gain on his prey to the point that he could hear that the old man was singing to himself. The song sounded familiar to Zellweger. After a minute, Zellweger recognized the tune. It was a Gregorian Chant that was nearing its end.
"Sis, Jesu, nostrum guadium,
Qui es futurus praemium
Sit nostra in te Gloria,
Per cuncta semper saecula.
Amen.

Caserta continued humming the chant as he came into a medieval, cobblestone walkway that led to some stone steps.

Zellweger moved silently up to Caserta and tapped him on his shoulder. Caserta turned quickly.

"Oh, my God, you startled me."

"I'm so sorry, *Father* Caserta, I see you no longer dress as a priest. You know, it was foolish of you not to change your name and return to your hometown. You made it just too easy to find you," Zellweger said. The Colonel towered over the five-foot-three Caserta.

"Now see here, young man. What do you want with me? Be on your way before I call for the *carabinieri.*"
"I'm afraid you will not have time for that, Signore. The time has come for you to sing your song to Jesus, if He will have you, but I doubt that He will. Remember what you did to those children? It was an abomination! Selling them to your sick priest friends, passing them around like little toys for their amusement."

Caserta opened his mouth to scream but even if he did, no sound would have come out because in an instant the combat trained Zellweger slit the old priest's throat from ear to ear with one motion of a sharpened, wooden crucifix. As Caserta dropped to his knees, the Colonel buried the cross deep into his victim's chest, then kicked the old man on the side of his head sending him down in an almost fetal position.

Zellweger calmly walked back to the piazza where Rocco Rotigliano was waiting in his car. The dark of night hid not only his victim's blood but also the deranged look in his eyes.

An hour later, Zellweger entered the main gate of Vatican City where he was saluted by two of his Swiss Guard. Business as usual.

CHAPTER 17

Angela decided to show them two of the remaining five suites that were open. The rooms were every bit as impressive as the common areas.

The first suite was ultra modern with Scandinavian furniture throughout, original productions of modern art on bright white walls, and plasma televisions in all of the three of its rooms. The window coverings were simple, blue mini-blinds.

The second suite was more classical with French country furniture with show wood sofas and high back chairs, antique coffee and end tables, landscape oil paintings, and French tapestries and Persian rugs that looked like the real thing.

"Angela, would it be at all possible, before we see your administrator to discuss details, if we could chat with the patient in the occupied suite? You know, to see if they are satisfied?" Raquel asked.

"I'm afraid that we cannot allow that. The privacy of the patient is of the utmost important to us," Angela replied.

Vic fumbled with his cell phone, pretending to take a call. He walked out of one room of the suite into another. In a flash he returned to join Angela and Raquel.

"Ladies, I'm afraid we must leave. An emergency has occurred back in the states that I must become involved via a conference call back at our hotel. Perhaps we can return tomorrow?" Vic asked.

"Oh, of course. Just call us before you plan to arrive. I will give you my card on your way out," Angela replied.

"You have been so sweet, Angela. Thank you for your time and hospitality," Raquel said.

"You know, we are new to Zürich. May we offer to take you to dinner tonight? I should be done with my business in a few hours. Our treat. We actually have no idea even where to go. Of course, you and your boyfriend as well," Vic said.

Angela turned to Raquel.

"How did you say that? Been there done that."

Everyone laughed.

"I would be delighted to accompany you. Does the offer go for my partner as well?" Angela asked.

Vic was momentarily stunned. "*I like her even better now,*" he thought. Raquel nodded affirmatively.

"Okay, great, and thank you. We don't get out too much. Living in Zürich is quite expensive. I'm actually starting to look for a better paying position. Let me check with Lisbeth and I will ring you up and tell you where we will meet. Say nine o'clock?"

"Perfect. Can't wait to meet Lisbeth," Raquel said. She looked at Vic and almost burst into laughter at the stunned look on his face.

Vic and Raquel finally checked into their hotel room. They had gone directly to the *Klinik* and the time difference was beginning to take its toll. They needed showers and rest.

Raquel booked a junior suite with a balcony and a view of Lake

Zürich at The Dolder Grand hotel. Raquel couldn't help but notice that one night's stay was more money than two months rent in her apartment while she was an NYPD patrolman, just a short few years ago. Life had been good.

"Baby, I need a shower and a shave, and some sleep. Oh, and a little sex wouldn't hurt," Vic said. He laughed at the sex comment.

"I guess you got all worked up following Angela around. And by the way, what was that dinner invitation all about? Was that from force of habit when you were single or did you forget I was standing there? Jerk," Raquel said.

"First of all, I have you. Why do I need anyone else? Second of all, she's only all right. Third of all she's a lesbian, and finally Miss Jealous Rican, we need to get as much information as possible from Angela and figure out a way to get in to see Deegan."

"Only all right, my butt. I almost slipped on your drool walking down the hall at the *Klinik*. Angela is drop dead gorgeous and a very sweet person. If I were gay, she wouldn't stand a chance," Raquel laughed.

"We need a plan to get into Deegan's rooms. Any ideas?" Vic asked.

"Why not just call him and tell him you figured out where he is?"

"Yeah sure… 'Hello, John, we were just in the neighborhood and thought we would stop over. I brought a cake?'" Vic asked rhetorically.

"Maybe we just go to the *Klinik* tomorrow, I wear a low cut something and my tight, leather pants with stilettos and keep Angela busy while you just knock on Deegan's door?" Raquel began doing a faux strip tease.

"Okay Ruiz, let's get into the shower. You need some attention."

Dinner that evening was interesting. Angela picked a local bistro that had great food a nice jazz trio and the price didn't even break the bank.

The more Vic and Raquel got to know Angela, the more they liked her. Lisbeth was a surprise. A pretty girl with very short, light brown hair, Lisbeth is much quieter person and more reserved than Angela. She could be described as cute and shy… and very bright. Angela introduced Lisbeth as 'my brilliant scientist,' and tried on several occasions to draw her into the conversations at the table, without too much success.

Lisbeth tried to explain what she did at work but Vic and Raquel had absolutely no idea what quantum physics meant, nor its application in real life.

"So tell us you two… what kind of work do you both do?" Angela asked.

"Well, Vic is in finance and I'm a stay-at-home mommy at the moment," Raquel said.

"Real boring stuff, you know… stocks, bonds, derivatives, options. Not much to talk about there," Vic said.

"My brother is an accountant in Palermo so I fully understand," Angela said as she looked up to the ceiling and laughed.

Lisbeth simply smiled.

"Angela, I'm a bit intrigued by the *Klinik* and what is done there. So, only if a person is wealthy they can afford the best care? If not, that's just the way things are?" Vic asked.

"On the contrary, Vic. In Switzerland, healthcare is universal. What that means is you must have private health insurance. Everyone in this county pays eight percent of their personal income. Should the cost of the insurance premium be higher, only then does the government pay a subsidy to the citizen and they in turn pay the insurance company. Anyone who needs to come to the *Klinik* is welcome. If they can afford the luxury of our concierge service that is, of course, the responsibility of the patient," Angela replied.

"The goal in Switzerland is to encourage general public health while reducing costs. It really works well," Lisbeth finally chimed in.
"Our country is a disaster with healthcare, a total mess," Raquel said.

"We are fourth in the world in life expectancy. The United States is thirty-sixth. Our doctors don't medicate, they seek a cure; forgive me for being so bold," Angela said.

"Are you kidding? I had a baby a year ago and I'm still getting bills from doctors I've never even met. It's what we called a cluster fuck when I was a cop," Raquel slipped.

"Oh, you were a police officer?" Angela asked.

"Ah... yes for a short time. Then Vic came and swept me off my feet and that was that."

"So interesting! Did you ever have to shoot anyone?" Angela asked.

"Only once and it was because Vic wanted sex on our first date," Raquel replied quickly to help defuse the line of questioning. Everyone laughed.

"Angela, I'm intrigued by the one patient you have in your suites. I know we can't meet him or her but can you tell us just a bit about his condition and prognosis?" Vic asked.

Angela looked behind her as if someone might be listening. It's a thing people do when they want to reveal a secret or tell an ethnic joke.

"It's a man. He is not very old, but not young either. I think about mid-sixties. Very jovial at times, yet very somber at times. I suspect if I had that disease my moods would be far worse. Anyway, he is here with his wife. They are both Swiss citizens but with an Italian surname. The man speaks fluent Italian with a New York accent. It's very cute."

"And the wife?" Raquel asked with an interested smile.

"She is definitely American although I heard her speaking Albanian on the telephone. She is quite lovely, but her sadness comes through… naturally.

Vic looked at Raquel. They had now confirmed Deegan was at the *Klinik*.

The dinner was fun. Vic danced with Raquel, Raquel danced with Angela, Vic danced with Angela, and Angela danced alone at times. Every guy in the place wanted to dance with Angela and Raquel and for good reasons. Angela was dressed is a tighter, shorter skirt than she had at the *Klinik*; Raquel in her form fitting, black, leather pants and spiked red heels. Lisbeth was dressed like she was going to work, but Vic could tell she was cloaking a killer body. Vic was good like that.

Back at the Dolder Grand, Vic and Raquel were relaxing on their balcony, gazing out at the moonlit lake. Vic lit a Davidoff *Robusto* and poured Marie Brizard anisette into two cordial glasses. The couple was sitting on a plush divan.

"Man, this is the life. I think we retire here. Live a longer life, make another baby or two, and live happily ever after," Vic said as he puffed away on his cigar.

Raquel draped her leg over Vic's, looked at the sky and purred. "And be closer to Angela," Raquel chuckled and took a sip of the cordial.

"Holy shit. I never knew it, but I think you may have tendencies!" Vic said excitedly.

"That girl exudes sexuality. Angela doesn't just dance she makes love to the music. I was soooo turned on when you were dancing with her."

Vic began to get aroused just thinking of the possibilities when his cell phone rang.

The illuminated screen read DEEGAN.

CHAPTER 18

Pope Francis could not sleep. His decision to resign was weighing heavily on his mind. Prayer, hot cocoa, and a boring Franz List concerto could not cure his insomnia.
His Holiness summoned his Secretary of State Cardinal Magnone.

"Giuseppe, thank-you for coming at this late hour. I feel I may have made a mistake with my resignation. It seems to me I have failed and am only running away from the insurmountable problems in our church."

"Your Holiness, I don't believe you are running. I believe you are simply trying to survive. Your position would kill any five men," Magnone said.

"I may have been better off dead than to feel the emptiness I now have."

"Your Holiness, your predecessor Benedict felt the same. We have sick cancers within our church, and they are slowly destroying us. There seems to be no easy answers."

"I confess I knew about the pedophile problems when I was a priest in Buenos Aries. We all protected Holy Mother Church and for what? Reputation? Money? Now the problem has escalated and is choking the life out of us," Pope Francis admitted.

"I have similar regrets, Your Holiness. I feel nothing but contempt for what I see and hear. Our own priests have run amok molesting children while their superiors cover for them. Perhaps there is an argument to end celibacy?"

"Perhaps you are correct, but the Curia will resist this to the last cardinal. Old habits die hard behind these walls, my friend."

"And the homosexual lobby is stronger than when Benedict resigned. Just the other day I called a meeting with Cardinal Bazzini. His two assistants are fragrantly shameless."

"Noted. One of the last things I will do is reassign Bazzini and send his two boyfriends to obscure parishes in Africa."

"Forgive me, Your Holiness, but that is what we always do. Send these so-called priests away to a different place, but that only perpetuates the problem. It has become a vicious cycle."

"You are correct that there are no easy answers, my loyal Giuseppe. It is making me grow more despondent day by day, and frankly, much weaker in spirit. Don't we owe the faithful of our Lord's church much better than we are offering?"

"Perhaps the next Pontiff will be better guided?" Cardinal Magnone asked.

"Who do you think will be elected?"

"Ah, that is a good question. Among the *papabili* there are several names that seem to be the most likely to succeed you. Cardinal Schonborn is a progressive. It seems when he speaks, he commands the respect of the *Cardinali*. The conservatives, who will do nothing to make serious changes in my view, Chaput, Napier, Pell, and that ilk, may bring us to our knees. And I do not refer to prayer, Your Holiness."

"Perhaps the Canadian?" Francis said.

"Cardinal Ouellet is highly thought of. Believe me, the politics of the election are already in full force."

"Benedict was very surprised when I was elected. He admitted that to me. And I may also be surprised at who the conclave elects."

"You are in a unique situation. You are among very few popes who will live to see his successor," Magnone said.

"And what pains me is I will be relegated to simply watch from the sidelines and hope for the best."

CHAPTER 19

"Hello great, international, celebrity policeman! Man do I love calling you that name. After all, I was the one who created you," Deegan said.

Vic put his cell phone on speaker for Raquel to hear.

"Hello, John. How you feeling?" Vic asked.

"Getting ready for battle. Soon my treatments will commence. Hello, beautiful Raquel. How is that beautiful baby?"

"Hello, John. Thank you, she is fine."

"And mama so far away in Switzerland looking for a bad guy," Deegan said.

Vic looked at Raquel in astonishment. He put both hands up in futile recognition of Deegan's information.

"I won't deny that, John," Raquel said.

"So when are you guys coming up to see me?" Deegan inquired.

"Give us an address, John," Vic added.

"C'mon Vic. I know you already figured that out. You haven't been in Zürich all day just wasting time. I'm encouraged that you even knew I was in Zürich and not Geneva, Lucerne, or Bern. Bern is very pleasant this time of year. So many Italian and German tourists."

"Join us for breakfast tomorrow. You will get to say hello to Gjuliana. She has some errands to run so try to get here early."

"I don't think that she would want to hear what we have to say to you," Vic said.

"I've already told you I had nothing to do with the episode at the Cloister. Why, don't you believe me?"

"How is 'no' for starters?" Vic replied.

Vic's cell beeped; he had another call coming in. It was Tony Frank of Interpol.

"Well, John, it's me that has to end the call now. See you at 8 in the morning," Vic said. He hit the end button and Tony was on the line.

"Good evening, Tony. How are things?" Vic asked.

"Vic, I hope I'm not calling too late."

"Not at all my friend, Raquel and I were just sitting here going over our notes," Vic lied and smiled at Raquel.

"There has been another homicide with the same M.O. this time in Italy. It hasn't made our I 24/7 just yet."

"I haven't had a chance to look today, anyway. Where in Italy?"

"A small town in the Abruzzo Provence. Pacentro. An elderly defrocked priest this time."
"Where is Pacentro?"

"About a three hour drive east of Rome."

"When did this homicide occur?" Raquel asked.

"Late last evening. The ex-priest's name is Emilio Caserta, we don't yet know why he was thrown out of the church, and we are working on that. Anyway, a wooden Crucifix was left in his chest. His throat was slashed."

"Tony, I'm one hundred percent certain that we have a copycat killer on our hands," Vic said.

"What brings you to that conclusion?"

"Because we know where Deegan is. He is and has been in Switzerland the whole time." Vic said.

"What? Where in Switzerland is he?" Tony Frank asked.

"You must forgive me, my friend. I can't expose his location to you. I promise to give you more information when I can."

"Vic, Deegan needs to be apprehended for his past homicides regardless of his not being involved with the current situation. You know our case against him is still open. You are impeding an investigation."

"Hold on. First, I gave him my word years ago he would not be bothered, and I'm not about to go against that word. If we determine that Deegan was the killer of these two men, I promise you on my word, you will be able to close your case," Vic said.
"Vic, be warned, you are on thin ice here. Deegan must be brought to justice at the International Court. I would hate to see you do anything you may later regret."

"Tony, thank you. I'll be in touch," Vic ended the call.

"Now where were we when we were so rudely interrupted?" Vic pulled Raquel close to him on the divan.

"Let's see... we were talking about Angela and the possibilities," Raquel chuckled.

"Mmmm, how about the two of us take this to the bed and discuss it a little further?"

The next morning, Vic and Raquel arrived at the *Klinik* at precisely eight o'clock. The sound of the roaring Mercedes engine and screeching wheels disrupted the serenity that surrounded the hospital.

Angela was at the reception desk in another killer outfit. A bright, orange jumpsuit with a zippered front, her ample breasts doing their best to break through.

"Good morning. I was about to text you to thank you again for last evening. Lisbeth and I had a fabulous time."

"Our pleasure," Raquel said. Raquel was dressed down in a modest, gray pantsuit outfit, her hair pulled back in a bun.

"Raquel your face is amazing. You look like a movie star or something," Angela said.

Vic cleared his throat. *I know which team she plays on for sure,* Vic thought to himself.

"Thank you, Angela, coming from you that is a great compliment."

"I will call our administrator. She is awaiting your visit."

"No need for that right now, Angela. We are expected for a visit with the third floor patient," Raquel said.

"What? Oh, my. I'm sorry. I thought I explained to you the

other day that I really can't let you up without their approval and I don't see a note to that effect."

"Please ring the room. I am certain we will be allowed up," Vic said.

Angela paused trying to absorb what was being said. She picked up the phone and dialed the suite.

"Good morning sir, I have…"

"Send them up, please," Deegan interrupted.

The anxious anticipation of seeing Deegan again made the elevator ride to the third floor seemed to take forever. When the door opened, Vic and Raquel were met by a man in a black suit. It was John and Gjuliana's houseman.

"Good morning. Right this way, please."

Vic and Raquel followed the man to the De Luca suite.

"Come in, come in, Vic, Raquel! It's so good to see you again," Deegan said.

Deegan sat in his elegant, high back chair with Gjuliana standing behind him. He looked both thinner and tired to his guests. John wore a pair of black running pants, a light blue t-shirt, and a pair of Chuck Taylor, hi-back, black, Converse All Star sneakers, the kind he wore on the streets of the Bronx when he was a kid.

"Vic and Raquel, may I present my wife, Gjuliana Deegan."

Vic bowed slightly. Raquel smiled broadly, tipping her head to her right.

Gjuliana was elegant in a long, black and red, peasant dress adorned with a pure gold, vertical, finger-length necklace. Her now auburn hair was pulled back in a tight bun much like Raquel's.

"Now, the introductions are all made. Let's go out to the balcony where breakfast will be served. Well, you three will at least be eating breakfast. I will be having something my Irish mother would call slum gullion or some variation thereof," Deegan laughed.

The morning was as beautiful as could be. The sun was brightly shining, the birds were chirping in the trees, and the warm breeze was heavenly.

The conversation at breakfast was pleasant. Just as if old friends were chatting and reminiscing. Gjuliana was especially interested in hearing about Vic and Raquel's baby and what the child was doing. Tying her shoes, knowing her numbers, colors, shapes, writing her name, and getting ready for pre-K were the hot topics. Raquel was very animated when she discussed her daughter, and her Bronx accent came out in full force. They spoke about all four of them growing up in the Bronx and how things had changed so much over the years. Gjuliana said she still missed the great food and pizza at Mario's restaurant and the market on Arthur Avenue, and how much fun she'd had at Aqueduct Park and the Bronx Zoo. Deegan talked about how great the Half Moon's pizza was and that he has never again tasted anything like it. Deegan changed the conversation to sports and talked about the great Yankee players he saw; Mickey Mantle, Yogi Berra, Whitey Ford, who was Deegan's favorite because he was Irish, and Roger Maris. Vic remembered the Yankee greats; Ron Gidrey, Thurman Munson, and Reggie Jackson.

Vic thought to himself, *Here I am, in Switzerland with John Deegan. You would never know this fucking guy was a serial killer.*

CHAPTER 20

His Holiness Pope Francis had a full day planned. After celebrating mass for the laity who worked inside the Vatican, he was off for a final visit as pope to A Chance In Life. Formerly called Boys and Girls Town of Italy just outside of Rome. An orphanage that was started for displaced boys at the end of World War II. The idolized pope would stay for lunch there, the food prepared by the young residents.

In the afternoon, Francis had meetings back at the Vatican with Cardinal Magnone and several other high-ranking red hats.

Early in the evening, the Pope would board the Agusta Westland AW139 helicopter manned by the Italian Air Force. The heliport at the corner of the Vatican Gardens would bring His Holiness, Zellweger, two additional bodyguards, the pope's doctor, and ten other clerics to Castel Gandolfo, just twelve miles south east of Rome. The Pope planned to rest and see several cardinals and archbishops for an informal dinner.

This would be the first night Francis would sleep at the summer residence. The pontiff found the place to be far too ostentatious and unlike his predecessors never stayed more than an afternoon at Gandolfo. Some locals say Francis was superstitious and didn't want to die in the Castle as Pius XII and Paul VI had.

Colonel Zellweger would be right beside His Holiness every step of the way. Zellweger would be staying up very late again, pouring over the blueprints and three-dimensional schematics of the key Vatican properties that Inspector Festa shared with him.

Zellweger was especially focused on the *Domus Marthae Sanctae* where the voting cardinals would be residing during the conclave, and the Sistine Chapel where the actual election of the pope would take place.

There were some inherent problems with Zellweger's plans and he knew it very well. Add to that the minute, detailed plans that were still yet to come, and you have one very stressed out mad man who, at the same time, is keeping everything all bottled up inside of him. While he felt he had a good plan, Zellweger knew he needed to have John Deegan's masterful mind aligned with his to pull this off. He couldn't do it alone.

Trying to maintain his stoic manner which was expected of him was also becoming increasingly difficult. If his master plan failed, his family's history within the Swiss Guard would forever be ruined; if he succeeded, well, nobody knows. All Zellweger knew was that either way he would be making history in and about the church he so dearly loved. In these times, he especially liked the etymology of the word *conclave* which comes directly from the Latin term *conclavis,* loosely meaning *with a key,* or *a room that can be locked.* Zellweger wanted to make certain that after the *camerlengo* announced '*Extra omnes!*' which is the order for anyone who is not voting to leave the chapel, he could begin his mass murder of the sex degenerate, homosexual, pedophiliac cardinals, and somehow be successful in preventing the doors from being easily reopened by his own Swiss Guard. One of Zellweger's main concerns was that if the older cardinals left the chapel, it would still leave over one hundred cardinals over the age of eighty, still alive. Customarily, these cardinals leave before the voting commences. Those remaining elderly cardinals certainly would be able to manage church affairs for a while, and the impact of his planned slaughter would have a lesser effect than he hoped. Zellweger wanted to really cripple the church all the way to its knees, and he wanted all of them, every last one of them, dead. It would take years, if ever, for the remaining archbishops and bishops to get the giant organizational machine of the Vatican up and running again. And by that time, hopefully the world-wide faithful would be awakened enough to ensure the church, *their* church, moved forward in a holy and proper manner. He would be a hero. A saint, or even be made a doctor of the church.

Zellweger just had to have someone of Deegan's genius to make a viable plan. Zellweger knew that with his own access to everything in the Vatican, he could execute any plan to fulfill his maniacal dream.

Alas, Deegan was not to be convinced. Zellweger felt his mind was slipping from all of the stress so he started to make lists to control and keep track of his thoughts. This much he knew:

1. Deegan would perhaps go deeper under cover since law enforcement thought he was back at the killing game.
2. Conversely, Zellweger thought that Deegan would capitulate and join him.
3. The Colonel was certain Deegan would soon be coming to an end, by either cops or cancer.

Pope Francis would spend the night at *Castel Gandolfo* and return the next day to Vatican City. Zellweger would also sleep at Gandolfo. The maniacal Colonel would not be able to work on his plan without the necessary blueprints for at least another full day.

Zellweger was becoming increasingly distracted by his obsession. When dinner was over and Francis was safely in his room at Gandolfo, Zellweger paced the shore of Lake Albano talking and humming to himself. His men thought Zellweger was deep in thought with the pressure of the upcoming conclave and felt sympathy toward their *Oberst*.

Eventually, retiring to his room, Zellweger quietly sang two Gregorian Chants, the one Emilio Caserta had sung before he was dispatched, and the Tantum Ergo, a Latin hymn written by St. Thomas Aquinas in the middle twelve hundreds, used for centuries during the Benediction of the Blessed Sacrament.

Tantum ergo Sacramentum
Veneremur cernui:
Et antiquum documentum
Novo cedat ritui:

Praestet fides supplementum
Sensuum defectui.

Genitori, Genitoque
Laus et iubilatio,
Salus, honor, virtus quoque
Sit et benedictio:
Procedenti ab utroque
Compar sit laudatio.
Amen.

Now nearing insanity, Colonel Zellweger did not realize anymore that his devotion to his Catholic faith was at odds with his attempt to destroy the Roman Catholic Church. He was a man who felt completely justified to do what he was about to set forth.

CHAPTER 21

On cue, Deegan's houseman announced that the car to take Gjuliana on her errands was ready.

"What a wonderful breakfast we've had. Now my love Gjuliana needs to do some marketing and run an important errand. It's a funny thing, no matter how much help Gjuliana has, she still insists on squeezing the fruit at the market," Deegan said.

"I know you need to extend your visit, so I will be on my way. I can't tell you how enjoyable and refreshing it was to spend this time with you two wonderful people. Vic and Raquel, it was truly a pleasure," Gjuliana said. Vic and Raquel stood to say their farewells.

"It was our pleasure, Gjuliana. I feel like I've known you my whole life," Raquel said. Vic smiled and nodded his agreement.

"Well that's what happens when Bronx people meet up. We have a common bond that is indefinable," Gjuliana said.

She kissed John on the top of his head. "Now don't exert yourself, John. Chemo starts is a few days. You must garner your strength."

Gjuliana left leaving John, Vic, and Raquel alone on the terrace.

"I know what was going through your mind, Vic. You are very easy to read, by the way. That expressive Italian face of yours gives up so much," Deegan said.

"Okay, I'm game. What was I thinking?"

"How could I be talking about the Yankees, in Switzerland, with a maniac, serial killer that I chased to the ends of the earth?"

109

"Pretty good, John. Except I never classified you as a maniac, "Vic said.

"I'm sure you did while you were on my tail. After all, what sane man goes around doing what I did?"

"A survivor. To many you were just as big of a hero as they thought I was," Vic said.

"And now you will be a double-survivor," Raquel added.

"I can only hope you are right, Raquel. Time will tell," Deegan said. He sipped a fruit smoothie and grimaced. "As we used to say in the Bronx, 'this tastes like shit.'" The trio had a good laugh.

"John, I've concluded that you did not kill either of those two priests?" Vic said.

"Two, now?"

"Yes. There was another priest. A defrocked one at that, and again murdered with your M.O. only two days ago in Italy."

"Well, I certainly could have certainly removed my tubes, taken a private jet and been back to this room in no time," Deegan said as he searched Vic's face.
"And I could dunk at basketball," Raquel added."

"Any idea who could have set you up?" Vic asked.

"That's the thing about copycats. You just can't trust 'em," Deegan said smirking.

"Seriously, now. Interpol is totally in motion to begin searching for you. If we could find you, so could they," Vic said.

"That is a possibility I've thought about. So then I die quickly in prison rather than in the comfort of my wife's loving arms and in my home. The hunter becomes the hunted. Not a very new concept at all."

"And why now, after all these years? What would be the motivation?" Raquel asked.

"That is academic. The killer is a survivor of priest sexual abuse. Let me guess. Both priests were mutilated?"

"The first was. Not sure on the last one," Vic said.

"Neither here nor there. Perhaps the latest, if he'd been defrocked, was not directly involved with molesting the killer. I suspect you will ultimately discover that to be the case," Deegan stated.

"So you have no idea who could have done these murders?" Vic asked.

"I didn't say that, at all. That would be lying to you. I'm a pretty good killer, but a pretty lousy liar. My Catholic upbringing, don't you know?" Deegan said using his perfect Irish brogue.

"So...?"

"That will remain a secret for the moment," Deegan said in his own voice.

"John, areyoukiddenmeorwhat? Now is not the time for playing chess with us. If we can help find who murdered these two priests, at least the heat will not be on you," Raquel said.

"You both know how I enjoy playing the intellectual game. Let a dying man have some fun 'fer fuck's sake'," he said again in the brogue.

"I tell ya, there is nothing worse than an uncooperative witness," Vic said smiling.

"So the copycat is setting you up for his own reasons. The question for us is to figure out is why," Raquel said.

"Warmer… you are getting warmer," Deegan teased.

"So you think you may know who the killer is?" Vic asked.

"*May* is too much of a passive word in my world."

"Then you *know* who it is?" Raquel asked, astonished by what she was hearing.

"With absolute certainty."

"So why not end the drama and let us help you?" Raquel countered.

"Because snitches get stitches?" John asked rhetorically.

"C'mon John. Quit talking in circles. Don't you know the game is now at a critical point for you? Interpol asked us if we knew of your whereabouts and we, for the time being, went deaf and dumb, but they are not going to quit until they find you. They are certainly pulling out all of the stops. You made them look pretty bad last time. Besides, if you have a death wish, what are you doing here in this hospital?" Vic asked hoping to challenge John into giving up information.

"And the Vatican especially is likely putting enormous pressure on Interpol. They don't want this killer going around offing priests right before the conclave, but John, they think the killer is you!" Raquel added. *I can't believe I'm pleading with a killer for his safety,* Raquel thought to herself.

"Boy, it's getting warmer and warmer out here," Deegan laughed.

"Hmmm…so the killer is someone associated with the Church?" Vic asked.

"There are one point three billion people associated with the church. Too broad my International police…

"Cut that out, John, it's growing old," Vic said.

"I get it. Someone at the Vatican!" Raquel said.

"That narrows things down a bit. Raquel how is your back feeling?"

"My back? It's just fine! Why do you ask?" Raquel asked, perplexed.

"I ask, because you are carrying Vic at the moment," Deegan laughed.

CHAPTER 22

Gjuliana wasn't going on a shopping expedition after all. The errand Deegan had asked his wife to fulfill was to go to the Bank of Switzerland's main office in Zürich to pick up a package of gold coins. He instructed her to have the houseman carry the parcel, as it would be quite heavy for her to handle. Deegan had made the appropriate transfer of Swiss francs into gold coins with his banker. All Gjuliana needed to do was show her identification as Gjuliana De Luca and sign a release document.

Deegan suspected he might need some gold just as a precaution. Gjuliana had always left all business matters to her husband often making bank transfers and deposits for him so she suspected nothing out of the ordinary.

While she was out, and Vic and Raquel were racking their brains to find the identity of the copycat killer. Deegan, meanwhile, sent a text to Colonel Zellweger's private cell phone. The message was somewhat cryptic and in Swiss-German.

In der vasammlung gerade bevor gie ture gescg lossen ist haben sie gehabt. Ubersehe wohnviertel. Studiene da luftungsystem. Werde nahere patentschridt. Spezifizeerung der heitungsrohre weiter leister. Versuche mich michy zu erreeicher werche bald weg gehren.

They must be had in the meeting just before door is locked. Ignore living quarters. Study the venting system of the masterpiece. Will forward specifications on the conduit. Do not attempt to contact me. Will be on move soon.

Seemingly, Deegan had bold-faced lied to Gjuliana. He had decided to become an accomplice after all. This was all that Colonel Zellweger had wanted from the beginning. Use Deegan's brilliant criminal mind, set him up for an arrest or better yet, to be shot dead by the police, and maybe with any luck, Zellweger thought he could get away with killing over two hundred Cardinals of the Holy See. An escape would be tricky, but Zellweger was confident Deegan would figure out a safe exit strategy for him.

Zellweger was on the AgustaWestland AW139 helicopter returning on the short flight from *Castle Gandolfo* with the Holy Father and the rest of the entourage, when his cell phone vibrated.

The Colonel glanced at his screen. It was Deegan's text message. Zellweger let out an audible *"fantastisch, vortrefflich."* *"Fantastic, excellent."* These words caught the attention of one of the other papal bodyguards. Zellweger just gave his man a thumbs up and looked away. The Colonel began ever so slightly, rocking in his seat while squeezing his hands together.

Now, Zellweger thought, *Now we will see if these "men", these cardinals will really not fear death! To watch them beg for their lives, to call their dead mothers, will be satisfying, or will they welcome death with chanting and song? Ha!*

As Vic and Raquel were leaving *Klinik Hirslanden,* Angela called out to them.

"Hey, you two. Not even a 'so long'?"

"How rude of us. I'm so sorry, Angela. We are so engrossed

with things," Raquel said.

"Not to worry. Will you be returning to see our administrator?"

"I don't believe so. We may return to see the people upstairs. They are such a nice, older couple," Vic said.

"And very generous. The De Luca's are a favorite of the staff. He is a bit odd, and sometimes crabby, but under the circumstances who wouldn't be?"

"Have you decided to take your father elsewhere, Vic?" Angela asked.

"Well, to be honest. He has taken a turn for the worst back home," Vic said. He felt his face redden with the lie.

"So are you going back to the states?"

"Well, ah…ah…" Vic stammered.

"Angela, Vic's dad has been dead for many years. We wanted to meet the De Luca's as we had some personal business with them. Sorry to have fabricated that story," Raquel said. She looked at Vic and rolled her eyes.

"I thought so. Vic, you don't seem like the typical finance guy and Raquel you are not just a stay-at-home-mom. You carry yourself with too much assurance and authority. But it's none of my business. I just like you both and hope we can go out again sometime. Are you staying in Zürich any longer?"

"Why, yes, we plan to stay at least a few more days. Why don't we make a date for dinner again with you and Lisbeth?" Raquel asked.

Angela looked down at her hands for moment and raised her head. Her eyes were teary.

"Lisbeth and I decided on a break for a while. She's moved out. It was coming," Angela said.

"I'm sorry, Angela. Are you okay?" Raquel said.

"I'll be fine. It doesn't hurt so much when you are used to being disappointed."

"How is tonight?" Vic asked. He seemed too anxious under the circumstance. Raquel looked at him with her Puerto Rican, dagger eyes.

"Tonight is not good for me, but how is tomorrow? It's Saturday, and I'm free. I can give you a tour of the city, if you like. Maybe a picnic by the lake? I know a great spot," Angela offered.

Vic held his tongue.

"That sounds like fun. Problem is our car only fits two," Raquel said.

"I have a car, that isn't a problem. How is ten o'clock? I can pick you up where you are staying."

"It's a date then. The Dolder Grand at ten," Raquel said.

"Wow, the Dolder! Wonderful, and I'll prepare the picnic," Angela offered.

Vic and Raquel made their way to their rented sports car without saying a word. Once they got in the car, and Vic gunned the engine, Raquel went Bronx. She sat with her back toward the passenger door window and faced her partner.

"Look it, mister I see you want the best of both worlds. You nearly jumped on her like a pit bull."

"What are you talking about? Angela is a nice girl and we had a great time with her the other night."

"And you want to get her under the sheets with me, Don fucking Juan."

"Hey hold it, you said that she was amazing and that if you…"

"*Cunjo*, I've never done anything like that in my entire life," Raquel blurted.

"Okay, take it easy, if you're not interested you're not interested."

Raquel paused for a while and calmed down.

"I'm curious, that's all I meant," Raquel said. She put her hands to her mouth like she wanted to pull the words back. "I guess I can't blame you. She is an amazing looking lady."

"And if she were an amazing looking man would you want him to do the both of us… you dog."

"Have you completely lost your mind? Hell, no. It's not nearly the same and you know it.

Tell me why? Why would you want that?" Vic continued to tease. "Ok, let's just drop the subject, Raquel."

"No, I don't want that. Another man, I mean."

"See, you understand the difference. Look, if you want to be with her I can understand… you know, an experience." Vic said. He became aroused again at the thought of his woman being with another woman.

"And here we are thinking that Angela is even interested in that kind of thing."

"Let's just have some fun, see the city, and have a picnic."

"Yeah, sure, but I think your idea of a picnic is a little more than deviled eggs and a brioche."

CHAPTER 23

It was a beautiful, Saturday morning, and Vatican Square was teeming with tourists from all parts of the world. By nine o'clock in the morning, the line for the Vatican Museum and The Sistine Chapel was already experiencing a two-hour wait, with visitors standing along the Vatican wall on the *Viale Vaticano*. Some twenty-five thousand visitors were expected today. Additionally, thousands of people were milling around St. Peter's square taking in the breathtaking, architectural beauty and historical significance of the Vatican.

Behind the scenes, Pope Francis had conferences with various cardinals of his church. A morning meeting with the President of the Governorate of Vatican City and his underlings, The Secretary and Vice Secretary of State. These are the cardinals who will be replaced by the next pontiff. They were, at the moment, Francis' key administrators of the Church.

Francis then planned to meet with the key members of the political factions within the church. Although the pope is the absolute, theocratic monarch of the Church, who the next Pope will be, conservative, liberal, or radical will shape the church's direction for perhaps decades. Francis wanted to add his say in the matter in spite of what is said about everyone in the process being guided by the Holy Spirit.

While Francis was busy inside the Apostolic Palace and no plans for His Holiness to see the light of day, Colonel Zellweger calmly busied himself with routine, security inspections. Later that evening the Colonel was to meet with Inspector General Claudio Festa and his major officers of the *Gendarmeria*. Today, however, there was more to Zellweger's routine rounds. In his briefcase were blueprints of the Sistine Chapel. Two of his Swiss Guard, in full regalia snapped to attention and saluted Zellweger as he passed through an arch on his way to the Sistine Chapel.

Zellweger noticed the incredible amount of people who were currently inside the chapel. No Swiss Guard or *Gendarmeria* was inside the Sistine as the Pope's security requirement centered on the Palace and the Pontiff's living quarters.

Only ushers circled the floor of the chapel reminding the tourists no photographs were permitted and "silence please… this is a church" command when the din hit a certain level.

Zellweger made his way to the sub-basement of the Chapel. He began mumbling to himself when the hidden entrance door from the chapel to the lower floors closed behind him.

"I have no idea what this man wants. Study the venting system he commands? This place was built, above an ancient hall. What did they know about ventilation in 1481? Anyway, this new air system is perfect. It controls the temperature, the humidity, the lights, everything. This is what this maniac wants me to see. I suppose he wants to gas them like Hitler did to the Jews. Who knows what goes through a mind like that Deegan?"

Zellweger began humming the Gregorian chant he heard his most recent victim, Emilio Caserta singing. Then the Colonel's mood turned darker.

"1492, that's when they started the voting here. When religion and the rules of conduct meant something. Now, the more you screw up the better you are. They made him a saint? A joke, I tell you. The sex abuse scandal blew up in his red, Polish face and he turned a blind eye to the victims. He was too busy dying to care. A saint? He looked the other away while his priests were raping the children of the world. And what did John Paul II do? He passed it off to that German fuck, and what did he do? Complicit I say! They are all guilty, all of them. They all know. On top of these loathsome pedophiles the place has become a gay nightclub besides. Enough of this! A tremendous black cloud has overcome this holy church. These idiots pay how much? Eighteen Euros to get into this place? They will all soon feel the Lord's wrath."

Colonel Zellweger spent the better part of two hours inspecting the medieval vents and concentrating on the new state of the art, integrated, ventilation system. Zellweger snapped a dozen or so photographs on his cell phone.

The Colonel then adjusted his tie, ran his hands through his short-cropped, military haircut to remove any accumulated dust and then returned to the main floor of the Sistine Chapel.

The *Oberst* of the Pontifical Swiss Guard looked up to the center of the Michelangelo's masterpiece, and smiled.

That same Saturday morning, the weather in Zürich was as magnificent as it was in Vatican City.

At eight o'clock that morning, Angela sent a text to Raquel. *"Did you bring bathing suits? If not, go down to the lobby and get them. You are in for a treat.*
Raquel replied… *"K"*

In a shop that was walking distance to the Dolmer Hotel Vic bought a European brief he was very uncomfortable with.

"This shows the family jewels way too much. How do these guys like these things?" Vic asked, his face turning red.

"I like them just fine, baby. Just relax, you have a great body for that bathing suit," Raquel assured.

Raquel modeled a revealing red string bikini for Vic.
"Forgetaboutit. Way too much boobage showing, but you look

amazing!" Vic said.

"I love it. This may be the only day off we will have in Switzerland. Chill out, you old school Italian."

Vic and Raquel wore their swimsuits under their tourist shorts. They both bought a pair of cheap flip-flops.

At precisely ten o'clock, Angela pulled up in front of the Dolmer in an old, Fiat sedan. Her halter-top and Daisy Duke, skimpy shorts exhibited her great figure.

"My father sent this car from Sicily. It's an old bomb but it runs and that's all I care about. Get in, and we are off!" Angela said.

Raquel jumped into the front seat. Vic shared the back with a picnic basket and an ice bucket with Peroni Beer and a few bottles of good, French Rose wine.

"Okay, let's not do the boring church and tourist sight thing. I want to show you my Switzerland. I will point out some sights and then we will drive about thirty minutes to the *Rheinfall in Scaffhausen*.

"What's that?" Raquel asked.

The Rhine Falls. It's the most amazing place. You will see white water falls that are simply spectacular. I know a great place to picnic and enjoy a nice swim."

"Works for me! Can I have a beer?" Vic said.

"There is an opener attached to the basket," Angela said.

The Fiat zipped passed the *Grossmunster*, a pair of high towers that overlooked Zürich, a protestant church founded by Charlemagne that opened in the year twelve hundred, then passed another large church and some other mundane sights Angela pointed out.

"They are all lovely but quite boring. It's like visiting Italy and going from church to church. Just dumb," Angela noted.

The trio chatted about Switzerland and the cost of living in Zürich and New York. Like clockwork in thirty minutes, Angela pulled into a park where dozens of people were enjoying the water.

"Let's take a tour of the Rhine by boat. I know a cozy place for us to have lunch a bit later," Angela announced.

At the dock along the beautiful, blue, Rhine River awaited a long, flat, red boat with Swiss flags and white, Swiss crosses that adorned the hull of the vessel. Vic rushed to pay the fifteen Euro charge, but Angela beat him to it.

The tour was serene at first and then became quite bumpy as the boat came into near rapids. Raquel grabbed onto Vic's arm. She wasn't too crazy about being on a boat to begin with, but she didn't want to spoil the mood. The sights along the trip were exactly as Angela described. White water cascading along the dark rocks, leaving a mist that was both cooling and invigorating. The trees along the river were full and they moved in unison with a cooling breeze. Raquel soon forgot that she was on a boat. An hour later, the boat returned to the spot where the trio boarded.

"Okay, all off. Is anyone starving like I am?" Angela asked.

"Famished," Vic said.

"Italians live to eat. But we eat less and drink more," Angela said.

"I can eat," Raquel replied.

Angela led them to a quiet spot under an ancient and giant weeping, willow tree. Next to the willow there was a communal, circular, stone pit with a grill that hung from a triangle of stainless steel.

"This is my safe place. There is a bridge over there, and an old, stone bunker down a bit that we can dive from later. But for now, I will start lunch," Angela said.

Angela laid down a small blanket and opened her basket. She had packed some *Bratwurst*, some blood sausage, corn-on-the-cob and sliced vegetables. There were no deviled eggs for this gal. Angela lit the charcoal briquettes she had packed and lit them with a bit of fluid. In minutes, lunch was sizzling on the grill.

"Here, try this local cheese and some olives with that crusty bread while we wait. Vic, will you open the wine?" Angela asked.

Vic poured the wine and made a toast to new friends.

"This place is heavenly, Angela. You are so right. I'd rather do this than the regular touristy things," Raquel said.

While they were eating, the trio talked about their lives a bit. Raquel said she missed their daughter and Vic agreed.

"I'm ready to start a family now. I've been through numbing hurt with Erick, I thought we would marry and have babies. He left me for a man, I'm almost embarrassed to say. So I think my time with Lisbeth was a way at getting back at him. Stupid, I know, but please don't judge me."

Vic thought to himself, *Wow. It's true, behind every gorgeous woman there is a guy sick of banging her.*

Angela continued, "So I guess it wasn't meant to be with Erick, and now I'm done with my girl stage. If my parents only knew I would be… oh, who knows? It wouldn't be pleasant. My mama and papa are very, old school Sicilians," Angela said.

"Are you ready to date again so quickly?" Raquel asked.

"If the truth be told, I've been dating for a while even when I was living with Lisbeth. Not sleeping around at all, mind you. I'm not like that. Old habits die hard, and I was brought up very parochially. Now, for me, it will be all about family," Angela replied.

"And your job? I heard you say you were looking for a change," Vic said.

"In Italian we say, '*Spazzatoio nuovo spazza ben la caza,*' '*a new broom sweeps the house well.*' Yes, I want to change my life and find what I'm looking for."

Raquel looked at Vic embarrassedly. They both realized their silly fantasy about Angela was unfair to this lovely woman.

Raquel said openly in front of Angela, "She's perfect!" Vic nodded his head to the affirmative.

"Perfect? In what sense?" Angela asked. Now she was embarrassed.

"We may have something for you Angela," Raquel said.

"That's if you are up for a challenge," Vic added.

"I am. What do you guys really do?"

"Again, our fibs have embarrassed us," Vic said.

"We own a pretty good-sized investigation company. We are based in New York but now we have an international business. We were both with the New York City police department. That was how we met. Tell you what, if you Google *Vic Gonnella*, two Ns, two Ls, our story is there for the world to see. But for now let's talk more about you," Raquel said.

"Is this a job interview?" Angela laughed.

"Well, yeah, I guess so. That's if you are really interested," Vic added.

"I would have to hear more about the duties. I'm really not sure if I qualify."

"As I said, we are now an international company. Centurion needs more visibility in Europe with a large office in London or Paris, not sure exactly where just yet. You certainly have the language skills and the education. We need someone to direct the administration of the office. Hiring the right people, marketing the company, dealing with the clients," Raquel said.

"Any training? I know nothing about the investigation business, but I pick things up very quickly," Angela boasted.

"You will train at our headquarters in New York for a month or so. You will have a budget to manage along with an office build out. You will work with me for a while, then in the field. During that time, we will decide to which city you will relocate," Raquel said.

"I would love to be in New York again for a while and learn something new. And if it doesn't work out for you?" Angela asked.

"It will work out. Your new broom, remember?" Vic said.

"I'm extremely interested. I really have no ties in Zürich. I want the position."

"Hold on, we didn't even mention your compensation," Vic said.

"If I have to worry about you two taking advantage of me, I'm a poor judge of character and I don't deserve the opportunity."

"Done. We will have a package sent to you from our HR director. If it's to your liking, when can you start?" Raquel asked.

"This is a God send. I will give my two week's notice tomorrow. They likely may let me go sooner."

"And then you can start your new and exciting life. Trust me, our business is amazingly exciting at times, and quite profitable. You are a dynamic person, Angela, and we are thrilled to have you aboard," Raquel said.

Vic poured some more wine and they all toasted to the newest member of the Centurion team.

When lunch was over, Vic, Raquel, and Angela dove from the bridge and then the bunker, swimming together in the chilly waters of the Rhine River for the rest of the afternoon. Just like teenagers.

"Raquel, this is Angela, I think there may be a problem with the De Lucas," Angela said.

It was Sunday morning and Angela reported to her position at the *Klinik Hirslanden*. She was getting prepared to speak to the administrator and tender her resignation, when she overheard that Mr. and Mrs. De Luca had checked out of the hospital. Angela called Raquel immediately.

"What sort of problem?" Raquel asked.

"It seems they are gone. Checked out. I have no other details, but I thought you and Vic should know immediately."

"Angela, see what you can find out. Don't mention anything about what we do at the moment. Vic and I will be there shortly."

Angela confirmed that the De Lucas left the *Klinik* in the very early, morning hours. They had a conference with Dr. Bauer and Dr. Eschmann earlier in the evening, but no one was aware of the results of the meeting or if the De Luca's went to another hospital. Angela relayed that information to her soon to be new employers.

"Looks like it's time to call Deegan," Raquel advised.

"And say what? John, you forgot to leave us your forwarding address?"

"He is on the run again, Vic."

"And will likely go deep this time," Vic replied.

"But Vic, he needs his treatments, the special diet, the radiation every day. Is it possible he's just giving up?"

"Possible, but not likely. He seemed pretty hopeful to get a few more good years in."

"I really don't know what to think." Raquel said.

"Let's just hash this out for a minute. Think like Deegan. We know he couldn't possibly have killed those two priests."

"What?" Angela was quite alarmed at what she was hearing. "What is going on, and who is Deegan?"

"Sorry. Just a minute, Angela. Ok, Raquel, walk me through this. He couldn't have killed the second one anyway. The first one he could have made the trip, but I highly doubt it. He *is* pretty weak. So let's just say he knows who the killer is. This killer has something on him, and he believes he is in great danger," Vic said. Raquel interrupted his train of thought.

"Yes, he is not afraid for himself, but he would be afraid for

Gjuliana," Raquel said.

"Good, you're right! Now he decides to get the show on the road. I mean, the man is a billionaire. He can afford to go anywhere for these treatments and have his doctors fly back and forth, or go with him, or tell other doctors what the course of treatment should be," Vic said.

"Precisely. And the special diet is easy. Just hire a nutritionist slash cook," Raquel added.

"Of course. But now where would he go? That's the piece of the puzzle we need."

"I still think you should call him."

"I think you're right."

Vic called the number he stored in his cell phone and pressed the speaker feature. After five rings the call went to voice mail.

"And all the king's horses and all the king's men couldn't put Humpty Dumpty together again."

The voice was Deegan's.

Zellweger had his meeting with Inspector Claudio Festa and his officers of the *Gendarmeria* at the Swiss Guard office inside the Vatican from nine in the evening until midnight on Saturday. Festa noticed that Zellweger's legs were uncontrollably moving up and down, bouncing on the balls of his feet. Zellweger was generally cool, calm, and stone stoic.

"Can we review our man power once more?" Zellweger asked.

"Certainly. The Guard has one hundred ten men. The *Gendarmeria,* well our normal contingent is one hundred thirty, but I've called in some retirees for the anti-sabotage unit and a few former officers for counter assault. We are now at one hundred twenty-seven for that. The Rome *Carabinieri* has several sharp shooters and I believe, a full squad of fourteen men we will borrow. The Italian Army has two hundred men and twenty vehicles, many of them armed; they will be posted in and around the Vatican City. More as a show of force than anything. Every time we use the army, all the men do is look at girls and smoke cigarettes. Finally, the Italian Air Force is bolstering the security of the helipad by an additional six men."

"I'm satisfied with the numbers. What about dogs?" Zellweger asked.

"Oh, I forgot, so sorry. As we all know the *Guardia di Finanza* are the best in the business. We will have twelve bomb-sniffing dogs, each with three heavily armed handlers. Another thirty-six sets of trained eyes inside and outside the walls," Festa said.

"When you said 'arms', Inspector, you reminded me of an explicit order I will be putting out tomorrow. Daily arms inspection will be done for every member of the Swiss Guard from now until the end of the conclave. The men find it a pain, but they have no choice. My officers will fulfill this order," Zellweger said.

"Good idea. We will do the same. No sense in having the hardware if they don't function properly."

Zellweger looked at his watch. "Good God, it's almost midnight. I believe we have covered everything."

The meeting adjourned and Festa asked Zellweger if he wanted to join him for a nightcap at a local restaurant a few blocks from the

Vatican walls. Festa thought to himself, *This poor guy needs a few drinks. He is wound like a violin string"*

Zellweger politely demurred citing the late hour and an early morning wakeup to accompany the Holy Father to say mass with Cardinal Bernard Law. Law, the now eighty-four year old American Cardinal who was brought to Rome during the Boston pedophile priest scandal, was a friend of Pope Francis' and a good temperature gauge for what the English speaking cardinals were thinking. The pope was doing his own political homework.

Zellweger pretended to walk to his quarters which was behind and to the right of St. Peter's Basilica, but instead of retiring the colonel nervously lit another cigarette and exited Vatican City, saluting two of his men.

Colonel Zellweger had other things on his mind this morning.

CHAPTER 24

While Vic, Raquel, and Angela were busy trying to gather information on why the Deegans fled the *Klinik* in Zürich under cover of darkness, and with any luck finding their whereabouts, the *Carabinieri* in Rome had their hands full with the murder of two gay men.

What really made these homicides more gripping, more compelling? The gay murder victims were both priests. And worse yet, both clerics were assigned to different positions *inside* the Vatican. Damage control from the Vatican spokesperson would be a gold medal performance. The most disturbing forensics at the gruesome, crime scene was something that shook the church to its foundation five years prior: two, sharpened, wooden crucifixes were found lodged through the carotid arteries of both the deceased. Was this a lover's quarrel or what was appearing to be another bloody killing spree by notorious killer John Deegan?

There are not many gay bars in Rome because the gay scene is not as accepted in Rome as it is in most other major European cities. Perhaps because the Pope still has influence over the police departments or, more than likely, gay men in the eternal city meet elsewhere, in places like restaurants and nightclubs.

Via di San Giovanni in Laterano is the closest thing to a gay zone in the city of Rome. Not so much during the daytime hours when the street is busy with tourists and business people, but *Laterano*, changes into the Bohemian center of the city in the evening. On summer nights, the streets around the popular gay bar, aptly called *Coming Out*, literally in the shadow of the Coliseum, is teeming with gay men of all ages, professions, nationalities, colors, and sexual desires.

Coming Out looks like any of the thousands of other *ristorante* and *trattoria* on the streets of Rome. A pastel, beige, almost pink, painted exterior on plaster walls, a dozen or so outside tables with the standard pasta and pizza menu, some rice balls, and *osso buco* as a special, very friendly and very gay waiters and bartenders help turn Coming Out into *the* place to be in the evenings in gay Rome.

Finally, and with subtle artistic flare, six, square, two feet by two feet tiles, with the colors of the gay flag are found over the bar's entrance.

Upstairs from the bar is a bed and breakfast that is well known in gay circles in Rome. This is where the bodies of the two young priests, Father Edwardo Ortiz of Buenos Aries, Argentina and Father John Wilde of Cleveland, Ohio, were found.

An apprentice chambermaid discovered the naked and bloodied bodies. The owners of Coming Out then summoned the police. Cardinal Magnone immediately received a call from the Commandant General of the *Carabinieri*. Magnone paged Inspector Claudio Festa due to his experience in these matters, and asked him to investigate on behalf of the Vatican due to the sensitivity of the homicides.

A strict warning Cardinal Magnone gave to Festa before he hung up. "Claudio, I don't have to explain to you why the media must be kept out of this matter. Especially now with the conclave upon us."

Inspector General Festa arrived at the crime scene less than thirty minutes after Cardinal Magnone received the call.

As he walked into the gruesome scene, Festa saw First Captain Vito Perna who was in charge of the homicide investigation and who was highly aware of the inspector was. Neither acknowledged the obvious: draped over the velvet, cushioned chair in the room were two pair of pants and two shirts, but on the table next to it were also two rosaries and two breviaries. The prayer books that priests use daily.

"The door lock was evidently picked, Inspector General. There are fresh markings on the lock panel. This is a professional job," Captain Perna said.

"Have we calculated the approximate time of death?" Festa asked.

"The *medico legale* is still here, I believe. He has the time between one-thirty and three o'clock this morning."

"Any blood tracks or markings?"

"The scene was untouched when we arrived. No, sir, nothing of the sort."

"Any defense signs on either of the deceased?

"No, sir. None."

"Any sexual mutilation? We often see that with homosexual homicides."

"Look for yourself, sir. None at all. The murder was done quickly."

"Captain Perna, Please recreate the homicide for me, will you? The best you can, if you please," Festa asked.
"Of course. It appears the murderer came into the room silently. There would have been some light coming from a street lamp outside so the room wouldn't have been completely dark. The two lovers, I'm sorry, the two men were in an embrace. What today would be called "spooning", please forgive me."

"Go on, Captain."

"We believe the victims were sleeping, sir, due to the identical stab marks into their necks. The thrust of the weapon looks as if they were done simultaneously."

"Why sleeping?"

"There are signs that they already had sexual contact, Inspector General."

" I see. Put those details into your report, please. And why do you think they were stabbed simultaneously?"

"The murderer stood above the victims, a cross in each of his hands, and he simply buried the weapon into both of their carotid arteries. Look how one victim's blood splattered on the ceiling here, that is the darker man's. He was hugging the lighter man from behind. The lighter man's blood shot to the ceiling and walls here and here. They never even had a chance to call for help."

"And you are so sure it was a male perpetrator?"

"Sir, respectfully, I believe the killer to be John Deegan himself. Almost the exact same *motes operandi* as before, with all of his killings."

"Okay, thank you." Festa was trying to remain calm on the outside but his head was spinning with wonder on how this was going to be played down for the public. *John Deegan again and we have gay, priest lovers inside the Vatican? Only a fucking magician is going to be able to get us out of this one! he thought to himself.* Calmly he continued, "I will be here for a while, so keep me informed if anything else comes up. But for now, when I came up here I saw some news reporters, one from *RAI*, and a few newspaper people, a couple of independent photographers you know, bottom feeders. They are not, under any circumstances, to know these two men were Catholic priests. You will now take their garments, put them in that black, evidence bag and give it to me. I will also take these articles back with me to the Vatican for proper disposal." He swiped the rosaries and breviaries and put them in his own pocket. "You know these things are personal items of consecrated men, and must be handled in a very delicate manner. As far as the media is concerned, this homicide was a tragic lover's quarrel. Just two, dead, gay men, that's all. It happens all the time. No talk of John Deegan, no crucifix murder-talk. Now, do you understand me, Captain Vito Perna?" Festa asked. "I will be leaving out the back."

"Yes, of course I do, sir." Covering up wasn't anything cops around the world hadn't done before for the deteriorating, Roman Catholic Church.

Festa stood nose to nose with the captain and gritted his teeth. "I'm telling you, I swear, if it leaks out that these two men were priests, and you and I right now, under God, know they obviously weren't even Catholic, for God's sake, you will be immediately be transferred to Naples as a school monitor, instead of being granted a promotion to Colonel. Which is what the Secretary of State of the Vatican and I will highly recommend for you."

CHAPTER 25

Angela Quagliata was now an employee of Centurion Associates, LLC. The administrator of *Klinik Hirslanden* graciously accepted her resignation and agreed her new position was an incredible opportunity for her. Angela would be paid for two weeks plus accrued vacation time and allowed to leave the *Klinik* immediately.

Her first assignment for Vic and Raquel was to get them an appointment with Drs. Baumer and Eschmann, no easy task for a Sunday afternoon. Angela used her friendship with both doctors and her charm to get a meeting at the *Klinik* at noon. They all met in a large, but Spartan, conference room with windows that overlooked a small pond with a few, white swans and some brown geese.

"Thank you both for seeing us on your day off, doctors. If it were not a matter of great importance we could have met tomorrow," Vic said.

"This is highly unconventional, Mr. Gonnella, as we generally do not discuss our patients' conditions with anyone other than close family members," Dr. Baumer stated.

"We understand, sir. However, we are not interested in Mr. De Luca's medical condition, only his whereabouts," Raquel added.

"That also falls under the scope of patient confidentiality," Dr. Baumer insisted.

"It's time to put our cards on the table doctors. As Angela has told you both, we are private investigators, and… "

Dr. Baumer interrupted Vic, "We are aware of who you are, Mr. Gonnella. At Angela's insistence we Googled your name and company. Quite impressive credentials, and congratulations on your great success.

However, you need to understand our position in this case. We have liability issues, as we're sure you know."

"Mr. De Luca is John Deegan, you understand that at this point I imagine. He is an international criminal who may very well be involved in two recent homicides which are currently under investigation, not to mention his string of murders from years past."

"Sadly that is not our concern," Dr. Baumer insisted.

"So you are not concerned with being charged with obstruction of justice?" Raquel said. Vic quickly glanced at Raquel for her cop like tone.

"Young woman, this is Switzerland. Our laws differ from those in your country. We are only concerned with the cancer treatment of Mr. De Luca. Beyond that we have no culpability or responsibility to assist you in this matter," Dr. Baumer said. He had now become quite irritated by the questioning.

"I understand and apologize for the manner in which this meeting is going. I would like to ask you a question about Mr. Deegan however. Is he planning to continue his treatment elsewhere?" Vic asked.

"Yes, he is."

"Can you be so kind as to tell us where he will be treated?" Vic asked. He knew what answer he would receive.

"No, sir, I cannot," Dr. Baumer said.

"Are you at least satisfied Mr. Deegan will be well cared for?"

"Assuming Mr. De Luca is your John Deegan my answer is yes. He will be in capable hands," Dr. Baumer answered.

"Dr. Eschmann, in your professional opinion, is the patient of sound mind and judgment?" Raquel asked.

"If I answered that question I would be going against the patient's rights to his privacy."

"We are not attempting to apprehend Mr. Deegan. That could have been easily accomplished by our telling Interpol that he was in your *Klinik* days ago," Vic said.

"So, why didn't you?" Dr. Baumer asked.

"Very simple doctor. We believe Mr. Deegan and his wife are in great, mortal danger and may be involved with a situation of potentially great disaster. Someone is trying to set him up, to frame him for murders he could not have possibly committed. We simply want to get to the bottom of why Mr. Deegan has gone deep," Vic said.

"Deep?" Dr. Baumer asked.

"Sorry, that is law enforcement jargon for under cover."

"On the lamb? I've seen some American gangster movies," Dr. Baumer said. He laughed at his wording.

"Yes, doctor, on the lamb is a very good way to put it," Raquel said with a giggle. Raquel was trying to get back to the good cop side.

"All I will tell you is that Mr. Deegan, or rather Mr. De Luca, was advised to stay here where we can better control his treatment, but the fact is he decided against our medical advice. Even that information I am uncomfortable telling you," Dr. Baumer said.

"Well, again, thank you taking time out of your family day doctors. We apologize for the intrusion," Vic said, ending the meeting.

Both doctors left on a cordial note. Vic, Raquel, and Angela stayed in the conference room.

"No sense pissing up a rope," Vic said.

"Pissing up a rope?" Angela asked.

"That's Vic's crude way of saying waste any time," Raquel said.

"What do you think?" Vic asked Raquel.

"I think Deegan paid them a lot of money. Under the circumstances, that patient confidentiality shield is total bullshit." Raquel said.

"I agree, but it still doesn't help us find Deegan. We don't know who we're up against and what they are capable of doing if they will find him before we do," Vic said.

CHAPTER 26

Pope Francis met with Cardinal Law that morning and con-celebrated mass at Law's former church, the *Basilica di Santa Maria Maggiore,* in Rome. Law was the former arch-priest at this cathedral. His Holiness and the cardinal then met behind closed doors for over an hour.

Colonel Zellweger found Cardinal Law reprehensible. Zellwe-ger tried to wait patiently for Pope Francis to finish that meeting and return to the Apostolic Palace.

Zellweger was mumbling to himself. *They throw him out of Boston and he is rewarded with this magnificent Cathedral. Do the people in the United States know about this? They even had this bastard officiate at the funeral mass of John Paul II. What courage this church has, thinking the world are all fools… sheep! Law protects pedophiles and his gay horde of priests, and he is never punished. All of them are beyond contempt. I would stomp on his corpse if given even half a chance!*

On the ride back to the Vatican, Francis was complaining about a severe headache. His physician, riding in the small Fiat with Francis did not like his heart rate and his sudden ashen look. The doctor decid-ed it was best to go directly to *Policlinico Universitario Agostino Gemelli* albeit over the objections from the Holy Father.

Colonel Zellweger, even though he was planning on killing every cardinal of the church, felt sympathy toward the man he swore to protect. He immediately contacted his second in command to reinforce security at the hospital. Zellweger began saying prayers in his mind for Francis' health and recovery.

The news wire announced the turn of events within the hour.

Corriere della Sera broke the news first.

This morning, His Holiness Pope Francis was rushed to Gemelli Hospital under observation. No further information available at this moment.

The global news media, already in Rome preparing for the conclave, rushed to *Gemelli* with their satellite news trucks. The media was already speculating on the pope's condition and suggested perhaps it was the real reason for his resignation.

One reporter from the United States was at the hospital and gave his report which was picked up on all American networks, interrupting early morning broadcasts.

"His Holiness, Pope Francis was rushed by car to *Gemelli* hospital in Rome. He remains under guarded condition. An exact reason for his emergency admittance is not clear at this time but rumors are pointing to a possible brain tumor." The announcer was practically shouting over the crowd that had now gathered, all with rosaries in hand. "The seventy-five year old Pontiff has officially tendered his resignation on July 12th of this year, becoming the third Pope to resign in the past six hundred years. *Gemelli* is the very hospital where the beloved Pope John Paul II was brought in 1981 after being shot four times in St. Peter's Square."

On the way back to the Dolmer Hotel with Raquel, Vic's cell phone rang.

It was John Deegan calling. Vic was driving and handed the phone to Raquel after hitting the speaker feature.

"Are we in for another nursery rhyme?" Vic asked to begin the conversation.

"I suppose I can recite me wee, Irish mum's favorite, Dirty Maryanne, but I think I may have fergotten all the words," Deegan said in his practiced brogue.

"What are you up to these days, John?" Raquel asked.

"Resting and recuperating at the moment."

"I suppose you're calling about Francis? It's all over the news," Vic said.

"Now why would I be calling about him? I really couldn't care less if he lives or dies. He's past tense anyway. No, I'm calling about the latest John Deegan killing."

"Another one?" Raquel asked in disbelief.

"Another two. Do you mean your friends at Interpol haven't alerted you already?" Deegan queried.

"I don't think we are on the must call list at the moment," Vic said.

"Anyway, my sources tell me that two gay priests were dispatched in Rome. Tragic ending, don't you both think, the crucifix and all?"

"You have sources?" Raquel asked.

"It's a funny thing about money. When you spread it out you get a lot of information otherwise unavailable," Deegan said.

"Like you did at the *Klinik*?" Vic countered.

"Very good, Vic. You are starting to think like a rich man! Guilty as charged."

"So where are you? Back home?" Raquel asked.

"I will tell you the truth. Not back home, but I will give you a little bit of a hint. We are in Italy."

"That's a pretty big country."

"I'll narrow it down with another hint. We are in just one of the twenty regions, in only one of the hundred and ten provinces. And they eat pasta a lot." Deegan couldn't help but laugh.

"That must have cost you a pretty penny to keep the *Klinik* on your side," Vic said. He chose to ignore Deegan's geography game.

"Delightful people. It's an interesting dynamic what some will do when they see the glitter of gold," Deegan retorted.

So tell us John, being you are in Italy, you may have had the opportunity to murder those two gay priests, yes?" Raquel asked.

"Very good try, my lovely and favorite Puerto Rican. What do you think?"

"Not sure what to think anymore, John. The world is becoming a more difficult place to understand by the day," Raquel answered.

"When I look closely at the world, it's no more brutal than I've seen in sixty-six years. Only the news gets to us a lot faster these days."

"John, seriously now, we are concerned that you and Gjuliana are in great danger. Whoever is trying to frame you is doing a fucking, damn good job of it," Vic said.

"Let me take care of the whoever. I'm not without skills, you know." Deegan ended the call.

CHAPTER 27

At the top of the famous *Scalinata di Trinità dei Monti*, is the Hassler Hotel, arguably the most elegant hotel in Rome. Just a few yards from the Hassler, the famed Spanish Steps are a steep, slope of stairs that go down to the remarkably busy *Piazza di Spagna*. Dozens of people sit on the steps enjoying a quick panini or pizza, or just people watching as the throngs of tourists and locals pass by. The *Fontana della Barcaccia*, the *Fountain of the Ugly Boat* sits a few yards from the bottom of the steps. Rome was about to get ugly in the days ahead.

John Deegan a/k/a Giovanni De Luca, now Sean Brady of Dublin, Ireland, paid for the Presidential Suite, at the Hassler in advance for thirty nights. At twenty thousand Euros per night, just do the math.

The luxury of the suite put the fancy digs at the *Klinik* to shame. Connected to the Deegans' massive two-bedroom apartment was a well-appointed, double room for the Deegans' loyal and trusted houseman. The breathtakingly, panoramic view of the city of Rome seemed more like a painting than windows. Renaissance tapestries, velvet sofas and chairs, antique furniture dating from late eighteen hundred Italian and French designers, and crystal chandeliers added to an experience of opulence reserved for the one tenth of one percent.

The classic Roman colors; Pompeian red and ochre ruled the motif of the suite, as well as the hotel's common areas.

"I feel so refined staying at the Hassler, my love. Not so bad for a poor, Irish kid who was molested when he was a kid. I could have really turned bad, you know," Deegan said. He howled with laughter.

"John, really please! Can't you not always allude to your past? Just be thankful for what you have and enjoy it, will you?" Gjuliana commanded. Gjuliana was still fighting her own internal battle. She'd waited for so long to be with the love of her life, and the thought now of him possibly dying soon left her a bit teste.

"I am thankful! I thank you for waiting for me, I thank the United States government for excellent training, I thank capitalism, and of course, I am ever so grateful to my sweet, dear, Irish mother, Maureen for making me the most compliant child you ever met," Deegan said, his voice tapering off. The compliant child comment put Deegan in a dark place. John's bright, blue eyes turned almost brown-green as he stared out at the eternal city. Gjuliana knew something had triggered the past agony he'd suffered by the priests and bishops who molested him, robbing him of his innocence and youth. She forced a smile for his sake.

"John, let's play dress up. I'll put on one of my classic, Albanian dresses with a bejeweled necklace and you can do one of your great disguises. I really want to go on a shopping spree at the *Via dei Condotti*. The stores are just at the bottom of the Spanish Steps," Gjuliana asked.

Deegan instantly snapped out of his funk.

"I don't know, my love. The stairs going down will be fine, but this bum leg of mine will never make it back up those hundred and thirty something steps."

"But you don't have a bad leg," Gjuliana laughed.

"No I don't, but the Viet Nam vet I'm going to be disguised as stepped on a land mine in the battle of Bok Choi."

"Bok Choi is a vegetable, you clown," Gjuliana was now doubled over with laughter.

Gjuliana had no intention of shopping. She knew John loathed going into stores and browsing, and she vowed to herself not to waste a moment's time for as long as she had him with her.

When they got to the bottom of the Spanish Steps Gjuliana saw a plaque on a house that interested her.

"Look Sean, the Keats-Shelly house. This is where John Keats lived and died. Percy Bysshe Shelly hung out there for a while, I believe," Gjuliana called Deegan by his new cover name. "I read they have all kinds of manuscripts and letters from Lord Byron, Browning, Wilde. Would you like to see it?"

"I would rather contract cholera. Unless, of course, you want to go in, my love," Deegan said.

"No, but I do want to go inside Babington's Tea Room right next door. Look at how beautiful that building is! I just love the pastel and brown colors all around us. Let's have a spot of tea," Gjuliana said in a put on English accent.

I hate the fucking English, Deegan thought to himself.

"That would be fun. Maybe I can have one of those scones with the raisins?" Deegan said.

"No, we will have plain tea with organic honey if they have it with lemon. We need to meet with your new chef in an hour, and you must call Dr. Baumer."

John and Gjuliana walked arm in arm for blocks and blocks enjoying the Roman scenery. John's dark blue with gold lettering Viet Nam Veteran cap got some attention from real Viet Nam vets who would salute and say some things about how they all need to stick together.

Gjuliana got a wink from a middle aged, Italian man who was sitting alone in an outside café with an espresso and a cigarette. She rolled her eyes.

Their afternoon together was glorious.

Back at the Hassler, Gjuliana poured herself a glass of mineral water and sat out on the terrace. Deegan called Dr. Baumer.

"Hello, Mr. De Luca. Are you feeling well?" Dr. Baumer asked.

"Feeling pretty good, just a bit tired after a long walk," Deegan answered.

"A nice walk is good for you. Keep that up."

"Have you made a connection for my treatments, Doctor?"

"Yes, we have. First of all, I want to thank you again for your generosity. You are one of a kind, Mr. De Luca."

"You're very welcome, Dr. Baumer. I am so delighted to help you and your family meet your goals. They really broke the mold when they made me, didn't they?" Deegan joked.

"Yes. At any rate, I have made arrangements with an oncologist colleague of mine, Dr. Davide Solarino to visit you daily at your location. He, along with a nurse, will administer the chemical treatments I have prescribed. I guarantee your anonymity. As far as he is concerned, you are Sean Brady, an Irish industrialist. I went to university with Davide; he is a great friend. He has two kids and a young wife he cannot afford. Davide has agreed with pleasure, to his compensation."

"And the radiation treatments?"

"I will be sending your houseman instructions via text. When it is time to commence radiation treatments, you will be going to *Instituto Nazioanale Tumori Regina Elena,* also under the direction of Davide Solarino. He is director of oncology there. You are in the best of care. Now to your diet and psychological condition. I believe that a nutritionist has an appointment with you sometime today, yes?"

"Yes, I believe my wife and houseman will be seeing her."

"Perfect. Also, Dr. Eschmann will be calling you daily via Skype. I insist you speak to him at least once a day. If you need him, he can always fly down to Rome for the day."

"Skype will be sufficient. I think we are ready to rock n' roll, Dr. Baumer," Deegan did his best Elvis Presley imitation, which was completely lost on the impassive Swiss doctor.

CHAPTER 28

Pope Francis was resting comfortably at *Gemelli*. Some light medication relieved him of his severe headache, but the doctors wanted to run some more tests. They all agreed the Pontiff was under an extreme amount of stress, and so they ordered complete best rest and quiet. No meetings, no calls, no politics - just alone time.

Many cardinals were already amassing in Rome for the conclave and were clamoring and bumping into each at the Vatican like a room full of expectant fathers. Just like in a horse race, pole positioning was essential and the major *papilla* were overtly vying for the attention of the other voting cardinals. The elderly non-voting cardinals were basically ignored.

Colonel Zellweger remained at *Gemelli* to be close to his charge, the Holy Father. Zellweger had not yet heard back from Deegan and was becoming increasingly anxious about what the mastermind had in store for his deadly plan.

Zellweger also had some unfinished business of his own needing attention.

Angela arrived at the Dolmer in Zürich to meet with Vic and Raquel. Even though she was dressed in tight, blue jeans with the chic, well-placed cuts and tears, a pair of black, high heels, and a white V-neck, t-shirt, Vic hardly noticed Angela when she entered the suite. He was busy checking on the Interpol I 24/7 site. Raquel was busy on the telephone with her mother checking on their baby daughter.

"Okay, let's get down to business," Vic said.

Vic continued, "Angela you need to get on line and read every-thing available on Deegan. Review the entire case, his life history, the murders, and anything else you can find. I want you to start to under-stand his mentality and what makes him tic. Raquel and I know, at least partially, how he thinks," Vic said.

"I've already started doing that. I think I know more about him than I know about my own father."

"Good. So now let's review what we already have," Vic ordered.

Raquel chimed in. "Angela, we think Deegan is in Italy. At least that's what he's told us. Where would he go for specialized, cancer treatments assuming he hasn't given up?"

"No way Gjuliana will allow him to quit. She adores him too much," Vic said.

"I believe he is in Rome," Angela said.

Vic and Raquel looked at each other in astonishment at the rookie's bold assumption.

"Okay, tell us. Why?" Raquel asked.

"In Italy, there are not too many great, cancer clinics. Milan, Verona, and Rome, but beyond that there is no survival possibility for Deegan. They are the only choices Deegan has. The public hospitals are an abomination here in my home country. Many hospitals, both private and public, require the patients to bring their own bedding, and the wait time to see even an average physician is intolerable. I doubt if a wealthy man such as Deegan would put himself in that environment. Italy is not like the States where you have choices in nearly every major city. He is in Rome because that's where the action is. Rome has quite a large selection of high end accommodations, a few excellent private clinics, and the best transportation hubs... should Deegan require a fast get-a-way."

"She makes sense, Raquel. I feel we are here in Zürich with our heads up our asses. Let's get to Rome on the first available flight," Vic said.

"I've already reserved the tickets. There is an Alitalia flight this afternoon at three thirty. We arrive at *Fiumicino* at around five," Angela said. Her manner was matter-of-fact.

"You already assumed we were going?" Raquel asked with a smile.

"Of course. It makes sense. Believe me, Deegan is in Rome; that is the smart choice for him," Angela said dryly.

"Perhaps a bit too obvious, though?" Raquel asked.

"He said he is in Italy for one reason and one reason only. He wants you to follow him." Angela was certain she was correct.

"Holy shit, I think she has something there, baby, I mean Raquel," Vic said, correcting himself.
"Now Angela, tell us you know where he is staying," Vic said.

"That will be a bit more difficult. A villa? An apartment? A Hotel? We have a lot of work to do," Angela replied.

In the meantime, back at Vatican City..:

Inspector Claudio Festa was summoned to the office of the Secretary of State of the Vatican City State, at his office in the Apostolic Palace. It wasn't very often Inspector Festa visited the pope's palace. Less than fifteen times in all the years he worked in the Vatican helping to protect and defend the leaders of his church. The Inspector could recall every visit he made to this palace. Festa always got butterflies in his stomach upon entering the palace, and once or twice he experienced an actual stomach ache.

It was nothing at all like having a meeting at the *Palazzo del Governatorato*, the Vatican government offices that were in the Papal gardens directly behind the great Basilica. An eclectic, tan colored, four-story, office building that was once three buildings and then they were joined together, the government building was almost like home to Festa. The Apostolic Palace was another story altogether.

To the right of St. Peter's square a variety of tan and copper colored buildings make up the Palace which includes the Sistine Chapel, the Vatican Museum, as well as the papal apartments. Over a dozen, palatial rooms surrounded by the finest European tapestries and frescoes from the best of the Renaissance masters adorn the walls and ceilings. Many popes and world leaders have walked on the white, brown, green, purple, and red marble which have been placed in various shapes and geometric patterns, prominently adorning the floors for hundreds of years. The furniture, mostly ornate Italian and French works of art in their own rite, are largely red velvet padding surrounded by gold-painted, show wood. The paintings on the ceilings tell the story of Christianity from its inception. Some of the ceilings within the palace are like three-dimensional woodcarvings, painted in gold and other rich colors, adding to the lavishness of the rooms they cover. There is nothing humble about the palace. Festa kept his eyes focused on the marble floors as he walked to meet Cardinal Magnone so as to be less intimidated by the sheer opulence of the sacred palace.

"Inspector, thank you for coming on short notice. His Holiness very much appreciates the manner in which you handled the unfortunate incident at *Via di San Giovanni in Laterano*. However, there may be a problem," Cardinal Magnone said.

"A problem, Your Eminence?"

"Yes. I received a surprise visit from the Archbishop of New York, who is already here for the conclave. It seems there has been a leak. Nothing surprises me about secrecy or shall I say the damn lack of secrecy within our walls. Anything that is confidential somehow always defies loyalty among our clergy."

"A leak? Regarding the incident?"

"Regarding that one and the other two priests who were murdered as well. Well, technically one is defrocked, but we must still consider him one of our own under the circumstances."

"A leak where?"

"The cardinal received a call from one of the members of his Cardinal Committee of the Laity, a devout catholic who manages one of the New York daily newspaper tabloids. They are about to print a story unless the cardinal can use his influence, and God help him, he may, about the four murders. They are claiming John Deegan is back doing the devil's work."

"That is very possible, Your Eminence. With the conclave about to start, what better stage can Deegan ask for?" Festa asked rhetorically.

"I understand. We have also heard from Interpol in Lyon. They agree that the manner in which these priests were murdered fits Deegan's methods."

"Forgive me, Eminence, with the conclave about to begin, my concern and my responsibility is here. I can ill afford to be involved with finding Deegan."

"I fully understand that, Inspector. However, I don't want to just pass this problem on to my successor. The public relations issues about to befall us are enormous. We can no longer escape the clerical sexual abuse scandal which has tormented the last three popes. Having to constantly do damage control is getting tougher and tougher. The laity, and especially the younger generation aren't buying it anymore. Having this occur now is extremely bad timing for the Holy See when all eyes are upon us anyhow."

"No doubt, Your Eminence. Don't worry. I am here to assist in any way you command."

"We think it best you contact Mr. Gonnella in New York and ask him to come to Rome and further ask him, as a paid consultant, of course, to work closely with Interpol and yourself. This Deegan mastermind must be stopped at any cost and Gonnella is the one man who may be able to defuse this… this maniac. Remember, Mr. Gonnella single-handedly saved our cardinal from sure death right here in Rome as you recall. Deegan has been a scourge to us all. I hope he rots in hell."

"I will contact Mr. Gonnella immediately, Eminence."

"It is best if Deegan is, how shall I put this gently, not allowed to be a martyr for his cause. If you recall, this killer became somewhat of a folk hero of sorts. We cannot abide this to continue, Inspector. Do I make myself clear?"

"Yes, I understand. We have the proper resources at our disposal to eliminate the problem."

"Very well, Inspector. I want you to keep me apprised on a daily basis, no matter the time."

Festa quickly left the palace, only peeking at some of the overwhelmingly, lavish artworks as he was escorted out.

Upon landing at Rome's, *Fiumicino* airport, both Vic and Raquel's cell phones had multiple calls from their New York Headquarters.

Vic called his assistant and learned he had received several urgent calls from Inspector General Festa. Vic decided to wait until they checked into a hotel before returning the calls.

Angela busied herself trying to find rooms, pounding away at her cell phone. With the summer in full tourist mode and the impending conclave, this was no easy task. Angela had tried to get accommodations for over an hour from Zürich with no success. Luckily, through good contacts in Rome, she was able to find two rooms at the *Parco dei Principi* in the Borghese Gardens. Not the most centrally located, the hotel was a mile or so away from midtown.

The trio hailed a cab from the airport. Angela knew a rented car was not the way to go into Rome, and taxis are always readily available throughout the city.

The two rooms were typically Italian. Very small, very clean, and in the Borghese Gardens, very quiet.

Before Vic called the inspector, he quickly checked his other voice messages to see if there were any from Deegan, but there were none. "Inspector Festa, this is Vic Gonnella. I hope your English is good. If not, my European director can translate," Vic said.

"No need, Mr. Gonnella, my English is good, if you can tolerate my accent."

"What can I do for you, sir?"

"Mr. Gonnella, I will cut to the chase, as you Americans say. The Vatican is in need of your services. I have been asked by the highest authorities inside the Holy See to ask for your assistance. How long will it take you to come to Rome?"

"What kind of services are you looking for?" Vic asked bluntly.

"We have reason to believe that John Deegan has again been targeting and killing our beloved priests again." Vic rolled his eyes and felt his stomach acid, but he said nothing. "There have been four homicides, two here in Rome. We can arrange immediate transportation for you. Your expertise is urgent and vital for us to put an end to this carnage."

"I can be at your office within the hour, Inspector. I happen to have just arrived in Rome."

"Uncanny luck! I will send my men to bring you. Where are you staying?"

"Inspector, with all due respect, we work quietly. How do you say, *sotto voce?* We will arrive at the Vatican on our own. Just tell me where we go when we arrive."

Vic, Raquel, and Angela freshened themselves and made their way to the Vatican. The taxi ride took twenty minutes. Angela admonished the driver to take the direct route across the River Tiber. She knew some taxi drivers in Rome are famous for running up the tab.

On the sly, Colonel Zellweger was also taking a short trip himself.

Pope Francis was sound asleep. His physicians had prescribed a mild sedative to calm their patient and allow for uninterrupted rest. Zellweger spoke with the pope's personal doctor himself, discovering that His Holiness would sleep through the night.

In less than an hour, dusk would settle over Rome, helping to mask Zellweger's nefarious deed.

Father Pasquale Ferrara, one of the two assistants to Cardinal Paulo Bazzini arrived at *Il Diavolo Dentro*, The Devil Inside gay bar on *Via Prenestina*. Father Ferrara, as was his habit, visited the *Dentro* every Sunday evening for an evening of anonymous, homosexual encounters.

At The Devil Inside, the customers pay at the door, cash only, and may opt to purchase towels, lubrication, condoms, and toys.

A low ceiling led to the dark labyrinth of glory holes and individual cabins that awaited horny men who were seeking a suitable partner.

Father Ferrara found an open cabin, placed his jeans and polo shirt inside, and in a pair of white, boxer shorts stood and waited for a new lover.

A few minutes later, a swarthy man, handsome with full, wavy, dark brown hair, well built with a thick chest and muscular arms stood in the doorway of the cabin. The man was clothed in tight jeans and an orange muscle shirt.

"Hello, there. I'm Rocco. You interest me."

"Hi, I'm Pasquale. What do you like?"

"I can tell you what I don't like. This place is filthy. Can you spend the night with me at my place?"

"Not the whole night, but yeah. Do you have a place nearby?"

"Two blocks away. A studio I use just for fun. I'm married, but my wife is as cold as witches' tits."

"I'm game. Give me a moment."

As planned ahead of time, Zellweger waited inside a vehicle in an industrial area a few blocks from the *Dentro*. The colonel had commandeered one of the official Swiss Guard automobiles. He had woven his way rapidly in and out of traffic for the thirty-minute drive. Now, he could see Father Ferrara and Rocco Rotigliano walking hand-in-hand toward him. A few feet from the car, Rocco gave a quick check around to see if anyone was near. Sadly for the young gay priest, there was to be no last minute reprieve.

Rocco pulled the scrawny, young priest close to him with his left hand, bashing his head with a short, leather, flap-jack he had kept hidden in his jeans with his right. The blows rendered the unsuspecting Father Ferrara semi-conscious.

"*Orecchione, fa schifoso, leccacazzi brutto,*" Rocco seethed into the priest's ear. Filthy, faggot, ugly, dick licker, or something in that vein.

Zellweger exited his car, leaving the driver side door open.

"*Vai velocemente,*" Zellweger said to Rocco. Rocco walked away from the scene quickly.

Zellweger took his weapon from the inside pocket of his suit jacket, holding it in his right hand but behind his back.

The Colonel slapped Father Ferrara to bring him back to consciousness.

"You? What are you doing here?" Ferrara asked.

"Me? No, Father, what are *you* doing here? You see, I've followed you many a Sunday evening. Always the same god forsaken place. Always doing the things you condemn in others. You are a hypocrite of the worst order, soiling the name of our Lord's church."

"Please, I've hurt no one. This is who I am," Ferrara said almost weeping.

"And I, as a messenger of Jesus Christ, need to clean my church of the filth that has polluted it," Zellweger said, his eyes bulging. The colonel's rapid respiration made him lightheaded.

With no compassion, Zellweger showed the young priest the pointed, wooden crucifix, holding it close to his victim's face.

"Merciful God!" Ferrara's final words were close to a whisper.

Zellweger buried the cross into the young man's larynx, pulling down hard, exposing his esophagus and stomach.

Unlike the way he rolled his eyes during his encounter with Zellweger at the apostolic palace, Father Ferrara rolled his eyes again but for his last time. This time they were rolled into the back of his head.

CHAPTER 29

The taxi dropped off Vic, Raquel, and Angela on the *Viale Vaticano* just across the narrow street from the Vatican Museum where Inspector Festa and two of his men were waiting. There was no long line for the museum as it was closed at this hour. Festa recognized Vic from his time in Rome and hurried to greet him.

"Mr. Gonnella, it is so good to see you again. Thank you for coming to Vatican City," Festa said. The men shook hands and the introductions were passed around.

"Inspector Festa, please meet my partner Raquel Ruiz and our Director of International Business, Ms. Angela Quagliata." Festa shook Raquel's hand and turned to Angela.

"Ah, Quagliata, *Italiana?*"

"Si, Inspector, I'm Sicilian. Born in Palermo," Angela responded.

"My mother is from Palermo. I'm sure we can discuss our common heritage at some point. For now, please let's all go to the *Gendarmeria* office which is inside the walls just over to our right."

Inside Festa's stark but bright office the trio was offered refreshments from a buffet table. Vic and Raquel took coffee while Angela made a plate of *biscotti* for the table.

"We Italians must offer something to our guests or we are thought of as rude," Festa said cordially.

"Reminds me of my grandmother's home. Without coffee and something sweet she wouldn't even talk with us," Vic said.

"I am so pleased you were all in Rome. What brings you to the eternal city?"

"We are looking for an office somewhere in Europe. We thought Rome may be a good place to start," Vic lied.

"Excellent choice. I am at your service if you need any help or advice. Perhaps the Vatican will be your first client. Let me start by saying we are in need of your services and expertise. I received word this morning that yet another priest was murdered last night, right here in Rome. It is very close to home. A young priest stationed in the Vatican was found killed with a wooden crucifix à la John Deegan. Many of the priests and visiting cardinals are a bit jumpy as you can understand. There have been no public reports or comments on this matter. The media is being kept out of this homicide for obvious reasons."

"Because of the conclave, I suppose?" Raquel asked.

"Yes, of course. We are not looking for any spectacular publicity that will mar the proceedings. We have enough of that as you can imagine."

"Can you tell us about this priest?" Vic asked.

"I will be frank with all of you. We must start with an open and honest dialogue if we are to apprehend the killer. Father Pasquale Ferrara was assigned to Cardinal Bazzini, the *camerlengo* of the Vatican. I assume you know the importance of the *camerlengo* to the conclave?"
"Yes, we know his role." Raquel said.

"Father Ferrara was killed near a known gay meeting place. It was no secret to us that he was homosexual," Festa stated.

"Was he ever implicated in any sexual abuse situations?"

"Not at all. No indication of pedophilia in his background, none at all."

"So, then what then makes you believe Deegan is the killer?" Vic asked.

"The crucifix for one, and the manner in which it was used. A classic Deegan killing, Mr. Gonnella. I will have photographs of the crime scene and the body within the hour."

"Yes, we would be interested in studying the photographs and any other forensic evidence, but I think you're making a broad assumption with all due respect, Inspector. Deegan has never murdered anyone who was not an abuser of children. Homosexuals have never been his target," Vic stated emphatically.

"Perhaps he is broadening his horizon?" Festa asked.

"Highly doubtful. Knowing his psychological profile, Deegan had no interest in this kind of person, a gay man."

Deegan is not your killer, Inspector. We have a copycat on our hands at the moment," Raquel added.

"We know of the killer's other recent homicides, Inspector. We are also aware Deegan was not able to perform these killings," Vic said.

"Not able?"

"John Deegan has terminal cancer and was in the hospital at the time those homicides took place. Frankly, he was not even physically able to carry out these kinds of killings," Vic said.

"It sounds like you have more knowledge of the homicides, Mr. Gonnella. What are you not telling us? Do you know of Deegan's whereabouts?"

"We know where he was at the time of the other killings," Vic responded.

"And now? Where is Deegan now?" Festa demanded. The Inspector was beginning to feel Vic was not being totally candid with him.

"Somewhere in Italy," Raquel replied.

"Hmmm, somewhere in Italy. So perhaps he is in Rome? Perhaps that is what really brought you here, Mr. Gonnella?

"Yes, we are assuming he may be in Rome," Vic confessed.

"So, in spite of your belief that Deegan did not murder Father Ferrara, he may have had the opportunity if he is in Rome," Festa stated.

"But no motive," Raquel quickly replied.

"And his physical condition precludes him," Vic added.

"I feel you all need to be more open about your intentions in this case. If you are to help us find Deegan we need to…"

"Inspector, forgive me for interrupting, but we have not agreed to work for the Vatican to find John Deegan. We will however, work with you to find the real killer. So let's just put that all on the table so we can begin our investigation. There are things you also are not telling us and frankly, we, too are holding our cards close to the vest as well," Vic said.

"*Alora*, I agree. I will give you what I have. As you say, my cards will now be on the table."

"Good, well, we haven't eaten yet, so how 'bout we buy you and your men some dinner?" Vic asked.

"We accept your invitation on two conditions. The Vatican will pay for our dinner, and I get to choose the restaurant," Festa said.

170

"Fabulous!" Raquel said.

"And Angela, where we are going you will think your grandmother was in the kitchen."

CHAPTER 30

Amid the beauty of Rome and the opulence of the Hassler Hotel, John Deegan was brooding. With all the magnificent aromas wafting from the hotel's five-star restaurant, the sight of the glorious pastas, pizzas, and plump cannolis at the *trattoria Pretoria* along the *Piazza di Spagna*, John was eating bland, unappealing things not fit for a man of his culinary experience. He felt well enough physically, but emotionally he was simply unhappy. To add insult to injury, the next morning Dr. David Solarino and his lead nurse would be visiting to draw blood and discuss his upcoming treatments.

John decided to call Dr. Eschmann on his cell phone.

"Good evening, my young, Irish lad." John said in his Irish brogue voice.

"And how are you, *John*?" Deegan could hear the tone in his voice but chose to ignore it.

"If I felt any darker, I would be a shadow."

"I can tell by your voice you are a bit depressed. Any particular reason?"

"Well, having cancer is bad enough, but eating like a cow or a rabbit is unbearable. Is this really worth it all?"

"Let me put it this way. Your diet is crucial to the success of your treatment. Now that being said, there will be a time, hopefully in the not too distant future, in which you will be able to enjoy the foods you like again."

"I'm in fucking Italy, Eschmann!" Deegan snapped at him. "This place is all about food and churches. I love food and loathe churches. I'm ready to bury my face in a dish of lasagna."

"A nutritionist I know says if you change your diet for twenty-one days it will become habit. In a short while you will get used to it and see that your body is reacting well to the change. Patience, John."

"I guess I just don't like rules."

"That is an excellent observation. And now that I know who you really are and have done some reading about you, it is clear you are not motivated by structure."

"How do you mean that?"

"You had the structure of a strict, parochial education, then religious training, again with all the rules about right and wrong, then the military, who has more rules than the Catholic Church, and finally Wall Street. If you broke rules, you went to jail," Dr. Eschmann said.

"I hate the word compliance. I have been compliant my whole, entire life. Not just with the priests who assaulted me. Submission, obedience, acquiescence call it any way you prefer. I was all of those things, wasn't I?" Deegan asked.

"And, now?"

"Exactly. Now I look at a stop sign or a red traffic light as simply a suggestion. I really hate to follow rules. You are one hundred percent right. So being put on a diet of hay and oats sprinkled with organic, raw, slivered almonds is a problem because I'm forced to do it."

"Let's avoid the word forced, for now, shall we? How about another way of saying it, John?"

"Let's see, not obligated, not compelled… how about choose? I choose to eat this shit because it will maybe help save my dumb ass life and get me some more time with my wife who needs and loves me."

"Choose is a great way to look at it, and doing it because of your great love for your wife is a wonderful reason and motivator. I'm sure she desires the very best for you; it's clear from what I've read that she loves you very much. And remember, you only need to do this for a short time. Not that you should go back to lasagna five times a week when treatment is over, but I promise you, you will be able to enjoy a great variety of foods in the near future."

"You're pretty smart for an Irishman, Eschmann."

"Half Irish, John. My dad was full German."

"So you never knew if you wanted to drink or invade a small country?" Deegan laughed.

"Very funny, and very close to the truth."

"This little talk helped me young, Eschmann. I'm grateful."

Deegan ended the call.

CHAPTER 31

Inspector Festa chose a typical, Sicilian *trattoria* that was an eight-block walk from the Vatican.

While several *Gendarmeria* vehicles with drivers were at the ready outside the office. Festa thought a nice stroll to *Sicilianbocca* would help the group bond together and perhaps break down any barriers he rightfully had sensed.

Along the way, Festa, flanked by his two men, pointed out places of interest to Vic, Raquel, and Angela.

"Vic, look at that street sign," Raquel said, pointing.

"*Via della Gjuliana!* Wow, that's a coincidence, isn't it?"

"I'd say. Maybe it's some kind of sign or something," Raquel responded.

"Maybe we'll run in to John and Gjuliana," Vis whispered.

"Alora, this is my favorite *trattoria* in all of Rome." Festa announced.

A yellow exterior with a few tables on the sidewalk, *Sicilianbocca* had a welcoming look about it, with no hawkers trying to pull tourists in for dinner.

Once inside, the owners of the *trattoria* greeted Festa by name and ushered the group of six to a yellow and white-checkered table in a quiet corner. Several, large, Sicilian marionettes decorated in medieval armor hung on the wall as the group entered. Sicilian sunbursts in copper-colored terracotta dotted the other walls, flanked with several, ceramic *trinacria* symbols, the three-legged head that is a throwback to the ancient island. The semi-oval, reception desk was made of multi-colored, ceramic tiles depicting Sicilian life from the middle ages with farmers, knights with swords, red tiled roofs on top of old stone houses, and fisherman displaying their catch of the day.

Appropriately placed throughout the restaurant were large planters, with faces of men and women in ceramic, and overflowing with beautiful yellow and red portulaca plants. Even the serving plates and dinnerware were hand painted, Sicilian ceramic with yellow sunbursts surrounded by tiny orange and red birds.

"Will you please all indulge me and allow me to order for the table... family style?" Festa asked, his hand across his chest.

"Order away!" Raquel said.

In perfect Italian, Festa ordered a variety of *antipasti* which included eggplant *caponata*, *cacciocavalo* cheese, *panelle*, deep-fried chick-pea patties, Messina salami, and roasted peppers with anchovies.

Festa's pasta course after the antipasti dish was *pasta con le sarde*, the signature dish of Sicily. He then asked the owner to surprise the table with the main course.

"Ah, *pasta che sarde*, my favorite!" Angela said.

"What is that?" Raquel asked.

"It's a long, thick, pasta called *buccatini* with a sardine sauce made of capers, fennel, and pignoli nuts. To die for when made properly, and something tells me they know how to cook here!" Angela said.

So as not to be rude, Vic whispered to Angela.

"I am not crazy for sardines."

"Believe me, if you don't love this dish you have no Italian blood, Signori Gonnella."

Carafes, ceramic of course, full of white and red, homemade wines were set upon the table along with bottles of mineral water. A bowl of ice was offered, as the owners knew the visitors of Inspector Festa were Americans.

"Angela, tell me, do you speak Sicilian as well as Italian?" Festa asked.

"Of course, I do. My *nona*, to this day, will only speak to me in Sicilian. She knew I would learn Italian in school but wanted me to preserve the Sicilian language, eventually so I can teach my children."

"Eventually?" Festa asked.

"I'm not married. But I hope soon, God willing." She blessed herself as she spoke.

"Today, the young people don't wait until marriage to have children. I'm happy to see that a beautiful woman such as you will be a traditional mother."

"Thank you, Inspector, for both compliments," Angela responded.

"And you, Raquel? Any children?" Festa asked.

"I'm one of those non-traditional mothers. Vic and I have a little baby, a girl. We have not yet rushed to the altar."

"Please forgive my *faux pax*, Raquel and Vic. It was a silly comment." Festa was as red as the plates.

Vic and Raquel both laughed.

"Inspector, we are way past any of that. Raquel is Puerto Rican, and her family reminds us every day to make plans for a big wedding," Vic said.

"And you, Inspector, do you have a wife and family?"

"I have a family, yes. Two boys and one girl. All grown now. I am even a *nono!* A baby girl as well. And I must admit, my daughter lives with the baby's father. Not so traditional."

"And your wife?" Angela asked.

"Sadly, my wife and I have been living apart for many years. We will not divorce because we are Catholic and of course, my position in the Vatican. We live apart because my wife felt I was married to the *Corpo della Gendarmeria dello Stato della Citta Vaticano,* as she bitterly calls it."

"The life of a policeman. Angela, you have heard this before. This is where we say in American idiomatic English, 'been there done that'," Vic said.

"Oh, so you understand? Your former marriage was also affected by your job?"

"Yes, and other things. Meeting Raquel, who was also a policeman, was the best thing that ever happened to me. On many levels, Inspector." He reached over and squeezed Raquel's sexy leg under the table.

The *antipasti* was served in large platters and passed around for everyone to partake.

"Forgive me, but I find it impolite to discuss business while we are having our dinner. Can we wait for coffee and dessert to get underway?" Festa asked.

"Certainly, Inspector. Thank you for your consideration as we are all three starved," Raquel said.

The *antipasti* were devoured as if locust had swarmed the table. Homemade, warm bread sopped up the oil and sauce in the platters, family style.

Next, a huge ceramic bowl arrived with the steaming, aromatic pasta. Vic braced himself for the sardines.

Inspector Festa stood and took the waiter's job, serving each of the diners with a moderate amount of the *buccatini*. His men, silent throughout dinner, felt awkward being served by their superior. Festa sprinkled toasted breadcrumbs atop the pasta.

"Do we sprinkle on the grated cheese now?" Raquel asked.

Angela and the Inspector simultaneously responded, "God forbid!"

Everyone laughed and tasted the sumptuous dish.

The entrée was an amazing selection of rolled swordfish, *bronzino,* and roasted lamb with fresh vegetables and potatoes. Two hours went by like it was twenty minutes.

"Okay, Inspector. May we discuss business yet or are we going to burst altogether?" Vic said. The entire group laughed at his sense of humor.

"I promised to be completely forthcoming to you all. There have been two more homicides I believe you may not be aware of. I ask that you all respect this information as confidential." Festa said.

"Absolutely." Vic said. He looked at the others who were nodding their heads affirmatively. None of them let on that Deegan had already clued them in.

"There were two homosexual priests murdered here in Rome a few days ago. They were in bed together at a well-known gay bar on *Via Laterano*. They were also murdered with wooden crucifixes. We put a blanket of silence and misinformation to deflect any negative publicity. We received word of a leak from the Archbishop of New York who is trying to keep a newspaper in his city from breaking the story."

"That guy knows me very well, Inspector," Vic said.

"We know that. It was he who recommended we contact you to help find Deegan," Festa said.

"It was not Deegan, Inspector. Mr. Deegan was in Switzerland having surgery for his illness," Vic advised.

"How sure are you?"

"We saw Deegan in the hospital. We had breakfast with him, Inspector," Vic admitted.

A waiter came by with plates of homemade cannoli and cassata and fresh fruit for dessert. For the moment no one looked at the sweets.

"Breakfast? I am stunned by this revelation. Why didn't you apprehend him?" Festa asked. The look on his face was incredulous.

"I have my reasons, Inspector. I made a deal with Deegan the night we found the cardinal from New York in his grasp. I don't go against my word, ever," Vic said.

"But… but we must stop him! Don't you see that he is slaughtering priests again? Right here, under the shadow of the Vatican walls!"

Vic was terse with the inspector. "Listen to me. There is another killer loose, and I believe he may very well have a close tie-in to the Vatican."

"Another *priest*? You think another priest is killing his own? That is ludicrous!" Festa retorted.

"On my word to you, that's truly what we believe. We just don't know with complete certainty yet. We need some more time," Vic said.

"Time is not a commodity we have much of. The conclave, remember?"

"We will find Deegan again. I'm going to ask you to stand down and allow us to do our jobs. If I discover we are being followed, or our phones are tapped, or our hotel rooms broken into, or any of that bullshit, we will be on the next flight back to New York, but I promise you two things: you will never find Deegan on your own, and if I am wrong and he is using those crucifixes again, when we do find him, I will kill him myself." Vic punctuated his last words.

Inspector Festa sat back in his chair. As he stared at Vic, almost unconsciously he took a cigarette from a silver case inside his jacket pocket and lit one. Festa took a long drag and blew the smoke high above the table.

"Alright, you have my word, Mr. Gonnella. We will not interfere. But I must tell the Cardinal Secretary about your progress. What in God's name shall I tell him?"

"Tell him what I told you. The murderer is not John Deegan. Also tell him Deegan knows who the murderer is."

"And if you are wrong and he is indeed the killer? What do I tell Cardinal Magnone then?" Festa asked.

"Tell him if I am wrong and Deegan is the killer... then I believe no one is safe."

CHAPTER 32

Just after Dr. Davide Solarino and his nurse left the Hassler Hotel, John Deegan became maudlin. Deegan was informed that his chemotherapy would begin the day after tomorrow, assuming the blood that had been drawn earlier had no significant, problematic markers.

Deegan's self-pitying could not be penetrated by Gjuliana's suggestion of a stroll, or a visit to a museum, or to see a movie. Deegan retreated deeply into himself. So deeply that he asked Gjuliana to return to their home in Lake Lugano leaving him in Rome. Gjuliana would not even discuss that possibility. Instead, she left her husband to sulk in the second bedroom where John kept his laptop computer.

The expression 'an idle mind is the devil's workshop' certainly never applied to John Deegan whose mind moved at warp speed. Deegan was already steps ahead of everyone that was looking to capture him, include him in a mass murder, or help him to survive his cancer.

Deegan obtained any and all information he could on chemical terrorism. He studied the biological, radiological, chemical, and high explosive threat spectrum in great detail. He eliminated nuclear from his studies due to the potential of human collateral damage.

There was one way, in Deegan's calculating, genius mind that Zellweger's concept of killing the entire field of Catholic cardinals could be executed. The serial killer had already figured out his agent of death. He chose hydrogen cyanide gas, one of the most deadly poisons known to man which in highly concentrated form can kill a human being in about one minute.

Deegan only needed a few more facts before he proceeded. The approximate total area in square feet of the Sistine Chapel, from wall to wall and ceiling to floor was essential. He mathematically calculated the theoretical amount of hydrogen cyanide concentration which would be required to bring the atmosphere in the Chapel to 2,000 parts per million. That amount of gas would obtain the toxicity level needed to halt the cellular respiration of over two hundred men.

If the new and sophisticated ventilation system at the Sistine Chapel could be made to emit the toxic gas into the environment, then all that remained was obtaining the necessary amount of cyanide cylinders and figuring out how to breach the security systems.

In spite of international bans against the use of blood agents as a means of chemical warfare, Deegan needed to make contact with various black market outlets... and be prepared to pay a heavy price for the product.

John realized that in spite of his deep disdain and lack of trust toward Colonel Zellweger, a face-to-face meeting was now imminent.

Deegan's first move, as in any high-level chess game, was to call Vic Gonnella.

CHAPTER 33

Pope Francis was released from *Gemelli* and returned to the Apostolic Palace with orders from his doctors to reduce his schedule and continue to rest.

Rather than live in the sumptuous, papal apartments, the Franciscan insisted on staying in the small, two-room suite, number 201, at *Domus Sanctae Marthae*, the building where the voting Cardinals would stay during the Conclave.

Colonel Zellweger met with Inspector Festa to help him transition His Holiness to temporary living quarters at Castel Gandolfo on the day his resignation took effect.

They met at the Swiss Guard office inside the Vatican.

Zellweger's office was a rather large room with modest furniture and a dozen live video monitors, which gave the colonel eyes at every key location in and around the Apostolic Palace and the *Domus*. Zellweger spoke with Festa, barely taking his eyes from the screens.

"I'm going to miss Francis. The man never complains and insists on living like a common priest," Zellweger said.

"Do you think the next Pope will stay in the Domus or go into the apartments?"

"Let me put it to you this way. For one hundred ten years the popes have lived in the Papal apartments. My guess is that Francis' successor will be moving up."

"You are likely correct. Let's hope your men don't have to carry the next Pope on that silly throne," Festa laughed.

"Oh, I have to find out where that gilded chair is, just in case,"

Zellweger said jokingly doing a pretend bow.

The two men discussed Francis' security at the Domus and Castel Gandolfo and reviewed a timeline for his relocation.

"Well, I need to get back to the *Domus*. I fear His Holiness is getting restless and will not be obeying the doctors," Zellweger said.

"And I, at the moment, am involved in finding the killer of our priests. I've been ordered by Magnone to make this my top priority."

"Finding Deegan will not be easy, my friend," Zellweger said as he perused the monitors.

"I have met with Mr. Gonnella who is here in Rome. He doesn't believe Deegan is the murderer.

Zellweger took his eyes from the screens and studied Festa's face.

"Gonnella? Is here?"

"Yes, we had a cordial dinner last evening. He seems to think we have a copycat killer."

"That's odd. It looks to me like Deegan's signature is all over each murder. Who could imagine that someone would be using the same techniques?"

"Evidently, Deegan has no issue with homosexuals. He always dispatched pedophiles, at least according to Gonnella. And that does seem to be his M.O., plus Gonnella informs me that Deegan in gravely ill."

"Gays, pedophiles, they are all the same slime to me! Can Gonnella prove Deegan in as sick as he indicates?" Zellweger asked.

"He said so with the utmost of sincerity. Matter of fact, he saw Deegan in the hospital."

"What? And he didn't apprehend him? It's looking to me, Inspector, that Gonnella is to blame for these homicides as well!"

"Don't be ridiculous; Gonnella has been hired by us to get involved with the case. He plans to stay in Rome until the murderer, be it Deegan or his copycats, are stopped."

"Where is Gonnella staying? Here in the Vatican?"

"No…no. Somewhere in Rome he said. Why are you so concerned about his whereabouts? He has his reasons not to divulge his whereabouts at this time. He said he works alone, with his lady friend and another woman. Very attractive women, I might add."

"Very simple then, have him followed."

"He is too smart for that. I've promised to give him a wide berth. We need his Deegan expertise at the moment so I don't want to step on his toes."

"Did Gonnella say if he has any leads or is this just more American cop theatre?"

"He gives up nothing. And his lady gives up less."

"I suppose he is looking for more fame and fortune on the back of the Vatican. I don't trust men like him. I think we are fully capable of doing our own investigation and search," Zellweger said, returning his attention to the bevy of monitors on his office wall.

"Time will tell, Colonel, but my patience isn't infinite. Matter of fact, I plan to personally escort he and his lovely ladies to *Fiumicino* at the end of the conclave, or sooner, if need be.

Zellweger walked briskly from the Swiss Guard building to the Dormus within the secure streets of the Vatican, where no general public is permitted. He dialed a number on his cell phone and spoke quickly.

"Meet me at the designated place. Nine tonight. There is a slight problem."

John Deegan's mood was lighter. Gjuliana gave him the space he needed, but he was still a bit restless. At six o'clock that evening, the Deegans had an early dinner, at least by Roman standards. Eight to nine p.m. is generally when dinner starts but John had other thoughts.

"My love. Let's take a stroll. The *Piazza Novona* is so very much alive in the evenings, and I think it will do me well to get some fresh air," Deegan said.

"Ok, but it's quite a long walk, John. If you get tired, we can always call for a car," Gjuliana advised.

"They have great *gelato* there. You can have one and I can have an espresso. I think that's allowed, right?"

"Tea, John, you will have a tea with a biscuit that the new chef made. You'll like it! I'll pack it in my purse."

"Oh, goody, a whole biscuit. I wonder if I can live through the shock of it."

"How are we dressing tonight?"

"You dress like a hooker and I will dress like a Harlem pimp from the old days."

"John!"

"Okay, I will wear a top hat and tails with long gray hair and you dress in an elegant, chiffon gown, as if we were going to the opera."

"I love it, and I love you. May we hum Madame Butterfly?"

Off they went into the early evening air of Rome, moving slowly so John could acclimate his breathing. He was still just a bit weak but yet stronger than after his surgery.

Along the way, John handed out twenty Euro bills to every street beggar they passed. Gjuliana stopped counting at ten. She noticed that every time John gave the poor, unfortunate person the note, his lips quivered. She wasn't sure if he was about to cry or if he was saying a silent prayer. She planned to ask him at another time.

Once in the square, John seemed to perk up to his old self. He especially liked the street mimes and their creative costumes and designs. Gjuliana would have to tug him along or he would have stayed in one spot forever. He was also generous to the pots and boxes the mimes and musicians kept at their feet.

"My love, let's have a seat. I'm invigorated and not really tired, but I think I need a rest," John said.

They found a café at one of the exits to the *Piazza*. The smell of street food was driving John crazy, but under Gjuliana's watchful eye he had no shot.

Under a red white and green, *Birra Moretti*, table umbrella, the well-dressed couple ordered espresso, tea, and bottled water. Gjuliana opened her purse and produced the golden treat for John.

"Just a moment, my love. I need to make a call. Be right back."

"John if you sneak over to that pizzeria I will make such a scene!"

John laughed. "I'll stay in eye shot. No worries."

John began walking and stopped at about twenty yards from the table. He tapped out numbers on his cell phone.
"Are you still in Rome, John or have you moved to Damascus or Moscow now?" Vic asked without even saying hello.

"There are no priests to kill in either of those cities," John laughed.

"Very funny."

"And what makes you think I'm in Rome, anyway, Mr. Detective? My only hint to you was Italy. You're trying to trick me, Vic!" John mockingly sang his last sentence.

"John, don't mess with me. I have not, nor should you, forget the promise I made to you. Rome is the most obvious choice, but I swear, if you are leading me on a wild goose chase again…, and don't you dare go hanging up on me and speeding off to another city like a scared little rabbit. If you are telling me the truth, it's just a matter of a day or two and we will be having a nice meal with you and Gjuliana again. Or perhaps a coffee or a drink or something, but you are not as hard to figure out as you used to be, John," Vic said with annoyance in his voice

"I'm slipping. It must be the medication."

Vic softened his tone. "Look John, you need to trust Raquel

and me. We are not looking to lock you up and be big heroes. At the moment that's Interpol's wish, so if there is a copycat, he may know more about you than you think. You and Gjuliana may be in danger. We are convinced from what you've told us that there is a Deegan imitator, and I am hopeful you will help us find this prick."

"All in good time, Mr. Vic Gonnella. Now can I walk with my lovely wife and have a nice evening? And one more thing."

"Shoot."
"You keep referring to the copycat as a him."

"What? What are you saying now, John?"

"I'll call you tomorrow." Deegan once again ended the call, and once again left his listeners with their mouths dropped open.

CHAPTER 34

The following morning, Colonel Zellweger was on duty at the *Domus*, adjacent to St. Peter's Basilica where Pope Francis was celebrating mass in the Chapel of the Holy Spirit.

"I thought I would never hear from you again," Zellweger whispered into the phone.

"Our last meeting ended very poorly, Colonel, perhaps we need a restart?"

"Depends on your commitment, Mr. Deegan. Without your mind I am not sure if I am able to fulfill my plan," Zellweger admitted.

"Not to worry. I have put a good deal of time into a viable plan. There is only a bit of information I need from you to complete the circle.

"I am encouraged by your call, however it is quite difficult at the moment to have this conversation, perhaps we can talk later today?"

"Are you free tomorrow? I have medical treatments in the early morning. I'm not certain how I will be feeling after they pour these chemicals into my system, but it seems to me time is our common enemy," Deegan said. Zellweger thought to himself that Deegan's voice sounded stronger than when he had seen him in Switzerland.

"Yes, I will make myself free in the afternoon. I have taken your advice and did my due diligence. I certainly want to hear what you have designed," Zellweger said.

"And what about trust? I still have the concern that you will apprehend me and make yourself the center of the Catholic world."

"And you could have very easily exposed my plans, Mr. Deegan, and I would be in prison by now. Obviously, you did not. If we join forces, we will change history together. I must go now, my duty calls."

"I will call you again, Colonel."

"Until tomorrow, then."

They ended the call simultaneously.

Vic, Raquel, and Angela were on the rooftop lounge under a lavender umbrella overlooking the deep, blue water of the pool at the *Parco dei Principi*. The rotunda of a church off in the distance, which popped out over the lush treetops was the only edifice in sight. Umbrella pine trees lined the border of the Borghese Gardens. The delightful sound of Indian peafowl from the nearby zoo added to the organic atmosphere of the hotel.

"This would be the perfect place for our European office, don't you think so Angela?" Raquel asked.

"It's a beautiful location. But I think it's too close to heaven for me to concentrate on business," Angela replied.

Towering palm trees and the amazing garden below wrapped around an ancient Roman wall with classic arches. Vic gazed at the scene thinking resembled an incredible oil painting. Fichus trees dotted the rooftop along with blue and purple, flowering perennials.

"The Borghese Garden has my vote so far," Vic mused.

A white gloved, tuxedoed waiter served American coffee and

Italian pastry and bread for breakfast.

"Okay, enough dreaming for a while, lets get down to business. Where would you be staying if you were John Deegan, Angela?" Raquel asked.

"Oh, there are so many possibilities in this city. If we assume he has taken rooms at a hotel, I would narrow that selection down to twelve or fifteen. Should he have taken a villa, or rented an apartment it becomes much more difficult. I know I have no experience, but I would not even know where to begin."

"Do you think he might be staying near the Vatican?" Raquel asked.

"Knowing what I know about him, I don't believe Deegan is interested in being close to all those Roman collars. He loathes the church for what was done to him and for what it stands for. Remember, when he was about to murder the cardinal from New York years ago, he had rented an apartment near midtown. But that was designed to be a quick stay. I think that his health would make him take a villa or a suite," Vic suggested.

"I agree, and I don't think Gjuliana would want him to have constant reminders by seeing a bunch of collars walking around," Raquel added.

"And we can't go to all of the finer hotels here. What would we do, wait in the lobby for him to show himself?" I don't think that would be practical, especially if he is feeling ill," Angela said.

"He is likely using another fictitious identity. We could describe him and Gjuliana to hotel personnel with a fist full of Euros, but that could be hit or miss, Vic added.

" I'm learning quickly, but as I said, I believe Deegan wanted you to follow him to Rome," Angela opined.

"I get that but I can't see us just sitting around waiting for him to call us…or for the next homicide to occur," Raquel said.

"So let's make a list of the best hotels within the city and at least start pressing the flesh. There are three of us, and we can work from the list and chip away at them," Vic said.

Vic continued. "And if we get lucky, no one approaches Deegan until we are all together, understood?" Vic said.

Raquel and Angela both agreed.

"I suggest you ladies dress in your finery to get the gatekeepers to pay close attention," Vic said.

Angela went online and began jotting down the names and addresses of the four and five star hotels in Rome. The list of potential Deegan hideouts was much longer than she thought. Vic decided to approach the five star hotels first.

Within an hour, the trio took taxis to the various hotels which were on Angela's list.

Raquel wore a skimpy, black skirt with a low cut white blouse with black, four-inch heels. Her long brown hair was flowing off her bronze bare shoulders. Angela wore those same tight jeans she wore when she and Lisbeth had their first dinner with Vic and Raquel. A simple, button down, brown blouse with the top two buttons open was finished with a pair of spiked, chocolate brown heels.

The streets of Rome were bustling with tourists and locals as always and the traffic was nothing short of chaotic.

After a while, Raquel called Vic on his cell phone.

"Vic, I went to two hotels not very far from each other. I couldn't get anything at the Hotel De Russie, but we shouldn't rule it out. The concierge thought I was a call girl. The mutt called me a *putana* and showed me the door pretty fast. But, Vic, I think we have company."

"What does that mean?"

"At the Grand Hotel, you have to see this place, the doorman told me something that's gonna knock your socks off! He said an hour before I got there a man was asking the same questions and the man described the Deegans to a T."

"You're kidding, right?"

"No! I asked him to describe the man, and he did one better. I tell you, these Italians love the feel of money. He called his cousin, who is the hotel's security guy, luckily they both spoke English, and I talked my way into seeing the hotel's exterior video tape in the security office." Raquel was almost breathless.

"And?"

"So after back tracking on the video a bit, and letting the knucklehead rent-a-cop leer down by blouse, I see this guy talking to the doorman. He is dark, fairly young, wore a nice suit, and talked with his hands a lot. He pressed some money into the doorman's hand."

"Are the Deegans there?"

"No, let me finish. Two hundred Euros later, I have a photocopy of the guy's face. As clear as can be."

"Okay, listen get back to the hotel right away. Call Angela and call her off as well. I have an idea," Vic said.

Vic met Raquel at the entrance of the *Parco dei Principi*. He looked up at the regal entrance to the hotel and asked the doorman what the words meant. Vic thought the answer was appropriate, Park of Princes. Angela's taxi pulled in moments later.

The threesome walked briskly through the lobby to a lavender granite staircase up to the second floor narrow terrace restaurant. They took a linen-covered table for four surrounded by heavy, wrought iron chairs with a greenish patina.

"I think I need a drink. Let's do something Italian. Any suggestions, Angela?" Raquel said.

"Try an Aperol spritzer. Or Campari and soda," Angela suggested.

Vic quickly ordered three spritzers and some peanuts from the handsome, young waiter. Vic was anxious to see what information Raquel had gotten from the Grand Hotel.

"Let's see that photograph," Vic said, as he impatiently wiggled his fingers.

Raquel produced the picture, pulling it quickly from her purse handing it to Vic. Angela leaned over in her chair to get a view. Raquel had already informed Angela of what had occurred at the Grand Hotel.

"Looks like a tough character," Vic said.

"Almost Spanish or Greek don't you think?" Raquel asked.

"Or Sicilian," Angela added.

"Here is my idea. First thing, I need to call Inspector Festa to see if he is double dipping and doing his own search for Deegan. Then, I will call Deegan and let him know what you discovered. Then, and this may be a tough one… I call Tony at Interpol and beg him to run this picture through their system. They have a very sophisticated facial recognition database which may at least be able to tell us who this guy is. Unfortunately, Tony was pretty pissed off at me on our last call so I may have to do some horse-trading," Vic said.

"Sorry, Vic, what is horse-trading?" Angela asked.

"We may have to tell Interpol what we are up to."

"That could go over like a fart in church." Vic responded.

"I think I understand what that means," Angela quipped.

"First things, first," Vic said, and he had already begun dialing Inspector Festa's cell number.

"Inspector Festa, Vic Gonnella here."

"Bonjourno, Signore Gonnella. Any news on Deegan?"

"You tell me, Inspector. I thought we had a deal."

"I'm sorry, but what are you referring to? You have lost me."

"We have information someone is trying to find Deegan. I don't believe Interpol is doing it so naturally my thoughts turned to you. And I trust that you recall our deal. Tell me you or your people are searching for Deegan and you are the fuck on your own."

"Please, Mr. Gonnella, on my word. We are doing nothing of the sort, as we agreed. The Vatican and I have the utmost faith in your ability, sir."

"Perhaps you have a rogue member in your organization who is looking to make a name for himself?"

"No one outside of my two trusted assistants, the Secretary of State and the Commander of the Swiss Guard is even aware of this search for Deegan."

"I take you at your word, sir, but if we have any leaks... forget it. I will update you soon." Vic ended the call.

Vic immediately dialed Deegan's cell phone.

"Your timing is very good, Vic," John Deegan said.

"Good morning, sorry, good afternoon, John. I hope you are feeling well." Vic did not put his phone on speaker out of concern that someone outside of the table could eavesdrop.

"I had my first chemo early this morning. It was great, we listened to Antonio Vivaldi and I haven't even puked yet. What's on your mind, Vic?"

Vic thought Deegan's voice was a bit stronger, but it just had to be his imagination.

"John, it's time that we spoke frankly. My suspicions you and Gjuliana may be in danger have gone to another level. High alert. I have confirmation there are people looking for you, and I'm not sure who they are. I don't believe that they are part of Interpol, and I'm pretty sure that they are not the Vatican police."

"Very good, Vic. Excellent work, as usual. So who do you think it is?"

"Areyoukiddenmeorwhat??? What the fuck are you talking about 'excellent work'? I don't have a fucking clue who the killer is. I don't have a fucking clue why he, they, she, or whoever the fuck, would want to come after you. If I knew, I wouldn't be on this call with you. Jesus Christ."

Raquel patted Vic on his arm to keep him calm.

"Oh, I am well aware of who is trying to find me. This is so much fun for me, you know the hunter and the hunted thing. I'm like that grizzly bear or that killer, Bengal tiger they always talk about who has doubled back around to stalk his pursuer."

"John, Please! These riddles and stories of yours… you may be playing in a different league, maybe someone that's your equal. Let's just meet and work on finding who the copycat is. Then you finish your treatments in peace and quiet, go back to your home and enjoy your life again and I get a nice payday from the Vatican. Everyone wins."

The waiter approached the table with the drinks atop a silver tray. When Raquel casually and politely waved him away, he stopped, shrugged, and went back inside the restaurant.

"Too boring. Let me say a few things to add a bit more action and fun to this game. Pay close attention to me now, my young and impatient protégé. My illustrious imitator has an axe to grind. He is closer than you think and will be killing again. Like me, he is on a mission. Like me, he is extremely good at what he does and is determined to make the world sit up and take notice. Unlike me, he is very healthy, but he has nothing to live for but an ideology. I at least have someone who loves me. And unlike me, he is not as smart as he thinks he is. Now, I promise you, we will be working together. We will meet quite soon as a matter of fact. But be warned, you are probably in more danger than I."

As he enjoys doing, Deegan ended the call.

Vic took the phone down from his ear and looked at the two puzzled women, "I recorded that whole conversation on my phone. We are going to have to listen to it again. I believe Deegan has given us a whole bunch of tips. First, I have to call Tony Frank."

Raquel motioned to the waiter to bring their drinks. Vic waited for the waiter to return and clicked glasses with Raquel and Angela. He took a long draw on his drink. "Wow, very nice," he said to Angela.

Vic called Tony Frank on his direct line at Interpol. Frank answered the phone on the third ring.

"Deputy Commissioner Frank."

"Well, the boss still answers his own phone I see," Vic said.

"Ah, the prodigal son returns. How are you my friend?"

"Hello, Tony. It's Raquel on the line, as well."

"I would rather talk with you, my dear. Vic is not on our good boy list at the moment."

"I hope it doesn't mean you don't still love me, Tony," Vic laughed.

"How could I not? You would have to do a lot more than be greedy with your leads for me to abandon our friendship, even though I only hear from you when you need something," Frank said.

"That's how he is, Tony. We used to call him one-way Vic at NYPD," Raquel laughed.

"All kidding aside, Tony. I do need a big favor, and I was hoping you would accept my call in good humor. I see you have and thank you. We are on Deegan's trail. I just want to know if you guys are as well. I would hate to be digging two tunnels," Vic said.

"Confidentially, and I mean that in the strictest sense of the word, the Vatican is an Interpol member as you probably know, and they are putting a lot of pressure on us to find Deegan and put an end to these priest murders. But with all of the terrorist attacks in Europe along with the normal craziness that goes on, we have temporarily decided not to spare our assets on the Deegan case. The short answer, Raquel and Vic, is that we have ordered our operatives to stand down on Deegan. We have reassigned our people to more crucial areas of our operation."

"Interesting. Did you have any solid leads as to Deegan's location?" Raquel asked.

"I was about to ask you that very same question, out of curiosity," Frank queried.

"We know he is somewhere in Italy, but we have not actually narrowed down his actual location. Which brings me to another special request, my friend. We have a photograph of someone who is nosing around looking for Deegan and his wife. Can we fax the photo to you? Perhaps you can identify the man?" Vic asked.

"I have a better way. Get the photo to our Rome office, I will text you the address right now. When you get there ask for the Senior Operations Assistant or the Criminal Intel Officer. Ask them to call me here in Lyon. They will electronically send me the document and I will run the photo through our facial ID database. If the photo is clear, or if he has a tattoo, we can usually get a hit fairly quickly. That is, of course, if the man in question has committed some crime in the past," Frank said.

"I don't see an obvious tattoo but the photo is very clear. You are amazing, Tony. How can I ever thank you enough?" Vic asked.
"Vic, we are friends and that's what friends are for... but my wife and I are coming to New York in a few months to see her family. You can take us on the ferry to see the Statue of Liberty."

"No ferry for you, my friend. We will take a helicopter service and see the entire city."

CHAPTER 35

John Deegan was feeling exceptionally well for his first day of chemotherapy treatments. He felt invigorated, his energy level surging. He also felt quite restless after having received the message from Vic. The master of disguise went into overdrive. Deegan encouraged Gjuliana to use the day spa facility at their hotel to relax and get her mind off of him for a few hours. Gjuliana accepted the invitation. The moment she left their suite, Deegan was out the door in his Viet Nam Vet costume.

Vic and Raquel raced the photograph of the Grand Hotel, unknown sleuth to the local Interpol office as Tony Frank instructed. Angela ran personal errands for the trio.

It was late afternoon by the time the threesome reconnected back on the second floor balcony restaurant at *Parco dei Principi* and awaited a call from Tony Frank.

"How about one of those Aperol spritzers? I can use one at this point," Raquel said. She had changed from her sexy skirt outfit to a pair of white tennis shorts she had just purchased in the hotel lobby store. A t-shirt, knotted at the bottom showing her bare midriff and the flip-flops she bought in Zürich finished her relaxed look. Four men offered a drink to Raquel as she walked through the bar to the restaurant. Angela also dressed down. A pair of gray gym shorts, a black *Roma* t-shirt, and sneakers without socks caught the attention of every woman and most of the men on the promenade. Angela was just amazingly sexy.

Vic got no attention at all. A pair of khaki jeans, flip-flops and a button down business shirt with its sleeves rolled up to his elbows was not breaking any hearts.

"I'm going with the Campari and Soda. How about you, Angela?" Vic asked.

"A really cold beer would be fine."

"On second thought make that two," Raquel said, changing her mind.

Vic waved down the busy waiter and placed the drink order. The drinks arrived within a few minutes.

"At this time in Rome, most everyone is drinking an *aperitivo*, *digestivo*, or their fifth espresso before going back to work. It's incredible how this country gets anything accomplished," Angela said.

Vic laughed saying, "And it's a wonder why in America we all don't drop dead from stress. Before we are fifty. Like right now, I'm wanting to pace up and down the damn halls until we hear from Tony."

An older man having his afternoon drink at the next table had a beautiful Italian accent that sounded like a song. The man interrupted the trio's conversation.

"I'm sorry to overhear young man, but perhaps this beautiful young Italian woman can explain to you, and to us all, what *la dolce fa niente* means?"

The man was an officer in the *politzia municipale*, the traffic control police. In Rome they are known as the *vigili urbani*, the urban watch. He was dressed in a nattily tailored, blue suit with for silver buttons that ran down the center of his jacket. A crisp, white shirt jutted just the right length out of the jacket collar and a blue-striped tie made the officer look like a banker. A silver cord ran from his jacket's right epaulette to a button on the jacket pocket, a gold badge prominent on the left side of the garment.

The pièce de résistance to the policeman's uniform was a pith-like, white, custodian helmet with a bulged out dome and a silver medallion affixed in front. The medallion had a red SPQR insignia in the center and a silver Romulus and Remus suckling on the She Wolf at its bottom. The policeman wore the hat over his brown, salt and pepper hair. The *vigili urbani* are unarmed, but a radio hung from an unseen belt under the jacket. A pair of white traffic gloves rested on his table.

"Of course. It is a classic Italian saying; *La dolce fa niente* is the sweetness of doing nothing. Just relax and enjoy life. This is the Italian way," Angela said. She and Raquel were taken by the policeman's uniform and charm.

"We have that *fa niente* thing in New York...it's called welfare," Vic quipped. Raquel spit a tiny bit of beer out of her mouth and nose.

The policeman did not get the joke and asked Angela to interpret for him, all the while smiling.

"Pensione!"

"Ah...fa bene, bene," the policeman said. His smile turned to a hearty laugh.
Finishing his *aperitivo,* the policeman excused himself again.
"Pardon me, but I must now return to my station. Traffic begins to build now. *Piacere.*"

Raquel and Angela gave the policeman polite smiles while Vic turned his attention to a bikini clad princess walking along the pool deck one floor below.

They enjoyed the serenity of the late afternoon for a while and watched how the shadows of the trees changed as the sun began to drop in the sky.

Still no word from Interpol. No word on who was stalking Deegan and his wife. Vic ordered a second round. When the drinks arrived, Vic's cell phone rang momentarily startling the group of three.

It wasn't the call they were waiting for.

Vic's phone screen read: DEEGAN.

He showed the phone to the two ladies and hit the green button.

"Hello, John. How ya feelin' now?"

"I just had my afternoon shot of some horrid, green shit, how can I be feeling?"

"C'mon now, a tough guy like you can hack this!"

"So Vic, tell me, how did you like my *dolce fa niente* line. I think the girls loved it. Man, Raquel is stunning, and that Angela will break hearts in the Roma t-shirt."
"What? What did you just say?"

"I hava to go an a wave-a my white a-gloves to the traffica," Deegan said mockingly in bad, broken English He exploded with laughter.

"Areyoukiddenmeorwhat??? What the fuck, John! How in the name of… how the fuck did you find us before we found you?"

Vic was pissed at himself for not recognizing his nemesis. He put his hand over the phone's mic and said, "That old cop was Deegan!" Raquel's and Angela's mouths were left agape.

Deegan was still enjoying his laugh.

"How did you find us John? Cut the bullshit! Ok, you had your fun at our expense, and you predicted you would be seeing us very soon, you genius jerkoff."

"Elementary, my dear Watson… *Pavo cristatus,* my darling Vic."

"Okay. I'm an idiot. Tell me, because I can't even spell that to look it up."

"*Pavo cristatus*, Indian Peafowl."

"I'm still lost." Vic was now seething mad.

"It's a peacock, you dullard. When you called me the other morning I heard in the background a peafowl calling to her mate or whatever they do. Only one place in Rome I know of that has that bird and it's the *Bioparco di Roma*, the fucking zoo, my friend!" Deegan was now belly laughing so hard Raquel and Angela could hear it through the phone. "And the only good hotel near the zoo is the place you and I shared a great moment years ago. Listen again to our last conversation, Vic. I think you are the one who is slipping, kid." Deegan ended the call.

CHAPTER 36

Vic fumbled with his phone looking for the app that held his conversation with Deegan, when he was interrupted by an incoming call. It was Tony Frank.

"Son of a bitch!" Vic said. "Yeah?" he said answering his phone quickly before the call went to voicemail.

"Vic, we have identified the man in the photo."

Vic pointed to the phone and put it on speaker with low volume. Raquel and Angela leaned in closer to hear the conversation.

"He is a known mafia soldier with the Salvatore Totò Riina family. His name is Rocco Rotigliano. He's a hit man and all around bad guy," Tony said.

Angela gasped and put her hand to her open mouth when she heard Riina's name. Vic and Raquel looked at each other wondering what she would know about hit men.

"Riina is the imprisoned leader of the _Corleonesi_ faction of the Sicilian mafia. Known for his violence and widespread murder, Riina was responsible for the brutal murders of the <u>Antimafia Commission</u> prosecutors <u>Giovanni Falcone</u> and <u>Paolo Borsellino</u>. Riina and his people also broke all traditional mafia code of conduct by killing women and children."

"The mob? Why would they be interested in Deegan after all these years?" For killing Catholic, pedophile priests five years ago? Mobsters brutally kill people, but are faithful to the church. Now _that's_ one of the mysteries of life, if you ask me," Vic explained.

"I would guess that he is a hired hand, and why they didn't kill him before, I don't know, but if they think he is killing priests now, well, I wouldn't want to be him. Cancer will be the least of his problems. You and I both know the Sicilian mafia is very good at fulfilling their job, and their front men who do their dirty work receive a sizable amount of cash, booze, and women, so you are correct that Deegan and his wife are in grave danger. There really won't be any place he will be able to hide. Their guy Rotigliano did a seven-year prison term for extortion in Palermo. He's been out for a year. He never ratted."

"So we need to find out who hired him," Vic stated.

"That is easier said than done, my friend," Tony acknowledged.

"What worries me is the mob actually knows Deegan and his wife are both here in Rome. No way they just guessed at that. Anyway, I promise to keep you apprised of the situation."

"Vic, be careful, very careful. If you and Raquel get in their way you are in great danger. Having to put a bullet through either or both of your heads would merely be a hiccup in their day."

"Thank you, Tony. Thank you for this information. We will be talking soon."

Vic ended the call and looked at Raquel and Angela.

"Angela, listen… you are the newbee here. If you want to get off this case we understand and will send you to New York to begin training. It's entirely up to you," Vic said. Raquel agreed.

"Thanks, but I have been around the mafia my entire life. They flourish by people's fear. My place is here with you and Raquel. I am not afraid, and will do anything needed to help. I was raised never to run away from problems."

"Thanks, Angela, you are tougher than we even thought. So, then, let's talk about who hired this Rotigliano character," Raquel said.

"I want to start by listening to Deegan's conversation with me and pick it apart," Vic said. *How did that mother-fucker even know I recorded the conversation?* Vic wondered.

Vic found the app with the recorded conversation of himself and Deegan, and played it.

"Too boring. Let me say a few things to add a bit more action and fun to this game. Pay close attention to me now, my young and impatient protégé. My illustrious imitator has an axe to grind. He is closer than you think and will be killing again. Like me, he is on a mission."

Vic put the conversation on hold.

"Is he trying to give us a message here?" Vic asked the ladies.

"He seems to know the killer will strike again. The 'axe to grind' may be a hint to something," Raquel said.

"Perhaps this is why Deegan is in Rome to begin with. He could have easily found another treatment center in Switzerland or stayed in Zürich for convenience to the *Klinik*," Angela said.

"Excellent point. Knowing Deegan, he is a step or two ahead of us," Vic said.

"What about the 'axe to grind' and the mission the killer is on?" Raquel queried. "Perhaps Deegan knows the copycat is anti-priest for a reason. Maybe the murderer was molested by clergy and Deegan knows this somehow.

"The 'axe to grind' may just be an expression. None of the recent killings had axes as their weapon," Vic said. "Let's listen to more."

Vic hit play on his phone to hear more of Deegan's taped conversation.

"... Like me, he is good at what he does and is determined to make the world sit up and take notice. Unlike me, he is very healthy, but he has nothing to live for but an ideology. I, at least, have someone who loves me." Vic stopped the recording at this point.

"May I? Angela asked. "The killer is about to kill someone very important. With the conclave coming to Rome, perhaps he is preparing to kill a cardinal, or Pope Francis, or even the new pope."

"That's my take, too. And Deegan confirmed that, remember? And 'he is not loved', what's that all about?" Raquel asked.

"Maybe a single man or a priest. Deegan clearly knows the copycat," Vic reasoned.

"And the ideology? Could it be a fundamentalist Muslim?" Angela asked.

"Hmmm, that could be a possibility but not likely. I think if anything the killer could be a fanatical Catholic. Or yes, another priest," Raquel said.

The waiter returned and asked if the table wanted another round.

"No, just some iced tea for me. And some coffee for the ladies?" Vic asked.

"Iced tea, also." Raquel said. "Espresso with sugar," Angela replied.

"Good, we really need to keep our wits about us," Vic said.

Vic replayed the next of Deegan's conversation.

"... And unlike me, he is not as smart as he thinks he is. Now, I promise you, we will be working together. We will meet quite soon as a matter of fact. But be warned, you are probably in more danger than I."

"That's the end of the tape. Any thoughts?" Vic asked.

"The 'not as smart as he thinks he is' is interesting. Perhaps someone in authority, someone who is smart but with flaws?" Raquel questioned.

"Compared to Deegan, everyone is not so smart. It sounds to me the killer is full of emotion, full of anger. Is that a stretch?" Vic asked.

"There is definitely a big clue here. Unfortunately, we can make many inferences from that," Angela said.

"And then Deegan said 'we will be working together'. This goes to Angela's point from the beginning. Deegan wanted us here in Rome," Raquel said. Angela smiled at the recognition from her boss.

"... 'And meeting quite soon'. This fucker played us like a deck of cards. That police crossing guard thing still has me questioning myself," Vic confessed.

"I'll be looking at everyone from now on, wondering if they are Deegan in disguise. Maybe this waiter? The taxi drivers? Who knows?" Raquel asked rhetorically. "Remember, Vic? He did the same thing to us when we were investigating the murder of Jonathan on the boy in the box case two years ago!" Vic nodded. He had to stop focusing on Deegan one-upping him and get his mind back on the clues. He would never forgive himself if anything terrible happened to John and/or Gjuliana.

"And the danger warning. How does Deegan know about Rotigliano?" Angela asked.

"Maybe he doesn't. Maybe he is warning us about the killer. We are in danger from the copycat if we get too close," Vic said.

"Just great! We are at risk from the killer and a mob hit at the same time," Raquel said.

The iced tea and the espresso arrived while the hair on Vic's neck stood on end.

CHAPTER 37

Zellweger met with Rotigliano again the next day at their designated spot.

The *Trastevere* section of Rome sits on the west bank of the Tiber River just south of Vatican City. The name *Trastevere* comes from the Latin, beyond the Tiber.

In this old section, with cobblestoned streets and mostly timeworn houses is the *Porta Portense*, one of the ancient city gates of Rome. There is an incredibly large and crowded flea market with thousands of stalls where locals go to find eclectic items from second had clothing, replica designer bags, household items, to collectibles, and antique pieces.

The bustling flea market is the perfect place not to be noticed, where no video cameras are snooping, and the bargain hunters are paying too close attention to items of their interest while negotiating with the vendors to notice anything out of place. Other than the locals, tourists walk through the market looking for inexpensive souvenirs and conversation pieces very often succumbing to expert pick-pockets and gypsies who run a variety of creative scams.

Rocco Rotigliano wore his typical, tough guy, muscle shirt along with his stereotyped, ruddy, tough guy face. Zellweger covered his head in a floppy hat and wide sunglasses wearing skinny jeans and gray, round neck t-shirt. They met along a busy aisle of stalls as planned.

"Any luck?" Zellweger asked.

"Nothing. Deegan may not even be in one of the hotels. We need to find a better way," Rocco said.

"So, find a better way! Remember, I don't want Deegan harmed at the moment. He and I may meet soon. I will contact you, and then you will follow him."

"Sooner or later he will surface," Rocco reassured. "We have people on the lookout, too. All they are to do is follow him and call me."

"I don't have time for sooner or later. You must find him, and soon. In the meantime, I have another problem. There is an American cop. He is here in Rome looking for Deegan, but for his own reasons known to him and God alone. He is with his girlfriend and another woman. An Italian girl. Find them and contact me. If I tell you to take the next step, the usual fee applies. Here is a photograph of Mr. Vic Gonnella and his woman. They should be easy to find."

Festa handed Rocco a folded, color photograph taken from the Centurion Associates website.

"Anything else?" Rocco asked.

"Yes, I have another job for you to take care of tomorrow afternoon. Go to the church of *Santa Maria della Concezione dei Cappuccini* on the *Via Veneto* near *Piazza Barberini*. Wear a better disguise. Wait for me on the steps at four o'clock."

Zellweger quickly walked away from Rocco and made his exit through the ancient, Roman door.

That evening after John Deegan appeared at the hotel disguised as a police traffic officer, Vic, Raquel, and Angela dined and relaxed at the hotel. They reviewed their notes and listened again to Deegan's telephone conversation with Vic. The trio again worked on possible theories in an attempt to break through Deegan's shrouded, obscure hints. Nothing new was really accomplished so Angela went to her room and Vic and Angela did some romantic dancing at the hotel's bar before turning in for the night.

Vic got into bed to the waiting Raquel who was clearly in the mood.

"You know something, baby? Who would have ever believed we would be here in Rome, once again, with John Deegan on our agenda?" Vic wondered aloud.

Raquel reached over Vic to turn the light on his nightstand out. Her bare breasts and sexy perfume alerted Vic to what was to come.

"Baby, I was just talking about Deegan and…"

Raquel shushed Vic with a sexy purr. She placed her finger on his lips to interrupt his thoughts and began to kiss and lick his lips.

John Deegan's night was not as pleasant. Upon returning to the Hassler after making certain he wasn't followed Deegan, began to feel a little weak and chilled. He rejected his dinner which was only a combination of tofu and steamed organic vegetables anyhow. Gjuliana made John some tea with organic honey and lemon, but John just wasn't in the mood. Although Dr. Solarino had prescribed anti-nausea meds, John still felt queasy and out of sorts. John decided to call Dr. Eschmann.

"Young Eschmann, it's your favorite and I hope your only manic patient."

"Good evening, John. Happy to hear from you."

"I wish I were happy to call you. I'm in a bit of a down period. Had my first blast of chemicals today. Felt like a thirty-five year old this afternoon, and now I fell like a ninety-five year old. This bit of the cancer ain't no fun, lad," The last line was in the Deegan brogue.

"Are you eating well?"

"Absolutely, I'm eating nothing tonight. Any thought of food makes me gag."

"Force yourself to have something. Remember that nutrition is a key to longevity for you."

"That's just the thing, Eschmann. Other than Gjuliana, who the fuck is gonna miss me? Don't have kids, grandkids, and only a few nieces and nephews who want to change their names because of me. Other than that, I'm really alone in the world."

"You have Gjuliana and that is a life's blessing, but why do you think you're so alone?"

"Because I am, damn it. Look, I would have loved to have had a normal relationship, you know, wife and kids and such. The only women I ever had were usually married and we rolled around a bit, then they went back to their husbands. And I was always left alone. It was always hard for me to get truly intimate with someone. Those rapist priests really did a number on my head, Doc."

"Naturally. You were abused at a young age. You were promised that God loved you and…"

Deegan interrupted him. "And told not to spill a drop of the priest's 'holy water' from my mouth when he had his smelly dick in there. After all, he was a holy man, and if I didn't swallow it all I was being disrespectful to him and to God. How fucked up is that, Eschmann?" Deegan asked.

"Very! Bad things happened to you, John. So bad I'm afraid you decided to take your genius to another place. A very, dark place. You removed yourself from reality at times and then when finally decided to deal with your pain, you did it in a way that was socially unacceptable."

"You mean shaving down a dozen wooden crucifixes is not the norm?" John responded with a slight lilt in his voice.

Eschmann ignored the sardonic question.

"Are you interested in my coming to Rome for a day and just having a long talk?" Eschmann asked.

"That may be what I am trying to do, isn't it. Talk this whole mess of a life out to someone. Let's wait a few days and see if I'm feeling any better. Good job, young Eschmann." Deegan hit the red button.

Deegan didn't sleep much that night. Between his reaction to the chemotherapy and his brain going into overdrive about Zellweger and Vic, John was quite clear as to what his next moves would be.

CHAPTER 38

Colonel Zellweger met Rocco Rotigliano outside of the church of *Santa Maria della Concezione dei Cappuccini* in midtown Rome at precisely four that afternoon. The mafia hit man had no idea what to expect but was a bit nervous about being seen on the busy *Via Veneto*, one of the most popular streets in all of Rome. There are many elegant stores and hotels along the wide boulevard-like street, along with the large and well-monitored, and secured American Embassy. Rocco wore a blue tracksuit, sneakers, and a baseball cap with a brim pulled down to cover his features. Rocco didn't recognize Zellweger at all. In a floppy hat, full gray and black beard, carrying a guitar case, and wearing an African-like *dashiki*, Zellweger looked as if he were on his way to play for coins at the *Piazza Navona*.

Zellweger sat on the steps of the church and mumbled his words, covering his mouth with his left hand. Rocco sat on the steps in front of him.

"Go inside the museum. Pay the six Euro entrance fee, and find your way past the chapels and down into the ossuary where the bones are on display. There should be one Capuchin monk at the desk. Walk around like you are a tourist. Pretend to say a few prayers. At this hour not many tourists enter the place, but just in case, stall for a bit. When it is only you and the monk down there, text my number. I will follow you and lock the door. You will cry out for the monk to come to your aid when you are down the narrow corridor. Knock him out and I will be there to finish him. You leave the same way as you came and I will lock up after you. Understand?" Zellweger said. His plan was well laid out and murder was becoming second nature to him.

Without speaking, Rocco headed into the church.

This particular church is among the most bizarre places in all of Italy. In the sixteen hundreds, a member of the Capuchin community, Cardinal Antonio Barberini ordered the bones of thousands of

Capuchin friars be exhumed and transferred to the crypt. Along with the bones of poor Romans who were buried in a lower chapel, the Capuchins arranged for all of the bones to be placed along the walls and knaves of the narrow catacomb- like space. The bones of over four thousand human beings are presented, some in full Franciscan habits, surrounded by dozens of skulls, and some with the bones from their spinal columns displayed in geometric patterns against the walls.

Rocco did as he was told. He paid the fee and quickly passed five separate chapels on his way to the ossuary. He never stopped to look at the various frescoes and paintings in each chapel.

The Capuchin friar on duty, in his Franciscan like habit with the brown and white hood around his shoulders, never looked up from his rosary as Rocco passed him.

The first thing Rocco saw sent the killer's blood cold. The full skeleton of a small child holding a scale in one hand and a sickle in the other adorned the entranceway to the crypt. Rocco made the sign of the cross and swallowed hard before moving on.

The hardened mafia hit man then came across a sign on the wall in three languages:

What you are now, we once were; what we are now, you shall be.
   "*Oh, Madonna mio,*" Rocco said aloud, blessing himself once more and spitting through the fingers of his joined hands to ward off the evil eye.

Seeing all of the bones in their macabre arrangements, some actual, complete skeletons peering down at an angle from the ossuary dressed in their hooded habits, was almost enough to send Rocco screaming from the building.

The crypt was empty except for the friar and Rocco. The hit man fumbled with his cell phone, his hands sweating profusely and texted the waiting colonel.

"Subito!" Rocco wanted out of this place a quickly as possible.

Colonel Zellweger entered the church and paid the fee to enter. He walked slowly past each chapel, genuflecting and blessing himself out of respect. He passed two, small, stone coffins of obscure saints and stopped at the third chapel. On the wall was a beautiful painting of St. Francis being given the *stigmata*. The saint was the first person in the Roman Catholic Church to receive the five wounds of Christ according to their folklore.

Some say that *stigmata* are self-induced or a result of hysteria. Others call it dissociative identity disorder. Colonel Adrien Zellweger, a devout Catholic, had an abiding faith that thought it was a miracle from the Lord.

Zellweger recited a devotional prayer in Latin to St. Francis then walked quickly to the ossuary.

The friar was still saying his rosary when Zellweger interrupted him.

Zellweger held up his cell phone and asked the friar, *"Posso? Foto?"*
In perfect English the friar said, "No photographs allowed… no."

Zellweger smiled at the unsuspecting friar and stood there at the desk. He could see Rocco down the dark and narrow corridor.

"Auita me, help me!" Rocco yelled.

The startled friar, his rosary attached to his brown rope belt let the beads drop to his lap. He looked down the corridor and could see a man lying in the floor. The friar looked at Zellweger for assistance but Zellweger shrugged his shoulders in apathy.

Zellweger quietly locked the ancient, wood door of the ossuary with a hanging rope, and then followed the friar toward Rocco.

The much younger and stronger Sicilian bashed the friar in his face with his strong, meaty fist, pulled him down onto the floor, and stood and stomped his head with his sneakered foot. The friar lay unconscious on the floor.

Zellweger hurried down the corridor to find Rocco looking up at the skulls as if they were silent witnesses to his assault. Rocco had a look on his face like a petrified child.

Zellweger quickly grabbed Rocco by his sweat suit jacket and pulling him toward the door near the friar's desk.

"Listen to me. Walk, do not run from the church," Zellweger held on to Rocco until he nodded yes.

The colonel let Rocco out and relocked the door.

Walking slowly back down the darkened strip, Zellweger laid his guitar case down next to the friar, opened it, and removed a sharpened, wooden crucifix.

CHAPTER 39

Angela talked Vic and Raquel into abandoning their idea of an early dinner. The 'when in Rome do as the Romans do' convinced the American couple.

Vic always wanted to eat in the famous *trattoria* where Deegan kidnapped the New York Cardinal. Angela made a reservation for nine-thirty that evening at the *trattoria Santo Padre*, not far from the American Embassy. For security and total anonymity, Angela made the reservation in her mother's name, Francesca Di Stasio. No chances were being made with all of the nefarious people on the lookout for the threesome.

The trio, dressed in gym shorts and t-shirts met at seven o'clock in hotel's gym. Raquel jumped on the stair master with her iPod buds snuggly in her ears listening to a mix of Latin music she had made. Angela's iPod played a variety of new American music she loved: Rhianna, Justin Timberlake, and Ariana Grande were among her favorites. She went to the mat to do sit-ups and light yoga. Vic hated to exercise so he went the easy route on a stationary bicycle while he watched CNN on a flat screen television.

At eight o'clock, just about the time that they were winding down their workouts, Vic's cell rang. It was Inspector Festa.

"Mr. Gonnella, I am sorry to bother you, but there has been another homicide in Rome."

"My God, tell me not with a Deegan cross." Vic said.

"Yes, the same M.O. but even more brutal this time. I am at the crime scene now. I think you should join me here."

"Absolutely, where are you?"

"Come to the *Santa Maria della Concezione dei Cappuccini,* The Church of the Immaculate Conception on the Via Veneto, just before the *Piazza Barberini.*

"We are at the gym, but we won't bother to change. Be there soon," Vic said as he abruptly ended the call.

"Ladies, there's been another homicide. Let's go!" Vic ordered.

The trio went to the front of the hotel to hail a taxi. Angela suggested that they not pull right up to the crime scene. It would be easy for anyone to find out from the cab driver where they came from. The cab whisked by the manicured hedges and colorful flowerbeds of the Borghese Gardens along the way.

It was a three-minute ride to the multi-arched *Porta Pinciana,* an ancient Aurelian wall at the top of the *Via Veneto.* They asked the driver to drop them there, Vic handing him 10 Euros.

Evening was beginning to darken the boulevard and the streetlights were already glowing. The three investigators walked quickly down the Via Veneto. As they passed the American Embassy, the lights from the *Carabinieri* vehicles and the crowd of curious onlookers was reminiscent of the many homicide scenes that Vic and Raquel experienced in the states.

Inspector Festa and his two assistants were waiting for the trio in front of the church.

"This is not a pleasant scene so I ask you to brace yourselves," Festa warned.

"We've seen a lot of homicides inspector. Angela, do you want to come in?"

"I work for you now, Vic. Of course; I am not a child," Angela said with a bit of irritation in her voice.

They all went into the crypt which was now fully illuminated with crime scene lighting. The sight of the skulls and bones of the Capuchin monks were even more macabre as the lights cast peculiar shadows.

The dead friar, his stomach exposed, his skull carved and flayed open to the bone was left hanging among several Capuchin skeletons, all wearing their Franciscan robes. Blood soaked his robe from his head to his open toed sandals. Two, fairly long, skeleton bones were protruding from each of his eyes. A wooded crucifix remained sticking out from his sliced open neck.

Several police officials were standing at the scene and the flash of a forensics camera added more drama to the scene.

Angela did her best to mask her revulsion. Vic and Raquel remained matter of fact in their appearance.

"This is the most brutal scene we have seen so far," Festa said.

"Tell us about the deceased, please," Vic inquired.

"He is a Capuchin friar who has been stationed here for nearly ten years. His job was a sort of punishment for past transgressions. A life of sacrifice and prayer was ordered to enable him to remain in the order," Zellweger replied.

"Past transgressions?" Raquel asked. Vic's heart began to race. Small beads of sweat were forming on his forehead.

"His name is… was, Father Brian Case. He is from the states, Wisconsin, I believe. The friar was accused of possessing and distributing child pornography along with several credible accusations of sexual abuse of young boys. The friary, of course, quietly battled to settle the case and move him here to Rome."

"Typical. Have there been any reports of him continuing his

actions here in Rome?" Raquel asked.

"None, as far as I can tell. It was reported he was being closely watched by his superiors," Festa replied.

"What do you make of the bones in his eyes?" Raquel asked.

"It seems to us that the deceased was not yet dead when the bones were rammed into his eyes. From the amount of blood, that is our theory, anyhow. The bones are arm bones from one of the skeletons over there," Festa said, pointing to a 300 year-old, armless friar.

"This copycat is very good, very thorough. Deegan gouged the eyes out of a child pornographer. I can't remember which number killing it was at the moment," Vic said.

"What is the significance of the guitar case?" Angela asked.

"We have reviewed video tapes from the restaurant across the boulevard and one from the *carabinieri* monitor looking up from the corner of the *Via Veneto*. The perpetrator, a bearded musician, spent some time sitting on the church steps before entering. The guitar case was his. There was also another man who entered the church just minutes before the musician did. No identification has been made."

Holy fuck! I bet it was Deegan! He is not going to fool me again! Vic thought to himself. "I want to see those tapes," Vic commanded.

"Of course, Mr. Gonnella. You can view them in the mobile unit outside when you are ready."

"I highly doubt he was really a musician," Raquel stated.

"Being that we know Deegan is here in Rome, do you still not think he is the killer?" Festa asked.

"Ok, first I want to examine the corpse and look for other

clues," Vic replied.

For the next thirty minutes, Vic, Raquel, and Angela looked over the crime scene wearing blue, paper booties over their gym sneakers. Angela found a footprint in the friar's blood that was otherwise undiscovered. She elbowed Vic.

"Inspector, please have a mold of this print taken. Also, I want a measurement as quickly as possible. Now, let's go view the videotapes," Vic ordered.

Outside on the crowded, posh *Via Veneto*, a uniformed officer manned a large, forensic truck unit. Festa ordered the video to be put up on one of the monitors inside the truck.

The trio looked at the evidence several times, playing it back at normal speed and then in slow motion.

One of the inspector's men knocked on the now crowded vehicle's door. He had the size of the footprint.

"*Quarantadue-quarantatre,*" The officer said.

"Forty two or forty three. In your sizes that would be about a size twelve," Inspector Festa said.

Vic was relieved and waited for a moment before he spoke. "Okay, good information. Now I can prove to you Deegan is not the killer of this friar. Deegan is short in stature. Five-foot six, maybe five-foot seven at most. This musician, as we will call him for now, is clearly well over six feet. I can't do the conversion into metrics but you can figure that out. Deegan's shoe size is exactly eight and a half, nowhere near twelve. We had found prints of Deegan's at crime scenes in both the states and in Dublin. And, look. See? The musician has squared off shoulders while Deegan's shoulders are rounded. Clearly, if we are hypothesizing, this musician is indeed the killer, and Deegan is clearly not the perp. And besides, Deegan is in no physical condition to lift the friar's body and hang it next to the other skeletons. He is too old and too sick to accomplish that task."

"I see. And what do you think about the other man who entered the church before the musician?" Festa asked.

"It's hard to tell. It looks to me as though the musician was communicating with the man in the tracksuit. His face is obscured by his hat though, so it may be difficult to identify him," Vic replied.

"May I say something?" Angela asked.

"Of course. Hey, you found that footprint which is hugely important to this case," Vic said.

"This may be a stretch and maybe nothing at all, but that man in the running suit and hat? Don't you think he is built very much like the man who was asking around at the hotel about the Deegans? It may just be a coincidence."

"Holy shit, Angela! I think you're right. Some people say there are no such things as coincidences," Raquel added.

CHAPTER 40

No one really knows what deals are made behind closed doors in the middle of the night between the Catholic Church, the media, and the police, but everyone knows it happens, so it came as no surprise when the sun came up The next morning there had been no mention of the Capuchin friar's murder in the media. The Rome newspapers and local television once again succumbed to the strong-arm power of the Vatican, orchestrated by the Secretary of State, Cardinal Magnone.

Inspector General Festa was once again summoned to the Apostolic Palace and again found himself face-to-face with Cardinal Magnone.

"Inspector, the conclave is mere days away. I asked you to handle this sensitive issue for the Holy See. I think perhaps I chose the wrong man to deal with this Deegan monster! Where is Gonnella? Why are we about to be ridiculed in the world press?" Magnone was furious and his voice was growing louder.

Inspector Festa stood rigid and still. He was having a flashback to when he was a young boy in Catholic school being admonished and embarrassed by the local monsignor and then spanked in front of his classmates. Festa did his best to remain calm but began hyper-ventilating.

"Eminence, we are doing the very best under the circumstances, however…"

"He who is good at making excuses is seldom good at anything else, Inspector! Let me be perfectly clear. We cannot, and I will not, allow another scandal to be laid at the steps of St. Peter's. This maniac Deegan must be stopped and eliminated. I thought I made myself understood to you! Now, I must use harsher terms with you. Your job depends upon a successful outcome, Inspector."

"But, sir, Deegan is not the killer."

"Pardon me, are you being…?"

"I am sorry, sir, but now, it is time for me to interrupt you, Cardinal Magnone, sir. I have more than thirty-five years of loyal service to the Vatican. I will not be threatened nor will I go back to being treated like a child who did not comply with every one of the rules in Catholic school. Now you listen to me and listen carefully. We have a much bigger problem. I am one hundred percent certain Deegan had nothing to do with the latest rash of priest killings. Mr. Gonnella has convinced me with clear and scientific evidence that a Deegan impostor slaughtered the friar. Using our resources to find an old and sick man is not going to stop these killings!"

"Now see here, Inspector, don't you raise your voice to me or…"

"You need to listen. Instead of covering up and hiding the facts, help us to flush out the true murderer. He very well may be a disgruntled priest, perhaps someone who has been laicized, or even someone right here, close inside the Vatican. Do you understand me? We truly have no idea at this point who the copycat is, but we are sure there is one, or maybe even two for all we know! You need to get your head out of the sand before our dead priest count surpasses that of Deegan's! You do realize there is a gathering of our highest ranks converging, um, sir? How long do you think before there will be a leak to the media and we will be able to suppress them from blabbing this story? At least with Deegan five years ago, everyone knew who we were after. This.. this..string of murders could be even worse!"

"Are you insane, Inspector? And what are you suggesting? That we actually turn to the media and ask for their help, telling them how pedophile and homosexual priests are once again being targeted for murder and we have no fuckin' clue as to who or whom is doing the killings? Sure! Perhaps a fucking prayer chain would work, also! Do you have any idea of the scope of that admission? And my God in heaven, do you have any idea how many homosexual priests there are today? The pedophiles are a whole other story. Our ranks are inundated with both of these degenerate types."

"Respectfully, Eminence, you know as well as I, the time to have cleaned our house is long past. We have all been guilty of looking away from what the faithful have been begging us to do and that is right the wrongs of the past, and weed out, help prosecute, and defrock any of these bullshit sexual deviants and those who cover up for them. Lying and hiding the truth has not worked well for the church. We need to embrace the problem now so perhaps the next pope, God willing, will put an end to this madness."

Cardinal Magnone placed his hands as if in prayer in the middle of his chest. His red robe almost matched the color of his face.

"Inspector, at the end of the conclave, I will make the next Secretary of State aware you will be resigning. Your disloyalty to Holy Mother Church is something I never would have expected. God be with you."

Magnone lowered his eyes indicating the meeting was over. Inspector Festa stood in front of the Cardinal Secretary's desk.

"There is no need to wait until the new pope is elected. You have my resignation now. I will continue to seek out the murderer on my own."

Festa walked out of the Cardinals office and was escorted to the exit of the Palace by two Swiss Guard in full regalia, which is customary. On his way out the inspector paused and took in the opulence surrounding him. The words of Matthew 7:27 came to his mind.

'The rain fell, the torrents raged, and the winds blew and beat against that house, and it fell--and great was its collapse!'

CHAPTER 41

John Deegan was feeling tired from his intravenous chemotherapy. On top of that, Dr. Solarino visited the hotel with his nurse and more blood was drawn from him. The following day Solarino returned with a prescription which was to help support Deegan's immune system. The blood test results showed a decrease in white blood cells. It was crucial he stay healthy.

"This injection is to bolster your white count, John. The drug is called *pegfilgrastim,* and it may have some side effects," Dr. Solarino advised.

"Will I get a four-hour erection like those guys who take Viagra?" John quipped.

"John! Really!" Gjuliana admonished her husband, but really she had all to do to keep from bursting out in laughter. Gjuliana always loved John's quick sense of humor going back to their school days in the Bronx.

"Not at all. Perhaps some dizziness, some mild abdominal cramps, and an achy bone here and there. They won't last long. I will likely prescribe this injection the day after each treatment. Your next treatment will be six days from today."

"Can I eat pizza yet?"

"I'll tell you what. My wife is from Naples. When you are able, she will make you the best homemade pizza you ever had in your entire life."

"I hear her pizza is to die for," Deegan said dryly. Solarino didn't get the pun. Gjuliana laughed so hard her side hurt.

Solarino and his nurse left, and Gjuliana got herself ready to go with the houseman to run some errands. The moment they left John was on his cell phone.

"Good morning, Colonel."

"Mr. Deegan, how are you coming along?" Colonel Zellweger asked.

"As well as can be expected, taking one day at a time, enjoying every day and all the rest of the bullshit cancer patients are supposed to say and hear."

"Are we able to meet soon? There is much to do."

"How is tomorrow? By that time my nausea may subside and my mouth sores will begin."

"What time works for you? Later in the afternoon perhaps?"

"I'll squeeze you into my busy schedule," Deegan joked.

"Very well, and where shall we meet?" Zellweger had no time for jokes. "Perhaps where you are staying? That may make it easier on you," Zellweger suggested. He was on a fishing expedition trying to make things easy for Rocco Rotigliano.

"I prefer a more public place. Let's make it a game day decision. I will let you know fifteen minutes before we meet, how is that?"

"As you wish. Until tomorrow." The colonel ended the call.

John spoke aloud to himself. "That rat bastard. He must think I'm a total fool... 'perhaps where you are staying?' John did a near perfect impression of the Colonel's voice and accent.

Deegan fluffed his pillow a bit and made a second call. The call was to a retired operative of the American CIA he had worked with and killed for during his military stint in Nicaragua. Deegan made millions for this friend, Carlos Baldwin, later on in his life when he hit it big on Wall Street.

"It's me, your old pal from the Somosa days," Deegan said.

"And you are still alive?" Baldwin laughed.

"Do you remember a line from the Godfather? Hyman Roth is the only one left because he always made money for his partners."

"I remember the line very well, and I remember the fortune you made for me. For that I am eternally grateful."

"I know you are. I didn't call you to set up a reunion dinner or with a stock tip. I am in need of hydrogen cyanide, in gas form, in canisters. I will let you know the amounts in a day or so."

"When is it needed?"

"In a few days, FOB Port of *Civitavecchia*."

"Shouldn't be too much of a problem. I have someone in the Middle East. A real player, but he's quite greedy, my friend."

"I don't mind getting fucked these days."

"I will reach out," Baldwin said.
"Talk soon," Deegan ended the call.

Deegan made a third call, but not before he had to go into his bathroom with dry heaves.

"Have you run into any *politzia municipale* of late?" Deegan laughed.

"Keep rubbing it in, Deegan. I'm still tossing and turning over that disguise," Vic said.

"So the murder of that degenerate friar hasn't hit the papers yet, and you still haven't found my imitator. You are really slipping, Vic. In the old days you would've been all over him like a cheap suit."

"How do you know about the friar?" Vic asked.

"His Holiness told me all about it at breakfast today. Man, can that Argentinian eat."

"Dumb question, I know. At any rate, I am working on a few leads, but I have to warn you about something John, so don't hang up on me like you always do."

"I'm all ears."

"There is a mafia hit-man, out of Palermo who is looking for you. Evidently he is the real thing, one of the best there is. It may be best if you clear out of Rome for a while."

"And miss the conclave? Not on your life. I can't wait to be in the square when that white smoke billows."

"Listen to me, will you? I'm pretty sure we may be on his list, too."

"Of course, find the hunter and you will find his prey."

"Have you had anything to do with the mob I should know about?"

"Hmmm, let me see. My mother bought a hot color television in 1964 from some oily guys in the Bronx, maybe she didn't pay up."

"Can't you be serious and answer a damn question ever?"

"Okay, no. No dealings with *La Cosa Nostra*." John mimicked an Italian accent.

"That leads me to believe you are being set up, Deegan."

"No shit, Sherlock! And it's probably by the same guy who is staging the fake Deegan murders. Boy, do I hate amateurs."

"Tell me who you think it is, John. This one time, work with me."

"We are working together, Vic. Only thing is you haven't figured that out yet. Can I hang up now?"

"You always hang up at the most opportune times."

Deegan ended the call.

CHAPTER 42

Inspector Festa spent the rest of the day cleaning out his desk, saying farewell to his men, and taking photographs down from the walls in his office. Thirty-five years of service and memories fit into two cardboard boxes.

Photographs of himself with the last five popes, various politicians, movie stars, Mother Teresa, and a picture of Pope Francis sitting in a chair in St. Peter's square hearing confessions. Festa admired Francis' humility even though at times he thought some of the pope's behavior was staged for public relations.

The inspector took his personal favorite photograph down from the wall last. In the photo were his daughter and two sons feeding pigeons in St. Peter's Square when they were all very young. Festa longed for these days and wondered at that moment if he made the right choice in his life, choosing his job over his marriage.

A knock on his open office door broke his melancholia.

"How can this be true?" Colonel Zellweger stood there with his arms outstretched in disbelief.

"Ah, I should have come to your office and told you. Forgive me, Colonel."

"After all these years? Why so suddenly?"

"Magnone and I had a difference of opinion. He has his ideas and I have mine and he wears the red cap. I'm ready to retire, anyway. I've had enough."

"And the conclave?" Zellweger wondered.

"My assistants are very good men. Perhaps one will be selected to take over my position, but this job is enough for two men. They know what needs to be done for the conclave. Everything is in motion."

"What will you do with yourself, Claudio?"

"Ha, I think that is the first time you used my name. I will look for something to do. I'm certainly not the type to sit on a bench talking politics with other old men. At the moment, I will be seeing Vic Gonnella later today. I'll see if he needs someone to help him find his killer."

"To find Deegan, you mean?"

"No… no, Deegan has not killed anyone recently. A Deegan impostor is on the loose."

"Yes, I heard about the homicide at the bone church. But I was told that a crucifix was used like Deegan's other jobs."

"The evidence clearly shows that the perpetrator was tall. A man about your height while Deegan is about the same height as me. Gonnella has convinced me that there is a copycat killer."

"I would like to meet this American one day. Perhaps I will ask him to lunch. Do you know where Gonnella is staying?" Zellweger's hazel eyes opened widely in the hope that he would learn Vic's whereabouts. He tried to keep his voice as casual as possible.
"That is a big secret. Gonnella works under a cloak of privacy, it seems."

"Can you arrange for me to meet him?"

"Certainly. I will speak to him about you. I know he would be honored to meet the *Oberst* of the Swiss Guard," Festa saluted the Colonel who returned the respect.

"I hope you are not digging the wrong hole, knowing Deegan is in Rome, and all. The coincidence leaves me still thinking he is the killer. Homosexual and pedophile priests in Rome are all in danger at the moment, but please don't look to my eyes for a tear, my friend, as I have no use for either of those types of scum."

"That is another one of Gonnella's theories, Colonel. He tells me Deegan never bothered with gays. His record is with pedophiles only. Incidentally, his victims were not always priests, if you recall."

"Ah… yes, I do. That's neither here nor there. Deegan is doing us all a favor. I'm about fed up with the whole church and they way they have handled these things. Those fucking priests need to learn to keep their cocks in their pants."

"Careful Colonel, this is the very reason I have resigned. I was no longer able to sit and listen to the bullshit from Magnone. You are still young and need your job. I'm old and I have a good pension and a bit of money saved. My life will be just fine."

"Old? You are in better shape than men half your age, Claudio."

"My mother, rest in peace, used to say in her Sicilian dialect '*gli acciacchi della vecchiaia*', *the aches of old age.* Time is catching up to me, my friend."

"Something tells me even with all their powers, the cardinals will soon be running to your door with their silly hats in their hands. Deegan will strike again, and this time it may be bigger than anyone has even imagined."

Festa noticed Zellweger's eyes had turned to a dark brown color and a peculiar smile froze on the Colonel's angular face. *Something is wrong with this man. What does he mean Deegan will strike again? How can he be so sure?* Festa thought to himself. *Perhaps the pressure has finally gotten to him.*

It was four o'clock in the afternoon and time for a much need-ed break. At the *Parco dei Principi,* Vic and Raquel went to their room for an afternoon love making session. The door of their room that led to the balcony was open and a beautiful breeze came off the trees from the Borghese Gardens. Vic held his hand gently over Raquel's mouth as her moans of ecstasy seemed a bit too loud.

Angela was also taking a break, lying down on a chaise lounge at the pool in her black, string bikini taking in the bright, afternoon sun. Her waiter was making too many stops to check if she needed another drink, 'or something'?

"What a beautiful day we have," a handsome young man said in English as he took a seat near her. His accent was American.

"It certainly is. The very best," Angela replied.

"Wonderful, you speak English. Are you here on vacation?"

"Yes, it's my holiday," Angela lied.

"I'm here on business, my name is Preston Shields."

He was just the kind of man that Angela was attracted to: friendly, foreign, tall, a full head of blond hair, blue eyes, and the all-American type with a slim, athletic body. It was obvious that Pres-ton Shields spent plenty of time in the gym.

"I'm Nora, Nora Bianchi. What kind of business are you in?"

"Freelance journalist. I'm here for the conclave, and you?"

"I'm in fashion. What are you planning to write about, Mr.

Shields? Angela was smart enough to know she needed to be the one asking the questions.

"Preston, please. You know, the pope retiring, the election of the new pope and the effect it will have on the Church. I write for a Catholic syndication back in the states."

"Oh, well, I was raised never to discuss politics or religion with strangers," Angela said.

"So, how about dinner tonight? We can avoid those subjects, no problem," Shields said.

"Perhaps another time. I have plans with friends this evening."

"Okay, I will hope for another time. May I have your number so I can make a date?"
"I'm not in the practice of giving my number, either, but I will take yours. Perhaps I will have a free evening before I return to Brussels." Angela had made a whole new identity for herself.

Shields gave Angela his number and she created a contact in her cell phone.

"I have to go. I need to prepare for this evening. It was nice to meet you, Preston," Angela said casually out loud, but she was thinking, *He is gorgeous!*

"Nice to meet you, Nora. Hope to see you again," Shields said aloud while he was thinking, *Man what a knockout!*

Angela put on her black, lace cover-up and left the pool. Shields did everything he could not to stare at her ass.

Angela met Vic and Raquel at six o'clock sharp in the hotel lobby. They were all going to meet with Inspector Festa at his request.

"How was your afternoon?" Raquel asked Angela.

"Delightfully sunny. I took a few laps in the pool, soaked up the sun, and met a man."

"Tell me, tell me!" Raquel said enthusiastically.

"Well, I felt like a man must," Angela said, "I did nothing but lie to him."

"Oh, geez, here we go… all men lie, I suppose," Vic said.

"Vic, quiet, will you?" Raquel said.

"'Hi! I'm Nora Bianchi, I live in Brussels, and I'm in the fashion business. What's your name?' How's that for lying?" Angela laughed.

"Smart girl. That fucker could be a plant," Vic said.

"Exactly what I was thinking, but I don't think so. Anyway, he is very hot, just my type!"

"You are catching on to our cloak and dagger style very quickly," Raquel acknowledged.

"My untrusting, Sicilian father always said *'nuddu nasci che causi ttaccati'* meaning *no one is born with his pants on.*"

"I've heard that, but what does that really mean?" Vic asked.

"Everyone needs to learn the ropes."

CHAPTER 43

In Deegan's devious and calculating mind, the time had come for him to meet with Colonel Zellweger to describe his plan to help him assassinate over two hundred cardinals of the Roman Catholic Church.

Deegan called Zellweger on his cell phone.

"I will meet you in thirty minutes," Deegan stated without an introduction.

"Tell me where, please."

"Let me be clear. If I get a whiff anyone but yourself is within a mile of me I will abandon you, and your plan will be trashed. And if you have me followed when we are finished, *you* will be finished. Understood?"

"Yes. But we need a modicum of trust if we will be working together."

"Fuck that trust thing. I trust my wife. You and I will not be 'working together', Colonel, as you put it. I will give you the plan step by step so easy even a child can do it. You will implement the plan. I am in no physical condition to participate, and frankly I would prefer to watch this whole thing unfold from the comfort of my home."

"So, where will we meet?" Zellweger was anxious to get the information he so desperately needed.

"Funny thing about that. I wanted to pick a public place. A public place with symbolic meaning but I thought what the fuck for? First I wanted the Circus Maximus, you know, that flat piece of shit park next to the Palatine hill where the Romans held their games, or the *Ludi Romani* where gladiators with swords and spears executed Christians, and wild animals tore the silly Jesus followers apart while two hundred and fifty thousand assholes cheered. From the magnificent edifice, the Circus Maximus once was to a flat parking lot in less than twenty one hundred years. What a shame. Now they have rock concerts there and kids smoke dope. Then I thought, oh, the Coliseum! Those Flavians really knew how to build a stadium. Eighty thousand people watched as five thousand animals were killed for a religious party. And Christians were toasted like marshmallows or used as a pin cushion for the gladiators' spears. Am I wasting this on you, Colonel? Do you see how fucking symbolic meeting in these places would be?"

"Yes, I do," Zellweger said. Zellweger's thoughts however were a bit different. *Deegan is truly a madman after all,* is what he was thinking.

"Then I decided on an even better place. A public place at the *Piazza del Popolo.* I love the names of these streets, *piazza* this, *strada* that. It sure beats Burnside Avenue in the Bronx. But I digress. The *Rosati Caffetteria.* Be there in thirty minutes.

Deegan left the Hassler, dressed in his Viet Nam Vet disguise without letting Gjuliana know he was going out. The walk to the *Rosati* was only eleven minutes even at Deegan's slower pace. John had calculated the distance from the Vatican to the café as a brisk thirty minute walk or an aggravating ten-minute car ride. Zellweger would likely jog in anticipation of their meeting and be there in fifteen.

The *Rosati* is arguably the best place in the whole of Europe to have an amazingly delicious coffee and something wonderfully sweet. The street level café is a throwback to Italy in the 1920's, complete with art deco-designed, wooden cabinetry and coffee bar, geometric designs in the mostly dark green and beige marble floors, and globe lamps that hang from the twenty-five foot ceilings by long, black poles. The outdoor tables are covered with white awnings and are perfect for people-watching or just to read a newspaper and enjoy the fresh, warm, summer air.

Deegan found a small table in the rear of the second room inside the café. Striped walls hearkened back to photos of European jet setters or Chicago mobsters found in old black and white photos.

Within moments, Zellweger found Deegan after he took a double take making certain the man in the Viet Nam hat and pilot sunglasses was his partner in crime. Zellweger wore his usual floppy hat and large sunglasses. He removed his jacket and tie and had on his starched, white shirt, albeit wet from his perspiration.

"A bit sweaty, Colonel. That tells me you likely jogged here." John's presumption was correct as usual.

"I needed the exercise," he said catching his breath.

"Here we are then, plotting to destroy the hierarchy of Catholic Church when all I ever wanted to do was whack out a few priests to make a point, no pun intended," Deegan grinned.

An overweight waiter came to the table with a pad and a white cloth draped over his chubby forearm.

"One, double espresso and a tea with honey. Organic if you have it," Deegan said.
The waiter shook his head no and promptly left.

"I need to know from you the total space of the Sistine including the height to the ceiling. I am sure you can get that information from your blueprints. The ventilation system can be rigged to expel the toxic gas I am working on. Once I have sourced the poison, you will arrange to pick up canisters at the port in Rome. It's up to you then to get the canisters into the basement and I will instruct you on how to release the gas into the atmosphere. The front doors of the Sistine must be closed to make this work effectively. If my calculations are correct it will take about five minutes for the odorless gas to permeate the chapel and do the job," Deegan said, in a matter-of-fact tone.

Zellweger paused to absorb the visual.

"How many canisters and how heavy are they?"

"Pay attention, Colonel. I need the dimensions before I can answer that."

"Understood. I will have that data for you in an hour. I do not want any of my guard poisoned."

The coffee and hot tea arrived along with the check.

Deegan paused to let the chubby waiter get out of earshot.

"I couldn't care less, Colonel. That is your job to keep your boys out of the chapel or they will no doubt be collateral damage."

"What is the cost involved?"

"That's my treat, and my pleasure. I suspect you want the canisters placed the day of the general assembly when all of the cardinals are in the chapel."

"Yes, there is a stationary engineer on duty at all times at the venting system. I will have to eliminate him."

"And how do you plan to escape? Or don't you?"

"If this is done correctly, I will not be suspected. I will walk into the chapel with my men to discover the carnage. If not, I am prepared to shoot myself."

"Why not shoot a couple of Arabs instead and blame ISIS?" Deegan laughed.

"I haven't thought of that, but that may be a good solution."

Zellweger's eyes moved to the ceiling in thought. *This man is truly devious and better than I give him credit for!*

"So, if there is nothing else, I will finish my tea and leave."

Zellweger left, leaving a ten-euro note next to the check.

Deegan pulled a map from his pants pocket. The *Piazza del Popolo* is on the edge of the Borghese Gardens. He calculated his walk to the *Parco dei Principi* to be about thirty minutes around the park. He felt well enough to make that trip.

CHAPTER 44

Vic, Raquel, and Angela met Inspector Festa at a small café along the Via Veneto. They followed the same drill of taking a taxi to the *Porta Pinciana* at the top of the *Veneto* and walked about three blocks. Festa was waiting on the sidewalk at a table for four.

"Inspector Festa, it's nice to see you again," Raquel said.

"It is now former Inspector. I've resigned from my position with the *Gendarmeria*."

"Areyoukiddenmeorwhat? So suddenly? And right before the conclave?" Vic asked.

"What they want me to keep doing, and how I was being treated was, well... let me just say I cannot abide the... yes, I am no longer there. So please, call me Claudio, if you will," Festa said. He was obviously upset and having a difficult time expressing himself.

"Relax. Let's have a nice drink and talk things out," Vic said.

A waiter was summoned and drinks were ordered. Three Aperol Spritzers and a *Campari Bellini* for Festa.

"They insist I find Deegan and eliminate him. Can you believe I'm in the Apostolic Palace, and I'm being ordered to kill a man? That stubborn cardinal didn't even want to hear a word that the newest killer is a Deegan impostor. 'Just find Deegan and make him go away' is all they said. I suppose I will be granted absolution. This regime is as bad as the Borgia's."

"Get on the list, Claudio," Raquel said.

"You are not the only one looking for Deegan," Vic clarified.

"I want to help you to find the real killer. I have a big reach here in Rome, and I believe my services can assist you. That is, if you will have me."

"Of course, but let's discuss this a bit more. You left right before the conclave. Don't you think that is abandoning your post, at the very least?" Vic asked.

"There comes a time in a man's life when he must finally do what is right for himself. I have sacrificed my entire life for the See, lost my marriage, rarely saw my children, and now I'm treated like a common criminal… a hit man. I had to say *basta, enough* of this."

"Look, we know Deegan is here in Rome. And we have no idea where he is, and the likelihood of finding him is remote," Raquel said.

"And the point of finding him is really not very important at this point. We need to find who is setting him up," Festa said.

The waiter returned with the drinks and everyone clicked glasses with the traditional *'chin-chin'* toast.

"Claudio, you are hired although the pay will not be what you might expect," Vic said.

"I don't want money. The satisfaction of finding this maniac and ending this craziness is worth more to me than a few euros. I don't need anything else."

"Let's put our heads together," Raquel suggested.

"May I?" Angela added.

"Stop asking that question. You have done very well so far," Raquel said.

"Thank you. We know the killer is good at killing. Evidently he is trained well or has had experience in that arena. He, like Deegan, is stealthy. He also has Deegan's method down as you Americans say, to a T. He probably has his own motivation for killing priests. This killer has expanded his victims to include homosexuals. Perhaps he is gay himself; perhaps like Deegan, he was molested when he was younger but in his mind attaches gays with pedophilia. He obviously knows more about his victims than the average person."

"What do you mean?" Raquel asked.

"I have studied the murders closely. The priests he has killed… their history for the most part, is not common knowledge. He has information only someone close to the inner workings of the church would have. For example, I did research on the Capuchin friar. There is no public record of his actions in the states. His case was settled by the archdiocese he came from without it ever going public. It's the same with the two gay priests in the hotel room. It is not public knowledge they are gay. Also, Cardinal Bazzini's assistant was a gay priest with a penchant for going to a gay, sex house. Who would know for sure he is gay? Most people have a sense their priests are gay but they decide to look the other way. And look at the Bishop Di Siena case. No one outside the church even knew why he was removed from his position. There is nothing online, nothing public about his sordid past. Only the ex-priest in Abruzzi has any public record, but the manner in which they were all killed is exactly the same. Our killer, our Deegan impostor, has information, or first-hand knowledge of these things… of the victims and of Deegan. I say the killer is a person inside the church somehow."

Vic and Raquel were momentarily blown away by Angela's profile of the killer.

"So where do we start?" Vic asked.

"The Vatican?" Raquel asked.

"It is very possible, but you realize there are over three thousand people who work behind those walls in some capacity, don't you?" Festa said.

"And who among those people are trained enough to kill?" Raquel asked.

"Anyone with a strong motive can kill," Vic assured.

"But it's not so easy to plan a homicide and execute a person in cold blood like our killer has," Raquel stated.

"The friar's killing was the most spectacular, with the most evidence left behind. Caught on video, we know the mafia hit man was with him as an accomplice. He left his footprint. Although the perp knows enough to wipe his fingerprints or wear gloves, he was very bold with killing that friar." This guy is pretty smart," Vic said.

"Okay, Inspector, I mean, Claudio... we need: a smart guy, somebody who is well-trained, and able to kill a man quickly and in cold blood. You're right, Angela, this is not your average, avenging cleric. I'll ask again, who among the three thousand people who work at the Vatican can we narrow this down to?" Raquel asked.

"Alora, my men in the *Gendarmeria*. They are certainly well-trained in law enforcement and some could easily be a suspect. The Swiss Guard, although they are very loyal, are trained first in the military and could easily kill a man with their *halberd* so why not with a crucifix? There are a few from the Italian Air Force who are well trained in combat and counter attack, and then there are other police around the Vatican as well."

"How about a former employee who was removed and is now disgruntled with the church?" Angela asked.

"That brings the potential field down to what? A few hundred men?" Vic asked.

"Certainly no more than that," Festa said.

"I wish you were back inside the Vatican right now, Claudio so you could snoop around!" Raquel said.

"Raquel, I still have access. Maybe not so much to the Apostolic Palace, but my men will always be my men. I can still maneuver inside the walls.

"Okay, but let's not be blinded by our own theory. Homicide 101 taught me one thing. Never believe your own bullshit. Our killer can be a fucking librarian. At this point, if Angela's theory is right, and I think she's on to something here, anyone inside the Vatican, except for maybe Francis and a few old cardinals is suspect," Vic said.
"Let's go to the wizard; he'll know!" Raquel said.

"What?" Vic asked.

"Remember the line from the Wizard of Oz? The wizard will know! The guy behind the curtain," Raquel replied.

Angela and Festa were lost in the analogy.

"Deegan?" Vic asked, looking at Raquel and tightening his lips as if she were crazy.

"Yes, the wizard!"

Thirty minutes after they left Festa, Vic, Raquel, and Angela took a fresh pizza and some beer back to their hotel. They decided to sit near the pool, have their pizza pie, and turn in early to begin their search for the Deegan copycat. The moon was full, casting its shine on top of the water, complimenting the lights from the bottom lit pool.

Angela wore her tight jeans, a sexy, white-below-the-shoulder blouse, and a Roma, soccer team cap, her hair pulled back in a taut ponytail. Raquel, sharing a chaise lounge with Vic and feeling the drinks, draped her bare legs over Vic's blue jeans. Her one piece short, black skirt, tight, red blouse and long, chestnut brown hair, and heels were an invitation for Vic to want to forget the pizza and get her upstairs to their room.

A voice came from behind their chairs.

"Hi, Nora!" It was Preston Shields.
"Angela was startled. Vic and Raquel both almost laughed knowing her fraudulent name. Vic took a long swig from his beer bottle.

"Ahhh. Yes, hello, Preston."

"Nice to see you again. Is this like an Italian picnic?"

"Preston Shields, please say hello to my friends, ahh…"

"I'm Lydia, and this is Ralphie," Raquel said.

Preston shook both of their hands. Vic looked at Raquel and mockingly mouthed… *Ralphie?*

"Nice to hear American English for a change. I've been interviewing so many people today, but I found only one American among them."

"Preston is a journalist here for the conclave," Angela said.

"Interesting. I always wanted to be a writer, but I can't type, spell, or conjugate verbs," Vic said.

"That's why they have spellcheck, honey," Raquel said nearly choking on the sip of beer she took.

"Preston, we are just wrapping up a business meeting. If you don't mind, I will try to call you when I have a moment," Angela said.

"No problemo." Preston waved to Vic and Raquel.

"Nice meeting you both. Nora, I will take that as a promise. Maybe the four of us can have dinner one night."

"That would be fun," Raquel said.

Preston walked toward the hotel, once again shot down.

"He is very cute, Angela," Raquel said.

"Maybe a double date would be a good idea. We can lie to him all fucking night and make up shit as we go along. I'll be a plastic surgeon specializing in boob jobs and Raquel can be a backup singer for Gloria Estefan."

"Why can't I be the surgeon and you the singer jerky boy?" Raquel said, a slight slur in her words.

Suddenly another voice came from the other side of the pool.

"They never respected us. We went to that piece of shit country to fight for our country and they spit at us when we came home."

A staggering drunk, in a Viet Nam Veteran hat and dark glasses was walking around toward the trio's side of the pool.

"Jesus Christ, I hope this fucking guy doesn't come over here," Vic said.

"Awww, poor thing. He can barely walk," Raquel noticed.

"Maybe I should go on a date with him instead of Preston," Angela said. They all laughed but not before Raquel spit out some of

263

her beer all over Vic's legs.

The veteran started getting closer, his head down and cursing.

"And another thing, fifty-eight thousand of us died and for what? To contain communism! There ain't no communism except for fucking Cuba. Fuck LBJ and that Dean Rush asshole."

"Don't even look at him," Vic said.

The vet passed by the trio's chairs without making eye contact and spewed his final offensive slur.

"And fuck that pinko, bitch Jane Fonda and every hippie puke who ever lived."

The vet walked toward the hotel and out of sight behind some high manicured hedges.

"What was that he said? Jane Fonda? She is an American actress, yes?" Angela asked.

"It's a long story not worth repeating."

Suddenly, the man came from behind the bushes, limping and staggering back toward the threesome.

"Act two," Raquel said.

As the drunken vet approached the two lounges he stopped and looked directly at Vic.

"You know, Gonnella, you really need to find another line of work, don't ya know?" The vet now had an Irish brogue.

Vic jumped up from the lounge while pushing Raquel's sexy legs off his.

"Deegan! What the fuck?" Vic said.

CHAPTER 45

Before his grand appearance as the Viet Vet at the *Parco dei Principi*, Deegan had the information he requested, in text form from Colonel Zellweger.

The Colonel sent the total interior space of the Sistine Chapel; 40.9 meters in length, 13.4 meters wide and 20.7 meters high. Deegan used his cell phone to find a conversion chart to feet. The Sistine Chapel is 134 feet long 44 feet wide and the height to Michelangelo's ceiling masterpiece is 68 feet. Deegan then calculated in his head that the total was approximately 400,928 cubic feet, including air space.

Although Deegan did the quick calculation, he would wait to confirm his math when he returned to the Hassler and by then a frantic Gjuliana.

The airflow through the United Technological Corporation venting system could handle a pushed maximum oxygen movement of five hundred and fifty pounds per square inch within fifteen minutes. John needed to calculate the amount of hydrogen cyanide cylinders needed. He also needed to design a quick and effective way to combine the cylinders and rapidly evacuate the toxic gas into the ventilation system as rapidly as possible. The logistics of placing the cyanide would be Colonel Zellweger's problem. John would call his ex-CIA buddy first thing in the morning.

"I'm sorry to have startled you Vic, ladies. I just like to have some fun and push the envelope a bit," Deegan said to the befuddled trio. This was the second time in two days a Deegan's disguise made them look like total amateurs. Angela at least had an excuse.

"I think you just enjoy embarrassing us, John," Raquel said.

"If truth be told, I think I do. Seeing the look on your faces is priceless. You see I've been doing pranks like this since I was around seven years old. It was my way of escaping reality. If I could be someone else, I could deal with that fucking priest and what he was doing to me. But as we all know, I got even, didn't I?"

"John, why are you here?" Vic asked bluntly.

"Can't you invite me to sit? Perhaps an organic tea with organic honey in an organic cup and saucer."

"Of course, let's all go over to that table in the corner by the pool so we can sit and be more comfortable," Raquel suggested. She sensed, and correctly, Deegan was in a talkative mood.

Angela waved at the waiter and placed an order for Deegan and a round of coffee for herself and the others.
Once seated, Deegan began the conversation.

"We are staying at the Hassler Hotel. I don't see the necessity to hide that from you three at the moment, for three reasons. First, I know you are not trying to hurt Gjuliana or me. Secondly, I think we may be leaving there as I'm getting a feeling being a nomad at this point is the right move. And thirdly, I'm getting tired of this battle and I'm starting not to give a fuck anymore."

"I get one and two but not three," Vic said.

"I couldn't care less if I live or die. I've lived a tormented life, so closing my eyes for good will not be the worst thing that ever happened to me. If some idiot puts two slugs in my brain or the cancer eats away at me, I'm prepared to go. I just want Gjuliana to be back at home and safe."

"What's going on, John?" Vic asked.

"The church won't rest until I disappear. I'm a public relations nightmare even though I've done nothing to them… of late that is. Look, on television today I saw the chimney was being installed on the roof of the Sistine Chapel. The conclave convenes in a few days. Francis will take his dramatic, final helicopter tour around that Vatican and yet another pope exits in failure. At least it's failure to those of us whose damaged souls have been left on their holy, dung heap. I believe in my heart this is all done because of some grand design by the Roman Curia. They keep buying time, and it's been going on for centuries! In our adult lives we've had all those years of JP II, the sainted Polack who won over the hearts of his sheep, then Ratzinger that fucking, conservative puppet, and now Francis, the smiling cherub, who is now running away licking his wounds. Wounds which are being imposed upon him by his very own cardinals!"

"John, …" Vic started to say something.

"Allow a dying man to stay on his soap box for a moment more. The church has been around for two millennia. A wacko killer like me, a copycat like what you have now, the fucking Internet and all the Catholic bashers out there are only like a pimple on a fly's balls to these people. The Vatican is too strong, too rich, and too steeped in evil to be defeated. So there, Vic, now you can have the floor." For the first time ever, Vic saw emotion in Deegan's eyes. They were glassy from welled up tears. Vic reached over to have Raquel hold his hand as he felt his own emotion from being abused as a boy rushing up inside him, as well.

The waiter came with the tea and coffee. Vic paused until he left the table. He was thankful for the interruption so he could take a deep breath and regain his composure before speaking.

"John, let's take one step at a time. You know who the copycat is. Now please enlighten us," Vic appealed.

"Well, unless I'm mistaken, you have already narrowed down the possibilities but are still no better off than a week ago."

"Jesus, fucking, Christ, John, enough of this game! Who is the killer?"

I will soon bring you under my tent but not at the moment. I have a job to complete. All I will say is if I figured you guys out correctly, you at least know where the killer sleeps. If I'm wrong, then it must be the chemo affecting my brain."

"You have a mafia hit man on your heels. Once he finds you it will be all over for you and Gjuliana. Is that what you want? Let us at least help you," Raquel said, trying to reason with John.

"I'll take care of the slimy Sicilian, my fair Raquel. You guys just keep your heads low and trust no one. If I can get this close to you so can that prick from Palermo," Deegan warned.

"Mr. Deegan, the mafia is ruthless. I know this first hand. They will not rest until they see your corpse bleeding from your head," Angela insisted.

"Vic, Raquel… please explain to this lovely Angela I am not as easy a mark as the mob is used to. And now, my friends, it is very late. I am without energy and am well past my bedtime. Do you really want to help me?"

"Of course we do," Raquel assured.

"Then get me a taxi, please."

CHAPTER 46

Completely exhausted, Deegan barely made it to the elevator at the Hassler. Once inside, he found the suite to be dark, but a light was coming from the bedroom. He called out to Gjuliana but received no reply. His shoulders slumped down and his breath nearly gone, Deegan made it to the bedroom door. Gjuliana was under the bedding with the table lamp on. She was propped up on two pillows reading a book.

"My love, didn't you hear me calling for you?" Deegan asked.

"I tried to call your cell no fewer than twenty times."

"I turned the volume off. I'm sorry."

"Fuck you, and your 'I'm sorry', John. Leaving here without a note, and without a text message to me? Just what the fuck are you up to?" The old Bronx flowed from Gjuliana like the white water torrents of the great Niagara Falls.

"I had some business to take care of with Gonnella, that's all."

"Bullshit. I'm sick of the cloak and dagger, John. Listen to me, I've been sick to my stomach with worry! Wondering, *is he dead in a heap? Is he out on a murder spree again? Is he floating in the Tiber River?* I waited for you for how many years, John? About forty, I'd say, sacrificing my family, my parents and brothers and sisters and their children. We finally are together for a few years of happiness and you get a deadly illness. Is this my lot in life to be trampled on by you? Maybe I need to go home. Not to Lugano but home to New York and live my life out in peace."

"My love, you are overreacting a bit. I'm here. I'm not dead somewhere, and I have something to do which you do not need to know about for your own benefit. Okay, I was inconsiderate and I should have called. I deserve your wrath. Can you forgive me, Gjuliana?"

Deegan collapsed on the floor of their bedroom.

"John!" Gjuliana leaped from her bed to run to her husband's side. Deegan was out cold but breathing. His shirt was soaked with perspiration and his face was bone white and sweaty. Gjuliana pulled a Pompeian, red, embroidered pillow from the ochre and brown settee and placed it under her husband's drenched head. She quickly ran into the kitchen and pulled a bottle of water from the refrigerator. She grabbed a hand towel that was hanging from a towel rack in the bathroom, soaking it with the cold water.

Gjuliana applied the cool towel to her husband's forehead then lifted his head to force a sip of water into him. Deegan came to immediately, but didn't know where he was. Gjuliana grabbed her phone and pressed the number one three times, which was Dr. Solarino's speed dial number.

The doctor summoned, Gjuliana told John not to move, encouraging him to drink the water from the green, glass bottle.

Thirty minutes later, Dr. Solarino rang the doorbell to the suite. His nurse was also on her way.

"I think he can sit up now, but I told him to not get up," Gjuliana said.
"Did he have a seizure?" Solarino asked.

"No, he simply collapsed."

"What was he doing when this occurred?"

"John was out for hours. He came in exhausted and just fell crumpled."

"Help me get him into bed, please," Solarino ordered. The doctor began to thoroughly examine Deegan.

Once he was on the king sized bed, the doctor removed John's shirt and took his pulse count. It was very low. At that moment, the nurse arrived. She moved Gjuliana away from Deegan's bedside then took his vital signs. Deegans blood pressure was abnormally low. The nurse drew blood for their records.

Deegan seemed as if he were in a trance, staring up at the ceiling. "John, its Doctor Solarino. Please, look at me." John complied.

"You've fainted, John. I think you are suffering from exhaustion and dehydration as a result of your chemo and your exerted activity. We are going to put you on a saline IV and see how that works for you. I want you to rest and drink as much water as you can stand. I don't think I need to admit you into hospital. We will stay here as long as needed."

John stabilized and slept. A few hours later, the doctor and nurse left. John awoke at eleven o'clock in the morning. Gjuliana was not about to recall her concerns and resume her argument, at least not for a while.

John was ravenous and had a double portion of his hot millet porridge and an organic pear. Gjuliana could only take coffee. They barely spoke except for John telling Gjuliana he was sorry and how much loved her.

When breakfast was finished Deegan took his cell phone into his bathroom and secured the door. He called Carlos Baldwin keeping his voice as low as he could to be audible.

"Any luck?" Deegan asked.

"I have the product."

"Can you give me the specifications?"

"I knew you were going to ask that question. The product is 98.6% pure. It comes in industrial-sized, steel, compressed gas cylinders. The cylinders are fifty-five inches high, about four and a half feet. They carry three hundred cubic feet of compressed gas per cylinder. Color yellow with double pressure gauges on each."

"Weight?"

"About one forty per cylinder. They come in three of four racked together, ready for a hi-low."

"I'll take four. How are they marked?"

"Oxygen, but at these prices, how do you want them marked?"

"Cooling liquids."

"Not a problem. When do you want them?"

"Three days, early morning."

"Don't you want the price?"

"I'm paying it, so I will need that."

"One hundred fifty thousand per. Cool half mil."

"I hope you stepped on it for yourself."

"Fuck no. Are you fucking crazy?"

"Of course I am. Do you have banking info for me?"

"Yes. It gets wired to our old friend in Rotterdam, he then fucks around with it so no trace to anyone, and then it goes to some frig in Iraq. Embarkation Port of Basra by container."

"I thought that place was knocked out during the war?"

"Reopened. Only eleven docks, nice and small. My guy is the guy."

"Okay, text me banking numbers. Done."

"Done, text me receiver name. One more thing. My guy has a guy at *Civitavecchia*. It will go through like shit through a goose. I'll spot you the 10K on my end."

"No interest, you fucker!"

Deegan laughed and ended the call. He flushed the toilet for effect, left the bathroom and joined Gjuliana in the afternoon sun on the canopied terrace.

CHAPTER 47

Colonel Zellweger was pacing back and forth in the Apostolic Palace waiting for His Holiness, Pope Francis to leave for a short trip, but the days of Francis' reign were dwindling down, and seemingly so was his health. Another headache forced him to cancel his brief sojourn. The official reason for the cancellation was Vatican State business rather than health. Another health scare would send what cardinals who already arrived in Rome for the conclave into a feeding frenzy.

At his doctor's orders, the Pope would retire to his bedroom in the *Domus* for the rest of the day. Two Swiss Guard men were stationed in the hallway outside his room so he would not be disturbed by any of his cardinal "friends."

Zellweger was now free for the day. The Colonel thought he would make a routine visit of the Swiss Guard barracks and the armory to check on weapon conditions. He would then wait until evening and carry out yet another one of his nefarious plans. His final killing before the conclave commenced.

As Zellweger walked from the Apostolic Palace, he once more checked the entrance door that led to the Sistine Chapel, confirming the lock configuration. On his was to the barracks, he spotted a familiar face walking behind the inner security walls. It was Claudio Festa.

"I knew it! You just can't keep away. Have you had second thoughts?" Zellweger asked.

"Hello, Colonel. No, not nearly. I am not one to look back. I'm actually here to poke around for some leads."

"Leads?"

"I'm working for Vic Gonnella now. We believe it is possible the Deegan copycat is someone within the Vatican itself."

Zellweger laughed a nervous laugh and tried to downplay the situation, but perspiration instantly formed on his forehead. "Oh, Claudio, another one of your conspiracy theories? Or a fantasy like St. Malachy and Pope Francis being the last Pope of Catholicism?"

"Well, let me put it this way. If the killer in not here where he may be privy to restricted and confidential information on the murdered priests then we are totally stumped."

"Oh, c'mon, who among the thousands of employees behind these ancient walls would be a suspect?"

"Virtually anyone with access to the files of these priests or someone who could possibly overhear certain information which has never been made public."

"That is still a very long list. What does your Vic Gonnella think, he is back with the New York City Police Department?"

"If that's the case he would have many more millions of potential perpetrators to choose from. We have a short list we will work from."

"Humor me, please. I would love to offer you any assistance I can."

"We postulate the killer could be a disgruntled member of the clergy. Likely a homosexual or perhaps a total fundamentalist who is very opposed to alternative life styles. Maybe a defrocked priest who still knows his way around the Vatican or lives nearby as Bishop Di Siena did. These are just theories, mind you. I must say, though, Cardinal, why are you so negative? Aren't you at all concerned for the safety of all the pope's men? They are dropping like flies around here. For all you know, you and I could both be targets of this nutcase murderer!"

Zellweger knew he'd better cool it. Calmly and reassuringly he stated, "Claudio, I am not at all concerned about the safety of this pope or the next one. Nor am I concerned for the safety and security of any of the cardinals for that matter. My Swiss Guard has, as you know, a nearly impenetrable ring around this city and the College of Cardinals. Zellweger's chest puffed up as he spoke. "Other than the public relations nightmare, another bad apple or two is really none of my concern."

"Colonel, if the killer is among *your* men or the *gendarmeria,* that one zealot with a mission will be difficult to contain. Wouldn't finding the killer put your mind at ease or don't you care?"

"Ahhh, of course I want to see the maniac caught. However, I am not of the same mindset as you and Mr. Gonnella. The infamous John Deegan is a brilliant tactician. He could easily mislead everyone with planted evidence, and I believe it is this kind of misinformation which has potentially cost you your job and sent you on a merry-go-round. I think finding Deegan," and he whispered, "*dead or alive...* is the key to this whole, sordid drama."

"I respectfully disagree," Festa replied with a strong degree of conviction.

"And to think the killer could be a member of the Guard or your former men is disloyal, Claudio! It's preposterous! I'm surprised you would even condone such an idiotic notion."

"Let an old man keep busy. If you are correct then no one has been harmed, and I'm an old fool. I've been called worse in my life."

"I hope you find what you are looking for, Claudio. Call if you need me."

The men shook hands and went their separate ways.

Zellweger, hands shaking, immediately called Rocco Rotigliano. *Fuck,* he thought, *we can't have another conversation like that again!*

A short while later, Deegan rang Colonel Zellweger.

"I am ready to share more details with you."

"It's about fucking time! Do you want me to stop by?"

"Don't be silly."

"Well, where and when, then?"

Calm down. Not until tomorrow night. I need to rest a bit and I have some finishing touches to complete. I should be all ready by then."
"Shall I call you?"

"Absolutely not. All your text messages to me the other night when I fell ill about gave all our plans away to my wife. You know I protect her at all costs, and when the time is right, she will know everything, but not yet. If you want to fuck this up, keep it up. No, I will call you thirty minutes before we meet. Believe me, you are going to enjoy what I have for you." Deegan hit the big, red button on his phone.

Zellweger retreated to his quarters to rest a bit, shower, and dress for his evening jaunt.

The colonel's room was austere to say the least. There was a six-drawer, plain, pine dresser, a comfortable, reclining reading chair, a side table, and a double bed made in military fashion, tight, and perfectly neat with a single pillow in the middle. This strict discipline had been with Zellweger from the time he was a six-year old boy. A very old and large, metal crucifix said to have been his Swiss Guard relative's property, hung directly over the bed. Zellweger's family member protected Pope Clement VII in 1527 during the sack of Rome. Ironically it was Clement VII who ordered the painting of "The Last Judgment" by Michelangelo in the Sistine Chapel.

A photograph of Pope Francis and Zellweger hung on an wall adjacent to his bed so it would be the first thing he would see in the morning and the last thing before he fell asleep. The side table next to his bed had a worn, family bible dating back to the fifteen century.

Zellweger untied his shoes and meticulously buffed them with a soft, shoe brush. He then took off his suit jacket and slacks, folding them neatly, and hung them in the only closet in the room. Before removing his starched, white shirt and straight, black tie, the colonel took his Glock 19 from his shoulder holster and placed in atop the pine dresser. Two extra clips were attached to the holster and were left untouched as the colonel hung it in the closet. Zellweger stripped naked and went into the small bathroom to wash his hands and face and urinate. He shook his penis exactly eleven times in honor of the twelve apostles, less the disgraced Judas Iscariot.

Zellweger slowly and quietly walked over to the pine dresser. He breathed in deeply and exhaled slowly opening the top drawer at the end of his respiration. Inside the drawer, there was a black, cylindrical container with the words FLESHLIGHT along its side in plain, red lettering.

The colonel, his eyes wide in anticipation, twisted the cylinder open exposing a long, pink, sack-like object. The top of the object came to a bulbous head with a soft rubber vagina in its center. Zellweger then removed a tube of lubricant from the dresser drawer and walked the few steps to his bed while applying the jelly-like substance to the fake vagina. His breathing growing heavier, he methodically lie spread eagle on his bed, atop of his neatly folded sheets and blanket, inserting his now hard, erect penis in and out of the rubber sex toy.

To aid in his ejaculation, Zellweger fantasized back to his childhood as his priests were brutally molesting him. As he came to the end of his masturbation, he recalled the faces of the priests he killed, moaning out in ecstasy as he emptied himself into the pink tube.

Zellweger's flaccid penis remained in the faux vagina as he fell into a brief slumber.

CHAPTER 48

Just above the *Trastevere* section of Rome where Rocco Rotigliano met Colonel Zellweger at the flea market is the neighborhood called the *Gianicoclo*, the *Janiculum* Hill. Although it is the second highest hill in Rome, the *Gianicolo* is not one of the famous seven hills of the eternal city, but is well known for its seclusion. The colonel had two meetings planned for that evening in the *Gianicolo* area. Zellweger asked for a meeting at ten o'clock in the evening meeting near the *San Pietro in Montorio* church with Rocco, and the second with a seminarian at the Pontifical Roman Seminary.

"My friend, I am not crazy about meeting you anywhere near a church. Seeing those bones in the last place we met has made me nervous," Rocco admitted. He was wearing a green, Team Lazio cap and a light blue windbreaker with jeans and pointed, brown shoes.

"This is not that kind of church, Rocco. I guess you have no idea what happened here, do you?"

"I don't give two fucks about history. Feeding my family is all I care about."

"It is here that tradition tells us St. Peter, our first pope, was crucified. Some say he was killed in Agrippina's Garden near the Vatican, but I like to think it was here on the *Janiculum* Hill overlooking the city."

"What do I give a rat's fuck? All these dead people will haunt my dreams!"
"Don't be silly. The dead cannot hurt you. Only the living can do that. Anyway, I have a job for you," Zellweger said, while lighting a cigarette with the lit stub of another.

"Ahh, but sir, I have to report on my work to my *padrone*. He has asked me to remind you of…" Rocco rubbed his forefinger and thumb together, the sign for money.

The Colonel, wearing a similar windbreaker to Rocco's but in dark blue and a touristy, Roma, baseball type cap, pulled a large, bulging, manila envelope from his belt.

"Tell your boss he will never come out second with me. This pays for the past job and the one I am about to offer. But if you are no longer interested, I have a member of the Camorra from Naples standing by."

"You are a very funny man, Colonel. What is the job?"

"I need someone put down immediately. If not tonight, then tomorrow for sure."

"Another fucking priest? Maybe I will pay *you* this time and have some fun in the meantime," Rocco was only half kidding.

Zellweger handed a second envelope to Rocco.

"No… no priest this time. Here is his name, photo, and his home address. I am not sure he is there tonight, but you need to find him at once. Do you understand?"

Rocco opened the small, manila envelope and looked at the photo.

"I've seen this man," Rocco said. He then scanned the paper and focused on his name. "Ah, yes, Claudio Festa. This man is a cop. The price is double for a cop."

"He is no longer in that position, and believe me, you will be satisfied with the amount. Any questions?"

"How do you want this piece of work done?" Rocco asked folding the envelope and placing it inside his front, jeans pocket.

"Quickly and as painlessly as possible. He is a good man who got mixed up with the wrong people. You do that. I have to do a 'piece of work' as you put it at the seminary a bit later."

"I'll contact you if I have any problems," Rocco said.

"Rocco, let me make myself clear. There will be no problems."

The hit man shrugged his shoulders and was on his way.

The view from the top of the *Janiculum* Hill, the eighth hill of Rome, is nothing short of spectacular. On this clear night, the lights from many church domes, bell towers, and monuments sparkle high above the illumination of various *palazzos*, the small apartment houses and homes. In the distance, floodlights dance upon the ancient arches of the Roman Coliseum. Zellweger stood, staring out and thought, *My plan is almost complete. I will be hailed as a hero for what is about to come! My family and its history could have never thought my mission in life was to fulfill St. Malachy's prophesy. I am sorry my dear friend, Claudio. Perhaps I should have given Rocco a message for him before he killed him.*

Zellweger blinked back into reality, composed himself, and headed to his next destination, the seminary where Americans called to the priestly vocation are developed for their ministry in the dioceses of the United States of America.

As the Colonel walked toward the seminary, he passed an area which was popular as a lover's lane. He stood for a moment looking at the small Lancias, Fiats, and Alfa Romeos with fogged windows wondering how far the occupants were going. Zellweger's emotion was anger instead of curiosity or arousal, as he could not relate to a normal sexual experience.

Zellweger could see the seminary in the near distance from the exterior flood lights which lit the paths between the buildings, a path seminarians and priests took on their nightly walks to help digest their dinner, pray their rosary, read from their breviary, or simply chat with one another.

The maniacal colonel waited in the dark like a leopard waited to pounce on his clerical prey.

A lone, young man, short in stature with a conservative haircut, dressed in mufti- ordinary clothes, rather than a white Roman collar or priestly robes- left Casa Santa Marie residence for a walk in the gardens.

James Joseph Troy of Providence, Rhode Island was about to become a third-year novitiate. He had taken his first vows, promising to offer himself to God and to enter the priesthood. He vowed to be poor, chaste, and obedient in the imitation of his Lord, Jesus Christ.

Under his left arm, James had his Syon Breviary, the daily office of Our Lady, a prayer book gifted to him from his proud mother and father during their recent visit to see him in Rome. James would take a walk each evening and find a well-lit bench, rock, or stone wall to sit on or lean against as he read his prayers for ten or fifteen minutes in solitude.

Zellweger followed the young man for about ten minutes as the seminarian sought out a quiet place to read his daily devotion from his breviary. The young, future priest settled on a bench along a path in the garden, quiet but barely lit by an overhead street lamp. A bronze bird bath topped with a statue of the outreaching arms of St. Francis stood behind the wooden bench. A small, metal, garbage can was next to where the seminarian sat. James took a stick of gum from his shirt pocket, taking in the fresh, spearmint taste he enjoyed during his prayer walks. James ignored the garbage can and put the used gum wrapper into his pant pocket.

James began to read, concentrating on the words which brought him closer to the Blessed Virgin and her Son. A crunching sound in the bushes behind the bench startled James. He sat up straight, closed the prayer book, and turned to look, peering into the area where he thought the sound came from. There was nothing there. *Must be a small animal,* he thought.

He returned his concentration to his prayers, snapping his gum unconsciously as he softly read the words. Suddenly, a shadow came over his beloved breviary.

Startled, James stood up, dropping his book to the grass below, his feet turning quickly to see what was causing the shadow.

As he turned, the Oberst of the Swiss Guard grabbed the top of the young seminarian's head in a vice-like grip with his left hand and stabbed him under the chin with a thrust using a sharpened, wood crucifix with his powerful, right hand.

The crucifix dug from under the victim's chin, through his tongue and palate, passing his sinus cavity, and into his brain. Through his black, leather gloves, his murderer could feel the warm blood rushing down the crucifix in a torrent.

The last thing seminarian James Joseph Troy of Providence, Rhode Island saw in this life was the piercing, hazel eyes and the engorged vein in the sweat-beaded forehead of his killer.

CHAPTER 49

The morning after the young seminarian was brutally slaughtered, Vic's cell phone rang. It was 7 a.m.

"Vic, there was another homicide. My former assistant called a few minutes ago," Claudio Festa said.

"Holy shit! Oh sorry, Inspector, excuse the language. Another priest?"

"Well, sort of. The victim is a seminarian at the Pontifical school. The Vatican has put a total blanket over this one as well."

"Where did it happen? Can we go?"

The School is in the *Gianicolo*, on the other side of the Tiber from Vatican City. I don't think we are welcome to investigate the crime scene but my man gave me the particulars."

"Shoot!"

"The victim is an American with no hint of scandal. His name is James Joseph Troy, from a good family in your state of Rhode Island. No record of child molestation whatsoever."

"Well, that doesn't mean he *wasn't* a pedo."

"Agreed, but the killer would have at least had some information on him, getting something from inside the Vatican before anything goes public, perhaps? But my man interviewed his roommate and a few, fellow classmates. Troy was not a homosexual. My man was sure to press them on that. This kid was a pious type, with a true, priestly calling."

"So what do you think? Sounds like it could be a random killing to me."

"Precisely my thinking."

"Same M. O.?"

"A crucifix under the neck into his brain, yes."

"So an indiscriminate but planned homicide."

"That's my take, Vic. The Vatican is taking this one as a sign of something bigger to come. It's very close to home and extremely upsetting all the way to the top. Cardinal Magnone had one of his assistants call me. He wants to see me at nine this morning. They're sending a driver for me."

"How about if we meet you there? Maybe we can talk some sense into this cardinal about Deegan."

"What can they say, get out of here? Then I will leave with you. Fuck them, as you say."

"Good, I can be at St. Peter's Square within the hour."

"Okay, I will find you."

Vic rousted Raquel and explained the situation. He rang Angela's room and told her about the murder. Vic advised both ladies to dress down as they may be going into the Apostolic Palace.

Fetsa showered, shaved, and dressed in his dark, business suit and tie. He made a quick cup of espresso and had a couple of *biscotti* for breakfast.

At eight o'clock, Festa opened the door to his flat. A short, well-dressed man in a suit and tie standing at his front door greeted him.

"Buongiorno," Festa said.

"Buongiorno a te." Rocco Rotigliano replied.

Rocco raised his Beretta PX Storm Subcompact pistol and pumped two nine-millimeter bullets into Festa's forehead. Festa fell back into his apartment. Rocco tapped two more shots into the inspector's head, and shut the front door as he calmly walked away.

It had really been Rocco who'd called Festa pretending to be the emissary of Cardinal Magnone.

Vic, Raquel, and Angela waited patiently for Festa near the Egyptian Obelisk in St. Peters Square. Vic wore his conservative business suit without a necktie. Raquel and Angela each wore below the knee skirts and shirts with collars which discreetly covered their breasts. They each carried a lace head covering in their purses.

"It's already past nine, Vic," Raquel stated.

"I know, these Italians sometimes can't keep track of time. If Festa was German he would have been here on time," Vic laughed.

"How can anyone be late for a visit to the pope's palace? I'm afraid something may have happened," Angela warned.

"Maybe he's just breaking balls. Let me call him," Vic said.

Vic called Festa's cell phone. It rang six times and went right into voicemail. He tried again with the same result.

"Maybe I misunderstood. Let's wait until ten," Vic suggested nervously.

The trio watched as workmen, under the scrutiny of the *gendarmerie*, unloaded aluminum, crowd-control barriers from three, flat bed trucks. Vatican City wasn't about to leave the electorate's safety to prayer. They prepared for the conclave and the election of a new pope with the most elaborate and expensive security devices known to man with money donated to them, of course, by their world-wide flock.

"Okay, something is wrong. Maybe Festa had second thoughts about us coming," Raquel said.

"Maybe, but I doubt that. Let's..."

Vic's cell phone rang. His screen read 'restricted'.

"Vic Gonnella, here," Vic answered.

"Mr. Gonnella, this is Monsignor Andriotti from the office of the Cardinal Secretary of The Vatican City State. Do you have a moment to talk with me?"
"Yes, of course, Monsignor."
"The cardinal would like to see you if this is at all possible with your schedule today."

"Yes, I would be happy to meet with his eminence."

"When can you be available, sir?"

"Well, right now my associates and I happen to be in St. Peter's Square."

"Where exactly in the Square?"

"At the Obelisk."

"With your permission, I can be there in three or four minutes," Andriotti said.

"Excellent."

Vic looked at the two women. "We are going into the palace. Festa must already be there somehow."

"I don't know; I have a bad feeling," Angela said.

"Me, too. Something is just not right with this whole thing," Raquel said.

"We never jump to conclusions, right? Our escort will be here in a few minutes," Vic stated.

"Maybe you can ask for an annulment, Vic," Raquel said jokingly.

"Fat chance. I would rather pay the two grand on our next vacation."

In the distance a handsome priest scurried toward the Obelisk. He waved to the trio. Vic returned the wave and the threesome walked toward the monsignor.

Andriotti moved like an athlete. Tall, with short, blond-grey hair, wearing the standard black suit and Roman collar, the monsignor's smile was friendly but subdued.

"Your Reverence, I am Vic Gonnella. Allow me to introduce my partner Raquel Ruiz and our head of European activities, Angela Quagliata."

"So nice to meet you all," Andriotti shook hands all around.

"*Piacere,*" Angela said.

"Nice to meet you," was Raquel's response.

"Please follow me. I am happy to see the ladies are dressed

appropriately."

"We are all products of Catholic education," Raquel said.

"So the nuns taught you well, I see."

"What's going on, Monsignor?" Vic asked.

"Let's discuss that with Cardinal Magnone. It is certainly a beautiful day, isn't it?"

Vic looked surprised at the way Andriotti changed the subject. He gave a quick glance toward Raquel with a look that said, *What the fuck?*

They walked toward the entrance to the Apostolic Palace, the ladies having a difficult time walking as quickly as Andriotti did over the cobblestone pavement.

They approached the Swiss Guard at the well-guarded entrance to the Palace.

"Forgive me, but everyone, no exceptions must be scanned before entering. We are taking all precautions at this time," Andriotti said.

A young, Swiss Guard, his halberd in one hand and an electronic, hand wand in the other ran the scanner over the three visitors. Another guard inspected the women's purses. A third and fourth guard saluted as Andriotti and his guests walked through the gate.

Vic again glanced at Raquel as they passed the guards. Raquel knew Vic was thinking of the Wizard of Oz and was afraid he would start humming the guards' song from that movie or blurt out a 'I'll get you, my pretty!' so she immediately gave him a cute smile but also the death stare at the same time. Vic stifled a laugh. Raquel was right. Vic's sense of humor was one of the things Raquel found so attractive about

Vic. They both cleared their throats and turned their attention back to the situation at hand.

Andriotti took two steps at a time, walking up a marble staircase toward the third floor office. His guests, lagging a bit behind, were breathless when they reached their destination.

"One moment, please. I will tell His Eminence you have arrived."

Vic and Angela looked around the hallway in sheer disbelief at the art and opulence. Angela kept her head bowed in reverence to the pope's palace.

"Please come in." Andriotti announced.

Both of the large, double doors, originals from the sixteenth century, leading into Cardinal Magnone's office, were opened. Cardinal Magnone was standing in front of an enormous, antique, golden-edged desk. The Cardinal was wearing his floor-length, red robe, and red, cardinal skullcap; a gold crucifix hung from his neck and rested on his ample stomach. His outstretched hands gave the trio a warm welcome.

"*Finalmente*, finally, I am honored to meet you, Mr. Gonnella." The Cardinal offered his ringed hand and Vic grasped it and shook it.

"The honor is certainly mine, Your Eminence," Vic replied, choking out the words.

"May I present my associates, Raquel Ruiz and Angela Quagliata."

The Cardinal offered his hand to the ladies. Raquel shook his hand while Angela made a curtsey and kissed his ring.

"Please make yourselves comfortable. Coffee and tea is awaiting."

The cardinal, Andriotti, and the three visitors made their way to an elegant, red and gold trimmed sofa and three low-backed chairs with matching upholstery. Andriotti sat on the sofa with Cardinal Magnone. An effeminate priest poured coffee into gold-rimmed cups from a silver server.

The cardinal got right down to business.

"Thank-you for seeing me this morning. I am sure you are all not aware of the latest two incidents that have befallen Holy Mother Church."

"Eminence?" Vic responded.

"Late, last evening, one of our seminarians at the Pontifical College was slaughtered in the gardens adjacent to the school. Like you, he is an American. He was a fine, future priest with an even brighter future. And just this morning, we have received word that our former Inspector Festa was gunned down in his home."

"*Oh Dio!*" Angela blurted. She raised both of her hands to her mouth. Her eyes filled with tears.

Vic and Raquel were in stunned silence. Deegan's words echoed through both their ears, *The killer may be closer than you think; trust no one.*

"I am aware Inspector Festa agreed with you that the recent killings were not the work of the insane John Deegan. This office does not necessarily agree with your learned opinion but we are in desperate need of your assistance still. Can you help our Church, Mr. Gonnella?"

"How was the Inspector killed?" Vic asked. He would not commit to the cardinal without further information.

"Our understanding is he was shot several times in his head."

Angela had composed herself.

"Again, that is further proof Deegan is not the killer. Forgive me, Eminence, but we believe someone deep inside the Vatican hired a Sicilian mafia hit man for a killing such as this. We also are fairly certain the killer of these priests is a Deegan impostor but perhaps trying to frame him for these homicides," Vic said. He nonchalantly added sugar to his black coffee like he was still a homicide detective in the 41st Precinct house in the Bronx.

"We are not in a position to second guess you, Mr. Gonnella. These latest murders have come too close to our doors. We are extremely concerned for the safety of our Holy Father and all of our cardinals. We are prepared to house you all inside the Vatican if it will assist you in determining who this maniac is. Payment, of course, is not an object. Please consider our plea for your help."

"We are fine where we are staying, but thank-you for the kind and generous offer. Yes, we will help you, conditioned on two things. We have full access to information the Vatican may keep closely guarded, and we have your full cooperation and authority to fully investigate anyone inside of these walls," Vic said. Everyone in the room knew that meant Vic would have access to all of the Vatican's secret files, always shrouded and concealed from the public, which has allowed its pedophile priests to continue to sexually molest children. He was playing hardball with a man who could possibly be the next pope.

"You have my sacred word, Mr. Gonnella."

Of course, anything to save your own ass, you motherfucker, Vic thought.

The office doors swung open. Cardinal Magnone immediately rose.

His Holiness, Pope Francis, dressed in his white, papal vestments entered the room with another cardinal, and a thin, tall man wearing a tailored, black, business suit.

CHAPTER 50

The leader of all Catholics on the planet entered Cardinal Magnone's office as if he were embarrassed for intruding. His friendly, happy face, and his soft manner made him look like any other average, older man who was entering a room with strangers.

Pope Francis greeted each of the trio, not by offering his ring but by extending his handshake. He took each of the visitor's hands into both of his own looking directly into their eyes without saying any words. Only Angela got on her right knee and kissed the Papal ring calling him *Papa*. Francis, almost embarrassingly, guided her back to her feet.

Cardinal Magnone asked the group to be seated. The pope sat on the sofa where Monsignor Andriotti had been.

"It is a pleasure to meet you all. I wanted to stop to greet you before I stepped out for a funeral mass I will be attending for one of our cardinals. I am a bit uncomfortable meeting you in this place. There is so much luxury here while so many of the world's people go hungry. I was voted to the chair and inherited this building. I'm not sure which was worse," Francis laughed. Everyone in the room chuckled except for the man in the black suit, Colonel Zellweger, his hawk-like look focused on Vic with an occasional quick side glance toward the women.

"Your Holiness, Mr. Gonnella and his associates have committed to help us in our hour of need," Cardinal Magnone said.

"Such terrible events have occurred. My heart aches for the families of the victims. I heard this morning about the tragedy at the Pontifical American College. That young man did not deserve to have his young life to be taken, and with such violence. I will offer mass for him and pray for his soul, as I have prayed for the others who have suffered violent deaths from this madman. Prayer brings us close to our

Lord and only He knows why these unfortunate trials have befallen His Church."

He turned to Vic. "Mr. Gonnella, I am pleased to hear you will lend your knowledge to us and intervene to help make this tragedy end."

"Your Holiness, we are all servants of God. And now we are your servants. We will do our very best," Vic promised.

He pulled that 'servants of God' line right out of his ass, Raquel thought to herself as she uncrossed and crossed her legs in the other direction. *And what the fuck? Why is he only addressing Vic? Does he think his misogynistic religious ways rule in the secular world, too?*

A photographer entered the room to memorialize the meeting.

"Ahh, look the photos. Some call me the publicity pope, so I guess they may be correct," Francis said.

Monsignor Andriotti scurried to set up individual photos of Francis and the trio.

"These may be nice to show your grandchildren someday," Francis said.

Over my dead body, thought Vic. *Maybe a bad analogy under the circumstances!*

Another priest walked in with a small box which he opened in front of the pope.

"These are rosaries made from the olive trees in the Garden of Gethsemane in Jerusalem. I have blessed them for you all. I understand you have a small baby, young woman?" Francis asked Raquel.

"Yes, Your Holiness. Mr. Gonnella and I are missing her very much at the moment."

"I will pray for her. Please give her this medal of Our Lady for me. When she grows up tell her the Spanish pope was your friend."

Raquel, as hardened as she had become as a police officer and as jaded as she was toward the church, filled with tears.

"And for you, young lady, I have a special something for your family in Sicily. A statue of *Santa Rosalia, La Santuzza,* the patron saint of Palermo."

Angela was over the moon. She could not wait to show her photograph with Pope Francis to her parents and give them the blessed statue.

Pope Francis said his goodbyes and left the room. Even the most cynical of people could not help but be touched by the presence of this charming and gracious man.

"I am so happy you had the opportunity to meet our Pontiff. I am sure it is a memory you will cherish all of your life. So, you have a lot of work to do. Please call Monsignor Andriotti for anything you need from this office. I fervently pray you will put an end to this nightmare," Magnone said.

The meeting ended and two Swiss Guard walked the trio back to the entrance of the Apostolic Palace.

Vic, Raquel, and Angela walked through St. Peter's Square toward an exit of Vatican City.

"It's not every day you wake up and suddenly you're with the pope," Raquel said.

"And it's not every day you lose a new friend and are put through a dog and pony show, either," Vic said.

"What? Don't tell me you weren't impressed, Vic," Raquel said.

Angela chimed in, "Impressed isn't the word. If I didn't enjoy sex so much I would sign up at the nearest convent." She did not realize what she had said until Vic and Raquel burst into hysterical laughter.

When the laughing and Angela's embarrassment subsided, Raquel returned to Vic's comment.

"What do you mean about the dog and pony show?"

"Okay, you have to look beyond the glitter and gold for a second. The Church has the whole world mesmerized with their pomp and circumstance. I just don't buy it. Here's what we really have, which, might I remind you through those rose colored glasses, the Vatican has squashed to the public: Festa is gunned down on his way to meet us. Magnone never mentioned a meeting so I suspect the hit man who shot and killed Festa is the same mutt you saw on the videotape at the Grand Hotel, and had no doubt set Festa up. That very same mob guy had to be the one on the steps of the bone church talking to the bearded musician. With me so far?"

Raquel and Angela simultaneously replied, "Yes."

"Now Magnone calls us, begging for our help even though Festa quit, because this jerkoff cardinal would not believe our theory that Deegan isn't the killer. So either the Vatican put the hit on Festa to stop him from working with us or the real killer knew Festa may have been getting close to figuring him out."

"Wow. Any more?" Raquel asked.

"Yes, they drag the pope into see us with all the gifts and photos and the rest of that whole drama to make us see how insignificant we are in their world. Festa devoted his life to them and they threw him out like yesterday's trash because he was no longer their compliant servant. They know that alone we have no idea what the fuck we are doing," Vic said.

"How did they know so much about us? Your baby and my parents in Palermo?" Angela asked.

"They are professional mind fuckers. They can find out the results of your last pap smear, and they love to let you know they can do that. For two thousand years the Vatican has perfected their game of illusion. Pull the sheep into the circle, sheer them of their wool, and then dispose of them when the time is right."

"Oh, now I want to smash that statue to the ground!" Angela said as she seethed in anger.

"Keep the statue and play their game. We need to pretend we are very taken in by the whole opera. That whole meek pope thing, 'the palace is too luxurious' my ass. They will be playing this game for the next two thousand years. The times change but the Church really never does. It's all about money and power. That whole faith thing is just a smoke screen," Vic said.

"Just as an aside, not that it makes any difference, but did either of you notice that guy in the suit?" Raquel said.

"You mean Superman, the guy who stared at me with his x-ray vision?" Vic said.

"And the fast glances he kept making toward me and Angela? That dude is strange."

"He made me feel uncomfortable. His eyes were creepy!" Angela said.

"He is perfect. Listen to me; the pope's bodyguard has a tough job. Just think of the pressure he's under with all the crazies looking to take out Francis or whoever else is in that chair. His mind must race as he listens to every nuance in people's voices and monitors every action that those around the pope make."

"So what's do we do now?" Raquel asked.

"We ask for a list of every name on the payroll just as Festa said. All the Swiss Guards, the other cops, any priest that has had a known problem with children, and any defrocked assholes. We can go through the list but for us it will be like looking for the proverbial needle in a haystack. We let them think we are up to something and try to smoke out the killer's next move," Vic said.

"And what about John Deegan?" Angela asked.

"Trust me, he will find us when he needs us." Vic assured.

CHAPTER 51

A few days passed with Vic, Raquel, and Angela busying themselves with personnel records they requested from Monsignor Andriotti. It seemed Cardinal Magnone had so far lived up to his sacred promise.

The trio was offered the use of a large conference room at the *Palazzo del Governatorato* building behind the great Basilica. For ease of logistics and in the interest of time, Vic and Raquel agreed to use the room.

The former NYPD cops also surmised their movements and words would be closely monitored. The Vatican, indeed, has perfected the cloak and dagger spy game. Vic and Raquel both realized Cardinal Magnone could not be trusted. Angela's inexperience did not yet register distrust.

Vic searched the room and found two microphones. One in a beautiful, antique crucifix that hung on the wall and the other device was tucked into a corner under the head of the rectangular, wooden, conference table. A sophisticated nanny cam took videos of the entire room. Vic spotted the camera in a ceiling vent and did everything he could not to make it obvious he knew. All Vic needed to do with Raquel was shift his eyes to where the bugs were. He passed a note to Angela advising her of the situation, telling her not to look around the room for the monitors. Angela folded the note and put it in her purse, the fury in her eyes told the others she fully understood.

Knowing they were being watched and listened to, inconspicuous notes were passed between the three, new, Vatican hired hands as they reviewed the files. Some files were in English but most were in Italian. The trio realized reviewing the files was nothing more than an exercise in futility. They were simply marking time. Raquel attached a blue, sticky note to one of the American priest's files. She passed the file, along with a knowing smile, to Vic. The note read: Look at this mutt. Accused of molesting a boy in Philadelphia. Moved to Milwaukee, accused again. Moved to New Jersey. A parent of twin boys attempted to shoot him in the church for sodomizing both kids. They moved him here. He is now working for the Pontifical Council for the Pastoral Care of Migrants and Itinerants.

John Deegan met with Colonel Zellweger inside the same café they had met before. Deegan gave the colonel the standard thirty-minute notice. They both wore the exact same disguises as before. Deegan sipped his cup of hot tea and Zellweger had a double espresso.

Deegan noticed the colonel was extremely jittery, his eyes fluttering around the restaurant, his legs bouncing up and down under the round table. Deegan fingered his pistol, flicking off the safety just in case Zellweger was setting him up somehow.

"I have some questions about the Chapel," Deegan said.

"And I have many questions for you as well. The conclave is in three days and I am anxious to put the plan together."

"That's why we are meeting, colonel. I am well aware of the date. I need to know if the windows of the Chapel will be open during the General Assembly of the conclave."

"The windows are all sealed. There is no apparatus for opening them."

"Good, that makes my plan easier. Now, on the third story of the chapel, what is up there?"

"That is a wardrobe area for the security guards. There is an open gangway which encircles the entire chapel."

"Will there be any Swiss Guard or anyone else up there during the assembly?"

"No. No one will be up there."

"Will the cardinals have any way of calling anyone outside of the room?"

"No. There are no telephones inside the chapel and all cell phones are surrendered when the cardinal moves into the Domus. They have no access to the outside word. Computers are also not allowed."

The perfect set up. Almost too perfect, Deegan said to himself.

"Tell me about the main door please, and the side exit door," Deegan said.

"There is no exterior door. The only access to the Chapel is the processional doorway which leads from the interior of the palace. The exit door on the right will be sealed and guarded from the exterior. There will be four of my men stationed at the main door. It is very important to me that none of my men will be harmed."
"I'm sure you have heard of the phrase collateral damage, Colonel. I cannot guarantee the safety of anyone who rushes into the chapel. You are about to kill over two hundred cardinals of the Catholic Church. A few Swiss Guards are not really my concern. I have an idea which may work regarding that, but we can revisit that issue later."

Zellweger didn't respond but glared with his hawk-like face. Deegan returned the stare with his piercing, blue eyes until Zellweger looked away.

"Now, the product is in the port, in a container marked Vatican City. You will need to arrange transportation from the port to the basement of the chapel. There are four cylinders which are quite heavy," Deegan said.

"That's not a problem."

"The cylinders are standard yellow and are marked "oxygen" and they are altogether in a manifold. The gas must be let into the ventilation system with the pump that is in the container. All of the valves must be opened to the maximum."

Deegan noticed Zellweger staring and nodding his head as if he were listening, but he seemed to be a million miles away wrapped up in his thoughts.

"Damn it. Are you paying attention? This is important! You fuck this up because of your inattentiveness and *you* will be the dead man. Do you understand?"

"Understood."

"Colonel, now listen. Unless you want to join the dead cardinals you must wear a protective gas mask in the event some of the gas leaks or is pushed back by the ventilation system. One whiff and you will be finished in a minute."

"I have such a mask at my disposal."

"Ok, and what do you plan to do after the gas cylinders are emptied? Have you thought about that yet? It's one thing to kill a bunch of people; it's yet another thing not to get caught, believe me. Follow through is everything."

Deegan laughed at his own comment and Zellweger joined him. "I feel like I'm training those who will come after me when I die," John said.

"Ok, back to business. Have you calculated the time it will take for the gas to permeate the room?

"Yes, I have. Approximately nine minutes."

"There is a secret door which leads from the basement back into the palace. I will have plenty of time to resume my post, while my men are outside of the ceremonial door. I don't know if we will be able to hear the pleas of the cardinals or hear them falling from their chairs. If we do, my men will begin to begin to smash the doors with their halberds."

"And where will the *camerlengo* be during the assembly?"

"He will be seated, with a few other priests who carry ceremonial candles, near the front of the chapel. The *camerlengo* then asks everyone who is not voting to leave. The doors are opened, and the procession of the older, non-voting cardinals slowly move single file toward the doors and they all leave. The camerlengo then sees to it that the doors are sealed from the inside. I will time the gas to be released during the invocations. I will be able to hear the prayers coming through the vents."

"It sounds to me like you have indeed done your homework, Colonel. I'm impressed," Deegan said.

"Yes, thank you. I have gone over the scenario countless times in my head since you planned the cyanide attack. Your plan is brilliant, and my execution will be flawless."

Deegan ignored the compliment.

"What will you do with the engineer in the basement of the chapel?"

"Your word collateral damage has covered that problem."

"Really? Does that man deserve to die? He did nothing to

harm anyone. He is just a working man who is happy to be working in the Vatican, and who plans to go home that night to his family."

"He will recognize me, and in the end…"

"So he will tell the world it was you who unleashed the toxic gas?"

"Precisely."

"Unless somehow you can figure a way to stealthily incapacitate him?"

"Why are you so concerned with this man?"

"Because he is innocent."

"I was innocent at seven years old when that fucking priest took me and raped me. Our entire destiny's change when these bastards abuse. The whole world. Everyone is affected. Why can't people see this? Perhaps St. Malachi knew more than we gave him credit for."

Deegan looked at Zellweger and finished his cup of tea.

"I will text you instructions on who to see at *Civitavecchia* tomorrow morning. Everything is taken care of so no money will change hands. Who will be picking up the cylinders?

"Don't worry yourself. I have that already figured out."

"Any other questions, Colonel?"

"Yes. Where will you be through all of this, Mr. Deegan?"

"I haven't figured that out just yet. Perhaps I will be safely out of Italy or perhaps I will stay in Rome to be witness to the destruction. I will play it by ear and see how I'm feeling.

Deegan stood to leave, placing a ten-euro note on the table. Zellweger firmly grabbed Deegan's arm.

"One more thing, Mr. Deegan. How will I be guaranteed there is really cyanide gas in those cylinders and you have not double crossed me?"

"Now why would I ever even think of that, Colonel? Even I am not that sinister."

Louis Romano

CHAPTER 52

His Holiness, Pope Francis, the two hundred sixty-sixth Pontiff of the Roman Catholic Church, the Vicar of Christ, could not sleep during his last night as the leader of the Catholic world.

He got out of bed at four-thirty, said his morning ritual of prayers, pretended to stretch and do a few squats, dressed in his white papal vestments and read yesterday's edition of *L'Osservatore Romano*, the Vatican newspaper.

At seven o'clock, his butler gently knocked on Room 201 in the *Domus Marthae Sanctae*. Francis opened the door with a wide smile, his eyes sparling like those of a child. He took one look at the butler and started to laugh.

"Paulo, if you are going to start crying now you will surely become dehydrated. Today is not so sad. I am doing the best thing for our church. Let's have a nice cup of coffee together."

Francis then said mass as he always did in the small chapel behind the Domus building. Many of the housekeepers and gardeners packed themselves into the chapel, as did several Swiss Guard in full regalia, several more in plain clothes. Oberst Adrien Zellweger was among the communicants.

Francis did not want a big, expensive, theatrical farewell. There would be no final blessing from the papal apartments he rejected at the onset of his papacy. No blessing from the balcony where he was introduced to the world as their new pope a few short years ago. He could hear the praise throughout the world of what a humble man he was. Really he was no more than a coward. Skipping out and passing the baton to the next guy to avoid dealing face-to-face with the enormous, sexual abuse crises and cover-ups himself.

A simple breakfast, an audience, and a short, touching final lecture on the importance of keeping their vows to a room full of senior cardinals in the Apostolic Palace, and a personal farewell to more of the Vatican workers was all that Francis would tolerate.

As the last maid kissed the papal ring and walked away in tears kissing the blessed rosary Pope Francis had given them, Colonel Zellweger spoke into his wrist letting the rest of the Swiss Guard know the entourage was on the move.

His Holiness decided a walk to the heliport would be good for everyone. He gazed around the papal gardens and old buildings replete with infamous history, smiling and waving to the few people who had gathered as he passed.

"The Pope's AgustaWestland AW139 helicopter was awaiting him with all of the Italian Air Force personnel standing at attention, snapping to smart salute on command as Francis approached. The humble pope approached each of the men and one woman, shaking their hands and pinning a miraculous medal on the lapel of their uniforms.

Francis was the first to board the 'copter followed by his personal physician and the rest of his retinue. Colonel Zellweger and two of his plainclothes men were the last to board. The door was slammed shut and locked from the inside. The whole time Zellweger felt as if he were on the verge of breaking down in tears. His chin had already begun to flutter during Francis' final mass as Pontiff.

The Italian Air Force pilot started the engines of the helicopter and within a minute or two they ascended into the sky above Vatican City. A church bell rang solemnly in the distance, signaling a fond goodbye to Francis for his trip to *Castel Gandolfo*, now out of his white robes and silky, white sash into history.

The pilot twice circled the Vatican as slowly as possible with Francis observing his city from his window seat. Francis was smiling broadly. Tears were flowing down Zellweger's face.

Francis said goodbye to the Swiss Guard at *Gandolfo,* pinning a small crucifix with the Vatican gold and white colors to each man's uniform. He met Zellweger last.

"You have served me well, Colonel. We have traveled many miles together, sharing memories I will always cherish. May God be always with you, my son."

Zellweger could not bring himself to respond. He knelt in front of Francis taking Francis' hands in his own and kissing the papal ring. A few tears from the Colonel's swollen eyes dripped onto the former Pontiff's hands.

Within two hours, the entire Swiss Guard that was stationed at the pope's summer residence retreated from *Castel Gandolfo* returning to the Vatican, several by helicopter and a few in two cars.

The pope was no longer there. An eerie silence was felt inside the walls of the Vatican, while swarms of the devoted flock filled St. Peter's Square and, of course, the gift shops. After all, the church getting a new pope is as big a business as the NFL's Superbowl.

That evening, Zellweger did his nightly step-by-step review of the scenario he was planning at the Sistine Chapel.

The Colonel returned to his small room, following his bedtime ritual.

This time however, his masturbation fantasy with his portable fleshlight vagina was different.

Zellweger imagined Raquel and Angela being tied to his bed about to bring him to orgasm.

CHAPTER 53

As Deegan returned to the Hassler, he began dreading the next day. Another round of chemotherapy with Dr. Solarino was scheduled for early morning.

Deegan didn't feel at all tired from his meeting with Zellweger. If anything, he was energized by the thought of the conclave beginning in two days. He was hoping he would not be sick to his stomach again. He was more worried about being sick and nauseous than he was of actually dying.

When Deegan arrived at the suite, he found almost every light in all the rooms on. The air conditioners were blaring and the place was chilly. He called out to Gjuliana with no response.

She's pissed off again. Now what? Deegan thought.

Deegan sheepishly went to the master bedroom assuming his wife was sitting up in bed reading and annoyed at him again for coming back later than he thought.

But Gjuliana was nowhere to be found. Her jewelry, pocketbook, and reading glasses were on the large bureau in the bedroom. Deegan thought perhaps Gjuliana was with Claude going over some details for the next day. He quickly went to the houseman's room.

"Claude, open up." Deegan tapped on the door. No answer. He knocked again this time a bit harder with the same result. Deegan tried the doorknob. It turned, and Deegan called out again. He opened the door to a mostly dark suite. The only light came from a lap top computer which was on a table in the small kitchenette.

Deegan let the door close behind him and waited in the dark for a moment to let his eyes become accustomed to the darkness.

He could see a lump of clothing on the floor in the living room area. Slowly moving to the pile of clothing, Deegan realized it was Claude.

Deegan flicked on the light and scurried toward the fallen Claude. Blood soaked the rug around the houseman's head. He was dead.

Deegan's heart began to pound as he quickly returned to his suite. He called down to the front desk.

" *Pronto, Si, Signore* Brady," the desk manager responded.

"*Buona Sera,* do you know if Mrs. Brady left the hotel this evening?" Deegan asked. He kept his breathing calm as to not give away and sense of panic in his voice.

"I am sorry, Mr. Brady, but I did not see her. We were very busy at reception tonight with registering a large group. I will ask the bellman and the doorman if you care to hold for a moment."

"Thank you. I will wait."

A few moments later the deskman returned to the phone.

"*Si, Signore,* Signora Brady left over an hour ago. A young man accompanied her; the doorman believed he was a tour guide or driver."

"*Grazie.*" Deegan hung up and pulled his cell phone from his pants pocket.

"Hello, John, how are you?' Vic asked.

"I'm in trouble. How soon can you get here?"

"Fifteen minutes."

"Don't come through the front door. I will meet you at the teahouse in the *Piazza di Spangna*. Bring the ladies. Please hurry."

"Raquel, get the guns from the safe, let's roll."

CHAPTER 54

Vic and Raquel strapped themselves with their pistols and extra nine-millimeter clips. Angela met them in the lobby minutes later, her black hair pulled back and still wet from the shower.

The taxi raced to the tearoom, Vic offering the driver an extra two, twenty euro-notes for not sparing the horses. The red lights along the Via Veneto became not much more than a suggestion as the driver only saw the paper in Vic's hands.

The pedestrian traffic in the Piazza di Spagna was wall-to-wall, as the stores along the *Via dei Condotti* were staying open until midnight for a special promotion. Vic ordered the driver to stop, paid the tab, and squeezed the forty-euro into the driver's hand. The trio walked the three blocks to the Babington Tea Room.

Deegan was pacing inside the restaurant, his face contorted with rage.

"I have arranged a quiet room in the back," Deegan said through clenched teeth.

A waiter followed them into the room where Deegan gave him a one hundred euro note telling him there was no need for them to order anything.

Deegan shut the door to the room and turned quickly to the trio.

"Someone has taken Gjuliana!"

"Oh my God... no," Raquel said, only a whisper of sound coming out of her voice.

"Our attendant Claude is dead in his room. Two shots to the brain," Deegan said. Vic could see that Deegan's hands were trembling.

"Mob style," Vic said.

"I agree. No note, no warning, nothing," Deegan said.

"Listen to me, John. If she is alive they will contact you. They probably want a ransom. You pay the fucking ransom with proof of life and get the fuck away from here," Vic said.

"What the fuck. What do you mean, 'if she is alive.' She'd better fucking be alive! There is so much more to tell you. I was waiting for the day after tomorrow to bring you all in," John said.

"Does this have to do with the conclave?"

"Yes. Now I will tell you who the copycat killer is. This prick has been setting me up for a month. I met him in Lugano, where I live. He sought me out with a plan to wipe out every cardinal of the Church. He double crossed me and I was going to double cross him… and now this!"

"Who the fuck is he?" Vic was practically yelling at this point.

"The answer is closer to the pope than you can ever imagine." Deegan paused, not sure if he was ready to name his imitator.

"Jesus Christ, Almighty, John, do you want to see your wife die or what? These mob guys are ruthless and you know it. They will clip Gjuliana and go have a spaghetti and meatball dinner a half hour later. No more guessing games or we can't help you," Vic said. He was staring into John's eyes that had turned from sky blue to almost black.

"Colonel Adrien Zellweger," John spit when he said his name.

"The head of the fucking Swiss Guard?" Raquel said.

"None other," John said.

"Is that the man we saw in the palace with Pope Francis?" Angela asked in disbelief.

"Yeah, that creepy bastard. No wonder he was acting so strangely," Vic said.

"Vic, I'm going to need your help. I'm no match for him in my physical condition, but I will outplay him every day of the week."

"What makes you think it's him and just not a coincidental kidnapping for money," Vic asked.

"Because it's a smart move. I never said he was a dummy. I'm just saying that I will out-maneuver him," Deegan said.

"John, with all due respect, he is playing with a full house here. As I see it, he has out-played you," Vic said.

"Tomorrow he is bringing in four large cylinders of hydrogen cyanide gas. He will jury rig those cylinders and when the conclave is in general assembly the day after tomorrow he will poison the air in the Sistine Chapel, killing the cardinals while they are in prayer."

"Holy shit!" Raquel said.

"If he pulls it off it will be the biggest murder in the history of the world. The plan is brilliant," Vic said.

"It's my plan," Deegan admitted.

"You would do this, John? I know you hate the church for what they have done to so many people, but is this the answer? This has gone too far," Raquel said.

"Absolutely not. That's where my plan to double-cross Zellweger comes in."

"Okay, explain, Vic said.

"I'm keeping that card close to my vest. Even to you three. I have a bigger stake in the game now. My plan right now is to get my wife back and expose this cocksucker. For once I wanted to be the hero but he put me into check, at least for now. His taking my wife was not part of my plan as you can well imagine. I'm simply asking you three to trust me and help me save my Gjuliana's life. You will be well rewarded."

"We don't want your friggin' money. Just tell us what we need to do," Vic said.

CHAPTER 55

Rocco Rotigliano was chain smoking Marlboro Red cigarettes as he paced in a dark and dank smelling warehouse near the *Piazza del Verano* in the *Collatino* section of Rome.

Rocco had conned Gjuliana Deegan into believing her husband had been hit by his taxi and was in the hospital.

Gjuliana rushed from the Hassler into a car where an associate of Rotigliano's was waiting. They drove away from the hotel and Gjuliana was threatened at gunpoint, slapped hard in the face, then bound and gagged, and blindfolded. She was forced to lie in the bottom of the back seat of the Lancia sedan.

Gjuliana was smart enough to know she could identify both men, which may have sealed her fate.

The warehouse was a mob storage depository for goods from hijacked trucks, and illegal drugs, mostly marijuana and cocaine coming in from Afghanistan and Albania, peddled throughout Italy via a sophisticated mafia distribution system.

An occasional torture and subsequent hit sometimes also took place at the one-story, steel-roofed warehouse, which sits adjacent to the *Cimitereo Campo Verano*, one of Rome's largest cemeteries and crematoriums. The warehouse was on a conveniently, secluded street, but just one block from a development of single-family homes that made up a quiet, working man's neighborhood.

A few old and stained mattresses lined one wall inside the warehouse. Gjuliana was on one of the mattresses. Her blindfold had been removed and plastic bottles of water for her to drink and a pail that acted as her toilet were next to her.

"I am sorry, Signora. Once things have been settled with your husband you will be free to go. But for now, this will be your home," Rocco said.

Gjuliana did not speak. *"nd my husband will slaughter you like a lamb,* she thought.

"I will be leaving for a while, but one of my associates will tend to you."

Rocco left two, young, Riina family soldiers to guard the prisoner and left the warehouse with the man who had tied Gjuliana up, the two of them driving away as if they were two pals on their way to go bowling.

Instead, Rocco and his sidekick drove the white van without any markings to the Port of *Civitavecchia* to pick up the "oxygen" cylinders as he was ordered to do by Colonel Zellweger. The mob hit man had no idea of the true content of the yellow containers. All he was being paid for was to return the tanks to the warehouse in *Collatino* and to wait for orders for his prisoner's disposition.

The transfer of the canisters went without incident. Carlos Baldwin's man at the port saw to it that the canisters were loaded into the van, even lending a hand to help load them with a forklift.

"What is this oxygen being used for?" Rocco's associate asked as they drove back to the *Collatino.*

"*Cornudo,* if you want to be part of the big game, keep your mouth shut, your eyes closed, and your ears deaf. You will last much longer in this life. Take my advice," Rocco said.

No other conversation ensued during the hour-long ride back to the warehouse.

The van pulled up to a loading dock at the depository and the four mobsters struggled with the bulky, wooden container, as they brought the four cylinders safely into the warehouse.

Rocco checked on his prisoner. The bound Gjuliana was now asleep. Rocco looked down at Gjuliana and thought of his mother back home in Palermo, as they were about the same age. That thought meant nothing to him should he be ordered to kill her.

Rocco walked back to the loading dock to use his cell phone.

"The goods are home," Rocco announced.

"No trouble? Very good. In an hour have your men bring them to the service entrance on *Viale Vaticano* where I showed you. I will escort them to their final destination and they will be finished," Zell-weger said.

"What do you mean asking if there was trouble? Was I out there like some pawn, you mother fucker? And what about my pay-ment?"

"Shut up, you asshole. You are fine. And I will take care of your payment when the job is completed. How is your guest?"

"Resting comfortably."

"Keep alert. Ciao."

Rocco put his cell phone back in his jeans' back pocket and turned to go back inside the warehouse.

"One move and I will put a fucking hole in your greasy head," Vic warned. His nine-millimeter pistol was aimed between Rocco's eyes. "Slowly on the ground, you motherfucker. If you flinch, you die," Vic threatened.

Vic held his gun to Rocco's head, frisked him, and removed the tough guy's stiletto switchblade, his pistol, and cell phone before tying his hands behind his back with duct tape.

Vic then pulled the hit man to his feet and walked behind him toward the warehouse.

John Deegan was hugging Gjuliana on the soiled mattress. She was sobbing into her husband's shoulder.

Rocco's associate didn't live long after all. His throat was sliced open from ear to ear. He was slumped over in the folding chair he was still sitting in, a blood soaked copy of *La Repubblica* newspaper on his lap.

John brought Gjuliana to her feet. The Bronx girl walked up to Rocco and slapped him hard on his face, the echo of which rang throughout the warehouse.

Deegan took his wife by the arm and walked her out of the warehouse to a Mercedes sedan which was parked in front of one of the homes a block away.

Vic forced Rocco to sit on the ground.

"Real professional! You don't have a chase car? No backup? Just you and this poor, fucking dead kid. No idea you were followed from the port. Just smoking cigarettes like a chimney and flicking the stubs out the window. I know the word for asshole in Italian is *strunzzo*. You popped Festa and now you will answer for that, you low-life," Vic said.

"You will die for this. The Riina family will hunt you like a wild boar," Rocco warned.

"Fuck you, and fuck Riina."

"Shoot me and get it over with. Unlike you I am not afraid to die."

"When that old man returns you will be begging to die. Right now, answer my questions so I can at least ask him to finish you quickly."

"*Non ditta ninda.*"

"What were you told was in those canisters?"

"Nice marinara sauce."

Vic slapped Rocco's head with the butt of his Glock 22.

"Can we try again, *strunzzo?*"

"Your mother is a whore."

Vic smashed his gun against his prisoner's nose, breaking it. Rocco's blood flowed like a torrent.

"Listen to me, tough guy. You can go hard, or maybe, just maybe, you can live. Go back to Sicily and tell your family the great killer John Deegan spared your life. It's entirely up to you. I don't care if you live or if you die, you piece of shit."

"I'm dead either way so I can die here and now and get it over with," Rocco said, the blood seeping out his mouth.

Deegan walked in quietly. He stared at Rocco for an uncomfortable thirty seconds.

"My wife? You come and take her and hold her captive? So, you would kill her at the order of your client, an innocent woman who would never even kill a bug? Is this what the mafia does these days? Now, you will tell me what Zellweger was going to do next!"

"Fuck you, old man!" Rocco yelled back. *Why the fuck did he just ask what Zellweger 'was' going to do next? Is Zellweger already dead? How am I going to get my cash now?*

"Very disrespectful," Vic said.

Deegan bent low bringing his head down to Rocco's bloody mess of a face.

"I learned to make men talk before you were born. There is no need for me to be brutal toward you unless you really want me to. Let me tell you the facts so you are fully aware of your client's intentions. Those cylinders are filled with compressed, hydrogen cyanide gas, enough to kill many people. Zellweger, the man who paid you to kill Inspector Festa and who used your dumb ass to help him kill a few priests is going to poison two hundred cardinals as they vote for the next pope. Do you want their deaths to follow you to the other side? Or will you help us to stop him?"

"*Sei potzzo*, you are a crazy man," Rocco said.

"Yes, many people would agree with you, but see how nice I'm being? I want to reason with you. Now, one last chance before I open your stomach and pull out your intestines and let you see how you digest your pasta. I can allow you to live if you help us. I need your time for one full day. After that you can leave Italy with a nice paycheck. Do I have your attention, or do I need to tape your mouth to stifle your screams?"

Vic's eyes were wide in anticipation. Rocco's eyes were blinking uncontrollably.

"I... I don't know how I can help you," Rocco said.

"Ah, you have finally become a reasonable man at the thought of money. I like that," Deegan said.

CHAPTER 56

Deegan left the warehouse and went back to the Benz to see Gjuliana. It was long past the time Deegan explained to his wife what was about to take place the next day in Vatican City.

When he approached the car he could see his wife was still crying, her head held high, dabbing away tears, trying to be stoic and strong. The trauma of being held by these Italian gangsters had overwhelmed Gjuliana's senses and sensibility.

Gjuliana waited in the front passenger seat; John moved behind the wheel. He needed to get to the story and was a bit clinical in his tone.

"Gjuliana, I'm afraid I have a lot of bad news for you so I am going to get right to the point. First of all, and sadly, our Claude was killed back at the hotel."

"What? Claude? Why?"

"There is a man who is trying to double cross me with some recent priest killings. He is the one who had you kidnapped to get leverage against me. Claude was just in the way. I'm sorry, but I never saw that coming. Secondly, that man who came to visit me and you were concerned and asked me about back at the *Klinik*. That man I said was a friend. Well, he is trying to kill the entire roster of cardinals in the Sistine Chapel tomorrow. Back in Switzerland, he sought me out to help him with his plan. So for now, I need to stay here and get some things arranged; Vic will bring you back to the Hassler. His girls will care for you and protect you until we can move you to a safer place. If I had my way you would be back in Lugano."

"Are you finished? Are you through giving me the God damn lists according to Deegan? I'm not at all interested in playing in your game, John. I don't care to be a bishop, or knight, or pawn, or rook. I refuse to wait for you to outsmart, out-maneuver, out-last, or out-kill the next piece of shit who has a game to play. I will go home to Lugano if and when I want. I may just go back to New York. I'm done!" Gjuliana declared.

"Why are you talking this way to me? I'm being totally honest with you."

"Did you see that I was almost killed by the latest contest that just happened to find you? Protect me? You should have figured that out before getting involved with this maniac. Not even cancer has stopped you, John, and speaking of cancer, you had a chemo appointment. Did you keep it?"

John put his eyes down.

"John! Oh, of course you didn't keep it! You are a gambler, John Deegan, and you always have been. You live on the edge all the time, and everything you do has to have some big risk involved. Since we were kids you've been that way except the stakes are a lot higher now. It was okay when you gambled and made a friggin' fortune on Wall Street but you can't help yourself even now in the face of your own death. I don't even feel sorry for you, John. I'm not even sure what I feel at the moment." Gjuliana's eyes were puffy and red even though she had stopped crying.

"Gjuliana, you need to leave now. Things are going to get a bit testy. We can talk tomorrow. Vic will be right out to take you back," Deegan said.

Gjuliana had no more fight left in her as her husband showed not the iota of a tell. Was he even listening? Did he even care anymore? Was John such a degenerate, game player, and gambler that nothing else mattered in life to him than to win? And to win at all costs, including at the cost of his own life?

John made no move to kiss his wife goodbye. No sign of affection or caring. Deegan had a stone cold, emotionless look to his face. Gjuliana thought for a second her husband's eyes resembled those of a shark. John's eyes had gone from twinkling, sky blue to dark and lifeless in the last week. John simply turned and walked toward the warehouse like a man possessed. Minutes later Vic was behind the wheel of the Mercedes heading back to the Hassler with Gjuliana.

"I don't know what to do, Vic. I think John has gone mad. He is no longer the person I once knew."

"He is not wrapped too tight, Gjuliana. To be perfectly honest with you no sane person would have done the things your husband has done. The murders he committed were brutal, more brutal than you know, evidently. Your husband is not that teenager you fell in love with on Grand Avenue in the Bronx. He has been so damaged as a child he is capable of anything at this point. I still don't know what he is up to with this Zellweger maniac. This is very much like the clash of Lucifer and Gabriel in the New Testament. Except I can't tell who's who."

"Why don't you just go to the police or someone and tell them what's about to happen? This is total insanity," Gjuliana said, sounding more angry than afraid.

"I've thought of that. I still may blow the whistle and play the role of the hero of the church role all over again."

"So just do it!"

"There is one thing holding me back. John had said to me he wanted to be the hero for a change. I'm hoping I'm not making the biggest mistake of the last two millennia."

While Vic drove Gjuliana back to the Hassler, Raquel and Angela were "cleaning" the room where Claude was murdered.

Angela had reached out to her close friends in Rome who would help remove Claude's body and dispose of any signs of blood or brain matter that was left on the rug in his suite.

Angela had promised her friends a full explanation when the time was right.

It was essential the hotel did not find out about the murder and report it to the local *carabinieri*. The houseman's body was wrapped in old draperies and put in a large, canvas, linen cart and brought down through a service elevator to the rear of the Hassler where a van was waiting.

Claude's body would be kept in a secure place until his family was notified of his death and he could be returned to Switzerland, and honored with a Mass of Christian Burial.

Vic arrived at the Hassler where Raquel was waiting under the hotel's canopy.

"We need to get her out of here, Vic. No way this place is safe," Raquel said to Vic as he stepped from the car. Gjuliana remained seated in the passenger seat.

"Let's get some of Gjuliana's things and bring her to our place. How did the cleaning go?"

"Everything is fine. Angela already packed a bag for Gjuliana and we are ready to roll. Where's John?"

"Angela is amazing. Deegan is finishing up a few things. I just hope he doesn't collapse before tomorrow morning when the conclave starts."

"I'll go get Angela and the bag and we can get the hell out of here. Vic, please keep your eyes open. These fuckers are dangerous."

"I think we've covered it all. Go ahead, honey. I'll be fine."

After a long five minutes, Raquel and Angela exited the hotel with Gjuliana's bag, surrounded by four of Angela's friends. No long goodbyes were exchanged, and Vic and the women sped safely away from the hotel. En route to the Borghese Gardens, Vic took every care they were not being followed. He turned onto the Via Veneto, then turned right at the American Embassy along the wide boulevard, then cut in and out of a half-dozen, small, side streets. In ten minutes they were back at the *Parco dei Principi* where Gjuliana would stay with Angela for the night.

"Hello, Nora, nice to see you again," Preston Shields said. The American reporter had been writing on his laptop in the hotel's lobby.

Oh, shit! "Oh, hi, Preston, this is my aunt. We are in a hurry so please forgive my not being able to chat," Angela said.

"Okay, I'm leaving in a few days and was hoping to see you."

"I promise to call you before you leave," Angela said as she and Raquel whisked Gjuliana to the bank of elevators.

"This guy will just not give up," Raquel said.

"He is harmless," Angela replied.

"Regardless, I will check him out the minute I get to my room. Now is not the time we can trust anyone."

Rocco's men had already delivered the gas cylinders. They met Zellweger at the service entrance to the Vatican on time and as planned. Zellweger jumped into the front seat of the van, waving at three plain-clothed guards with Swiss made Sig 552 assault rifles hung from their shoulders, and entered close to the Apostolic Palace.

Zellweger watched as the two Sicilian mob associates struggled getting the four cylinders out of the van and onto a large, push bar, four-wheeled, platform, truck dolly. Once onto the dolly the crate was easy to move and the pair followed Zellweger to a large door. Zellweger carried a small box which contained the remote pump and his gas mask he would need the next morning.

Getting the cylinders down a winding, wooden staircase into the basement of the Sistine Chapel was no easy task, but the strapping young gangsters made the work look almost easy. Zellweger breathed a sigh of relief as the cylinders had made it close to the ventilation system, their ultimate destination. One of the two men went back to the top of the staircase and managed to bring the dolly down without any assistance.

The basement of the Sistine Chapel, like the design of the Chapel itself, is a large rectangle with very high ceilings. Zellweger had found a place to hide the dolly and its deadly cargo in a corner room of the basement. All that was left for the colonel to do the next day was to wheel the cylinders over to the ventilation system, dispatch the stationary engineer on duty and connect the valves as Deegan had instructed. Zellweger's heart began to pound with unrestrained anticipation.

CHAPTER 57

While the still-restrained Rocco waited for the return of his two, young, wanna-be mafia, made men, Deegan sat quietly trying to garner his strength. Deegan's body was feeling depleted, as if he had just walked five miles in a blazing sun. His age, along with his condition, no longer enabled him to compete with the physical demands of the young man's game in which he found himself.

Angela and Gjuliana sat on the balcony of the hotel room looking out at the Borghese Gardens drinking espresso and bottled spring water.

"This is probably the worst part of my life other than pining for my husband for over forty years," Gjuliana said.

"You actually waited that long for him?" Angela asked as she sipped on her coffee.

"I fell in love with him as a teenager and no one could ever come close to making me feel the way he did. And the funny thing about it is we were never intimate back then."

"And you waited for that, too?"

"Oh, God, no. There were other men but they could never touch my soul the way John did. It's very hard for me to explain Angela."

"So, no children, I suppose."

"None. That is probably my biggest regret. Years ago women didn't have kids and raise them by themselves, especially in a strict, Albanian family like I come from."

"I know all about that. I think the Sicilians and the Albanians have a similar culture. My father is not happy I'm not married with a bunch of kids by now. When I left home I thought he was going to die of a heart attack."

"And nobody has won you over yet?" Gjuliana asked.

"Not even close. My friends tell me my standards are way too high, that I'm looking for the perfect man. Maybe I am."

"John is far from perfect as you probably know. If you knew him when he was young I think you would understand why…" Gjuliana's eyes filled with tears. Angela went into the room and brought out some tissues.

"And now he is very sick. I suppose he was always mentally ill from the trauma of his childhood, but this disease doesn't leave too many survivors. His time will be short and the agony of watching him suffer and wilt away is almost more than I can bear," Gjuliana said.

"What are your plans?"

"I can't plan even one day at this point, and planning ahead is a fool's game anyway. I have to take one day at a time and trust in God as I always have."

"You seem to be a very strong woman. Someone who has control of herself and her life."

"That's just a façade. A defense mechanism, if you understand my meaning. I am afraid. Afraid to be alone, afraid John may not make it past tomorrow, afraid he will wind up dead, or in jail."

"Just stay calm, and let's think about other things."

"Good idea. How about that young man who approached you in the lobby? He seemed nice." Gjuliana tried to snap out of her funk and had a lilt to her voice.

"I met him at the pool here. He is very nice, a journalist from somewhere in the states. This is no time for a budding romance for me, as you can well imagine. So, not in this life anyway," Angela said.

"The power of destiny is an amazing thing."

"Maybe I should go back to Sicily and marry a policeman and make my father proud."

"Ahhh, I don't think that will make you happy, young lady. You seem too, I don't know, too…"

The room's doorbell rang that gravelly chime most European hotels have, interrupting Gjuliana's thought. Angela looked frightened, which sent a scare through Gjuliana.

The younger woman walked softly and slowly to the door and looked through the door's peephole. It was Raquel.

"Oh, it's you! My heart is in my mouth. Maybe you should give me a gun," Angela said.

"For what? So you can shoot yourself? Are you sure you want to stay on this assignment with us? This is definitely above and beyond," Raquel said.

"Are you kidding me? And go back to Sicily and marry a policeman. Is that what you want me to do, too?"

"What?"

"Gjuliana and I were just discussing that very thing. Don't worry. I'm in for the duration, boss."

"How is she doing?"

"Only okay. She's out on the balcony."

Raquel led the way and the two young women walked out on the balcony with big smiles for their charge.

"Oh, great, coffee and tissues. A real girls' night out. Let's get some pizza and ice cream and all get fat," Raquel joked.

"That buzzer scared me shitless," Gjuliana said.

"Now, that is a real Bronx saying if I ever heard one." Gjuliana and Raquel laughed; Angela was lost in the cultural and idiomatic translation.

Raquel sat and poured some water into an empty glass.

"Well, I checked out Mr. Preston Shields your American admirer. I have the poop on him," Raquel said.

"Poop, like caca?" Angela asked.

"No, the word on him, the skinny, the… oh, just listen," Raquel said opening up a small, brown, notepad she had taken from her pant pocket.

"Preston Shields, age thirty-one, born in Cleveland, Ohio, masters degree in English from the University of Chicago, worked for a while for the New York Times, freelance writer, and a very well known one at that, plus lots of awards, and no arrests. So, at least we can pretty much rule out he is not a bad guy, and he may not shoot us all in our sleep."

"Well, that's a relief," Angela said.

"One problem with your All-American, dreamboat though. He got separated from his wife of sixteen months about four months ago."

"That's a problem?" Angela asked.

"Ooh, I suggest you get him on the rebound Angela, that is always very sexy," Gjuliana said.

Angela looked at Raquel, and they both looked at Gjuliana. All three women broke out in hysterical laughter.

Dusk was falling over the *Collatino* and the warehouse. John didn't feel any better or any worse, just tired.

A light from the van came through the small, barred window which was high up on the warehouse wall. John got up from the folding chair he had commandeered from under Rocco's dead friend. He felt his back twinge and his knees ache, which was an everyday occurrence since he turned sixty.

"You just stay quiet. Don't take this personalyl. It's not that I don't trust you, but I don't trust you," John said to the wide- eyed Rocco as he put a fresh piece of duct tape around his mouth and neck.

John waited in the dark while the two mob guys opened the lock and came through the door.

"*Oh! Rocco! Dove sei? Cosa stai facendo?*" One of the men hollered.

Deegan appeared out of the darkness and into the dim light that came from a street lamp through the high window.

John had his 40mm Heckler and Koch semi automatic pistol aimed in the direction of the two men.

Instinctively, the former Sicilian street thugs spread out away from each other.

"I played this game in the Bronx when I was a kid. Let's see if I can remember how it went. Eeny, meeny, miny, moe, catch a tiger by the toe. If he hollers, let him go, Eeny, meeny, miny, moe!"

The two, befuddled Sicilians looked at each other just as John shot one of them in the side of his head spraying his brains and blood all over the warehouse wall where he stood.

The survivor raised his hands over his head.

"No, please!"

"Ah, very good, you speak English!" John said.

"Yes, a little, from the school and movies.

"Just let me finish my rhyme if you don't mind; this was always my favorite part:

Not because you're dirty, not because you're clean, just because you kissed a girl behind the magazine."

The Sicilian closed his eyes and flinched waiting for the pain.

"Where did you put the cylinders? And don't you fucking lie to me," Deegan yelled.

The gangster looked at the bound and gagged Rocco for guidance. Rocco's eyes gave him none.

"Okay *paisano*, one more try and don't pull that Sicilian, *omerta* bullshit right now. Where are the cylinders... you know the oxygen... ossigeno?"

"In the chapel. In the basement. Behind a door. All together, good job, all finish."

"Did you say a prayer in the chapel?"

"No signore, I don't say no prayer."

"That's too bad."

John shot the *paisano* twice in his chest killing him instantly.

John dropped the HK to his side and made a face of disgust.

"Oh, Jesus Christ, what is that fucking smell? Rocco, did you shit yourself? You will be staying in your crap until it hardens."

John approached Rocco and ripped the gray, duct tape from around his mouth and neck in one violent move. The tape pulled enough skin and hair from the back of Rocco's head to make him scream in agony.

"Now to finish the deal we made. You will call your pal, Colonel Zellweger. Depending on what transpires, I will either leave you with one hundred thousand euros worth of gold coins or I will shoot you in the head. Make the call, Rocco, and if you say the wrong words the last thing you will hear is the loud noise from my pistol."

Deegan took Rocco's cell phone and dialed Zellweger's speed number that he'd given to Rocco.

"Pronto!" Zellweger said.

"Is everything complete as you requested?" Rocco asked.

"Yes. The merchandise arrived and is ready to be sold," Zellweger replied.

"Do you require any more of my services?"

"Yes. I am not certain, but I may need you and your men to meet me outside of the Vatican walls and escort me to a nearby airfield. I just may be leaving my position and will need to fly out of Italy."

"Where and when, Colonel?"

"I will text you the exact time and location in the morning. Most likely at around the noon hour."

"And you will have the correct payment in full before you leave, correct?"

"You're starting to annoy me with that question. You will be paid immediately and in full."

Deegan heard every word of the conversation between Zellweger and Rocco. He now knew the Colonel was planning to escape. Deegan's genius mind went into overdrive like never before. He stood motionless, his plan going through his mind faster than a computer.

Deegan then looked at Rocco through his intense eyes and furrowed brow. Rocco knew he was dealing with an absolute maniac.

"You know, you're doing pretty well on this deal, my friend. You get the gold I've promised you, plus this joker's loot. You can set yourself up real nice somewhere on a beach, open a small shop to keep busy and live life in peace and tranquility."

"Sure, until someone recognizes me and they come and cut out my tongue before they choke me."

"Well my dear, Rocco, we all must die of something."

CHAPTER 58

The morning of the conclave found the Eternal City, Rome, in general, and Vatican City in particular, abuzz with anticipation.

Vic and Raquel showered together after a night of steamy sex that was one of the best sessions they ever had as a couple. While Vic shaved, Raquel worked on her hair and makeup. It was too early in the morning for Raquel to call her mother back in New York to check on the baby, and she realized it would be near impossible to call during what was sure to be a hectic day.
They would both stay up late and Skype back to the States later on.

Gjuliana never slept that night as she lie worrying about her husband. Dozens of scenarios ran through her mind. None of them being good kept Gjuliana staring at the ceiling. At this early hour in the morning RAI television was broadcasting from St. Peter's Square awaiting the pomp and circumstance of the procession of cardinals at the great Basilica. Gjuliana's bleary eyes became transfixed to the flat screen television on the wall of her room while Angela scurried to prepare to join Vic and Raquel. It was decided Gjuliana would be secure and anonymous in Angela's suite for the day. If things went bad, Gjuliana had already decided her next move would be back with her family in New York City. For the time being, though, her concentration was on the papal ceremony.

Under the watchful eye of an intense army of security, the cardinals amassed in procession into St. Peters Basilica for an early morning *Pro Eligendo Romano Pontifice Mass* to bless the conclave. Plain clothed members of the Swiss Guard carefully monitored metal detectors at the only entrance to the spectacular cathedral. Traditionally, this mass is open to the public, and the camerlengo felt it necessary to continue the tradition in spite of the abnormal threats to the Holy See. Any variation from the norm would throw the media into a firestorm of speculation, and even though lives might be in danger, nothing was more important than preserving the pristine image the Church had.

Oberst, Adrien Zellweger, stood at the door to the basilica with his men, looking into the faces of the potential congregants for signs of abnormal behavior or any familiar face who had previously threatened the pope or had interrupted any mass or celebration. The colonel was also looking closely for any person who could be the disguised John Deegan.

Sharp shooters were in constant, radio communication with Zellweger from their perches around the basilica and from the *Domus Marthae Sanctae* where the cardinals had all slept the night before, incommunicado from the rest of the cyber world. Technicians had blocked any form of computer, cell phone, television, or radio communication into the *Domus* even though such devices were forbidden. Newspapers or magazines of any kind were not allowed to be seen by the cardinals.

With St. Peter's Basilica at full capacity, the procession of the entirety of the cardinals of the supposed One, Holy, Catholic, and Apostolic Church walked slowly in single file on either side of the wide, marble aisle.

Dressed in full cardinal, Episcopal regalia, their vestments contain hidden symbolism which are lost to even the most faithful onlookers. The cardinals wear below the waist, white *rochets* in linen or lace which are covered by scarlet red *Mozzetta*, capes which are adorned with twelve, silk-covered buttons representing the twelve apostles of Christ. Long, form-fitting, watered silk, scarlet cassocks, the color symbolizing the blood the cardinals would shed for their church, not Christ, mind you, but the Church, are adorned with thirty-three, silk-covered buttons for the years Jesus walked on earth, reaching to their black shoes. The sleeves of their cassocks have five buttons memorializing the five wounds of Christ. The cardinal's heads are covered with the *zucchetto*, the widely-recognizable cardinal-red skullcaps, which are concealed by a tall, white, *mitre* covered by layered, pure white, damask silk, finishing the dramatic and almost overwhelming, awe-inspiring appearance.

The procession of the entire two hundred twelve cardinals, some in wheelchairs, some using canes or forearm crutches were mostly somber due to the daunting task of electing a new pope after yet another disgraced, papal resignation. With the exception of the arrogant and pompous cardinal of New York who was smiling and waving to some congregants as if he were at a Yankee baseball game, the mood within the procession of cardinals was solemn and subdued. The gas dispersing into the chapel would for sure be breathed in heartily by this fat, New York slob.

Colonel Zellweger, his hands clammy, his stomach filled with adrenalin butterflies, and his knees twitching slightly, entered the basilica behind the last man in the procession, Cardinal *Camerlengo* Bazzini. Zellweger knew the time to fulfill his historic role as the pro-creator of the new Catholic Church was only hours away.

Raquel and Angela were in different parts of the basilica. Angela was part of the standing room only crowd nearest the main altar, while Raquel was in the third row of faithful spectators. She entered the basilica with Vic, having special permission and clearance from Cardinal Magnone to carry their concealed firearms. Vic roamed freely around the massive church as the celebration of the Mass began.

The cardinals were in straight chairs in a semi-circle at the altar above where the bones of St. Peter have rested for centuries.

Humpty Dumpty sat on a wall,
Humpty Dumpty had a Great Fall;
All the King's horses and all the King's men,
Couldn't put... Zellweger was humming to himself.

The mass was much like any other solemn celebration before a conclave, with special prayers recited in Latin invoking the special guidance of the Holy Spirit for the cardinals to choose the next Vicar of Christ to lead His Holy Church.

The Swiss Guards stood at rigid attention wearing their traditional and impressive dress in Medici blue, red, and yellow stripes which ran all the way down to their leggings with a fluffy white collar and white gloves. A white plume of feathers sat atop their metal, high-crested, open helmet with the front and back edges turned dramatically upwards. A coat of arms of Pope Julius II who established the guard in the fifteen hundreds is embossed on the helmet.

The guards' weapons are the halberd and the broadsword with their chest and arms protected by a striking, polished silver armor.

At the end of the hour and a half mass, the cardinals made their way back down the aisles as the procession made its way toward the Pauline Chapel, a side sanctuary adjacent to the Sistine Chapel, for a short prayer before the final procession.

Colonel Zellweger made his way toward the Apostolic Palace ahead of the procession. His destination was the basement of the Sistine Chapel.

Raquel started looking for Vic and Zellweger through the crowd of onlookers. Her heart rate began to quicken, as Vic was nowhere to be found.

CHAPTER 59

The cardinals exit the Pauline Chapel wearing their *biretta,* the cardinal red square hat, which replaced the white silk *mitre.* They enter the procession by prominence and seniority based on the day they received their red hat. First the cardinal deacons, followed by the cardinal priests and finally the cardinal bishops, and the patriarchs.

From a side door next to the Pauline, the procession to the Sistine Chapel is led by four papal Master of Ceremonies all in white lace vestments over black cassocks, one carrying a large crucifix and the other three carrying foot high candles. A Gregorian choir follows them with a cantor chanting a prayer.

The Litany of Saints evokes the blessing of the Holy Trinity, The Blessed Mother, and every saint, to intercede on behalf of the cardinals to guide them while they are making their decision on the election of the new Pope an acceptable one.

The chanting, mesmerizing in its cadence, is responded by the cardinals with the Latin words *Ora Pro Nobis, Pray for Us.*

"Sancta Maria...," the cantor began.

"Ora pro nobis," sang the cardinals in unison.

"Sancta Dei Genetix... "

"Ora pro nobis," again the echoed reply.

Hundreds upon hundreds of saints and martyrs of the church are named in this lengthy, solemn prayer.

On the marble floors, and passing renaissance frescos on the walls, the procession passes fifteen Swiss Guards standing shoulder to shoulder who are in full attention with their halberds held straight up. One looks like a replica of the next.

Finally, the one hundred twelve voting cardinals walk in single file, past Swiss Guard who are posted on either side of the doorway, taking the two marble steps up into the Sistine Chapel. Among the cardinals, it is known which ones are the *papabil*, the ones who pass through the enormous, wooden, double doors. What they never know is who will win the two thirds votes to become the next pope and get to walk into the 'room of tears' to change into his white papal vestments. And at this particular conclave, they have no idea who among them will be the first to succumb to the poison, cyanide gas which will emanate from the ventilation system.

The chanting continued:

"Sante Gabriel... "
"Ora pro Nobis."

"Sante Raphael... "
"Ora pro Nobis."

Forty-five minutes would normally pass for this invocational prayer.

But as the cardinals walked up a small ramp past the gold painted, lattice-work wall and into the main part of the chapel where the voting takes place, Colonel Zellweger could hear the monotonous litany as he looked around the basement for the stationary engineer. To Zellweger's surprise, the engineer was nowhere to be found in the large basement.

The colonel removed his suit jacket draping it over an old pew which was used for the staff during their lunch breaks. Zellweger moved with catlike precision as he opened the door to the storage room where the gas cylinders were secreted. In Zellweger's inside, jacket pocket was a shaved, wooden crucifix with which he intended to use to murder the stationary engineer. One final and hopefully lasting, blame-shifting, double-cross on John Deegan.

The dolly made the job of pulling six hundred and fifty six pounds of steel cylinders filled with toxic gas to the state of the art ventilation system easier than he thought. Zellweger felt his strength had become almost super human, which he took as a sign from God.

The cardinals, now nearly all filed into the chapel, began to take their seats on the straight-back, cushioned chairs. Two long rectangular tables, one elevated behind the other, with a beige covering and purple bunting were situated on either side of the aisle. The tables are marked with a plain, white, folded, paper nametag for each cardinal. On the table is a green book with the rules of the conclave, and a second, larger green book with a roster of all of the cardinals of the church and a red folio with voting papers.

"*Sancta Lucia...* "
"*Ora pro Nobis.*"

"*Sancta Agnes...* "
"*Ora pro Nobis.*"

"*Sancta Caecilia...* "
"*Ora pro Nobis.*"

Knowing the Litany of the Saints, Zellweger knew the prayer was nearing its end. He calculated there were thirty or thirty-five minutes more before the doors to the Sistine Chapel would be closed and locked by the Cardinal *Camerlengo.*

Zellweger attached the manifold valve pumps Deegan ordered and then attached a larger, main valve to an existing output regulator of the ventilation system.

All Zellweger needed to do now was wait until the Latin Hymn *Veni Creator Spiritus, Come Creator Spirit* was sung and listen as each cardinal took his individual, solemn oath of secrecy before the doors were finally sealed and he could release the toxic gas sending the world reeling in panic.

The final prayers of the Litany of the Saints were being chanted by the cantor and responded to by the cardinals. The cardinals were now all settled in their seats and given a few minutes to reflect on the enormity of their task.

As the hymn began which called the spirit creator to bless the room and its occupants, Zellweger's throat dried up and tightened with anticipation. He fingered his gas mask and awaited the next and final ritual before the doors were locked.

Under the bright, blue and beige hues of Michelangelo's masterpiece ceiling and side frescos, the sub-dean of the College of Cardinals awaits saying the final prayers as each cardinal stands in the middle of the Sistine Chapel, placing his right hand on the Gospel, and in Latin, states his name and proclaims an oath of secrecy on the voting of this conclave. On the third finger of their hand is a gold ring, given to each by the Holy Father. This elegant piece did not diminish the cardinals' thoughts of how boring and daunting this whole process was, but they knew in order to keep their sexual inclinations alive, be it sex with little boys and girls, their homosexual lovers, or abuse of vulnerable adults, they had to play the holy, publicity game.

Down below, Zellweger suddenly heard a noise on the far side of the chapel's basement. He walked back to where he hung his suit jacket and put it on, now covering his shoulder harness and pistol.

Zellweger listened attentively but could not hear the cardinals swearing their oaths. He looked at his watch and tried to calculate how long it would take all one hundred and twelve of the participants complete their pledges of secrecy.

Nearly thirty minutes later, about what Zellweger had anticipated, the colonel heard the words from the chapel declaring *extra ominus* from the Cardinal *Camerlengo*. This was the warning that everyone who was not a voting cardinal must leave the chapel so the voting process could begin.

The master of ceremonies, priests, a handful of nuns who manage the *Domus*, the choir, cantor, doctors, photographers, and assorted Vatican insiders quickly moved to the doors of the chapel. A senior Swiss Guardsman, dressed in a purple uniform with a purple, plumed helmet was the last to exit the chapel.

In dramatic fashion, while photographers and videographers focused their cameras on the door of the Sistine Chapel, the Cardinal Camerlengo took each of the two doors and closed them to the outside world. The clanging sound of the doors locking echoed throughout the hallway.

The Conclave had begun.

The gas continued to hiss thorough the pump and into the conclave.

"They should all be dying at this point. At least I lived long enough to see my dream fulfilled. This is what they get for passing me around like a play toy when I was just an innocent school boy."

The hissing of the cylinders suddenly stopped. The gas was successfully sent through the ventilation system and into the Sistine Chapel.

Instead of hearing choking and the screams of mass confusion and hysteria, Deegan and Zellweger could hear voices and laughter coming through the vents.

Zellweger looked confused and became quiet. He put his ear close to the ventilation system to verify what he was hearing.

"*Il protossido di azoto, gas esilarante.* Nitrous Oxide you stupid fuck. It's also known in some places as laughing gas. There is just enough gas in these containers to get these old men a little high and remove any anxiety they may have. Some of them will laugh their asses of for a few seconds while some will take a quick nap. The worst these fucks will feel is a bit confused. That's better than being stone dead, am I right?"

"You double-crossed me, you bastard!"

"Ahhh, yep. I just loved fucking with you and now I will watch you squirm, you double-crossing prick. Karma is a bitch as they say."

Zellweger thought of reaching for his gun but thought twice. The Colonel grabbed a brown, attaché case which was on the floor near him and ran for the door that led up to the Sistine. Instead of a scene of total carnage he had dreamed of, he saw some of the cardinals wobbling out of the now opened doors of the chapel. The Swiss Guard who remained at their posts were leading some of the more affected prelates from the chapel. Other cardinals were being assisted by clerics who were still milling around the hallways of the Apostolic Palace.

Zellweger rushed toward the exit of the palace, unnoticed due to the confusion of the abruptly curtailed conclave. The colonel sprinted toward the *Viale Vaticano* looking for Rocco Rotigliano. The sound of the boots of the anti-terrorist brigade of the *gendarmeria* on the cobblestones mingled with the piercing sound of ambulances which were rushing toward the Apostolic Palace.

Before his quick exit from the basement of the Sistine Chapel, ahead of the security forces who finally had the sense to realize where the gas had come from, Deegan opened the door to the closet where the stationary engineer was tied.

"Sorry, buddy. Maybe someday you will realize I saved your life," Deegan said.

The Italian worker had no idea what Deegan said to him as he neither spoke nor understood English.

Zellweger spotted Rocco's van driving slowly down a side street toward the *Viale Vaticano*. He jumped into the passenger seat of the van, the attaché case clinging to the side of his chest.

"Drive quickly; get me away from here," Zellweger commanded.

The van came to an abrupt halt nearly sending the colonel through the passenger side front window.

"Now why would I want to do that?"

Vic Gonnella was driving the van, wearing one of Rocco's hats. Vic placed the barrel of his handgun on the side of Zellweger's head.

"You! What is the meaning of this?"

"You are, as we say in New York, fiddle-fucked, Colonel. Now don't move a muscle or your brains will make a mess of this nice van," Vic said.

Rocco was hiding under a tarp in the rear of the van. He jumped into the back seat grabbing Zellweger around his neck.

"Where is my money, Colonel?" Rocco demanded.

Unable to speak, Zellweger pointed to the attaché.

Rocco pulled the case into the back seat and opened it with his free hand. It was filled with cash and bearer bonds. The source of the bonds was the Vatican Bank, and the euros were bound in Vatican Bank note wrappers.

Rocco eased the pressure around the Colonel's neck. "How much is here?" Rocco asked.

"A little over a million," Colonel Zellweger gasped.

"And all you owe me is fifty thousand. Incredible!"

"Nice little payday, Rocco. Between this million and what Deegan paid you, dude, you can own a chain of pizzerias in Brooklyn," Vic said.

Zellweger stiffened at the sound of Deegan's name.

Vic turned the van onto a side street that was lined with parked cars and Vespas. He found a no parking area and pulled in. Putting his gun back into his ankle holster, Vic turned to Rocco.

"Here's where I get out. Take care of yourself, Rocco. Nice doing business with you. If you ever open a pizza shop in New York, give us a call."

Vic turned his head and looked at Zellweger.

"Your mistake was trying to fuck the guy who's unfuckable. Have a nice trip."

Vic exited the driver's seat of the van, closing the door behind him. He began to walk toward a main thoroughfare when he heard three muffled popping sounds coming from the van.

Vic never looked back.

CHAPTER 61

Vic called Raquel on her cell phone to tell him he was alive and well. He said he would meet her back at their hotel promptly. Raquel went off on him in her rapid Puerto Rican fashion.

"Mira canto de cabrón! Nunca piensas en mi! De verdad que estas pasaó! Que hacias?, "comiendo gofio?" So anormal! Me tienes por el techo con precupación."

Loosely translated, "You bastard! You never think of me! You're really something else! What were you up to? Wasting time?! You idiot! You had me worried through the roof!"

Before he hung up Raquel could hear Vic laughing which infuriated her even more.

Deegan was slowly walking along the *Via Veneto* near the American Embassy compound, where it was prearranged to meet. Dressed in his Vietnam veteran disguise. A taxi pulled over near Deegan.

"Hey, need a lift old timer?" Vic asked.

"You're fifteen minutes late, jerkoff. Our wives are gonna be pissed," Deegan joked.

In minutes Deegan was in the arms of the sobbing Gjuliana in Angela's room.

Raquel stood near the sliding glass door of the balcony, her hands on her hips. In a Spanish accent mimicking Ricky Ricardo, Raquel had all to do but laugh.

"You got a lot a splainin' to do, Gonnella!"

Vic moved slowly toward Raquel and they embraced tightly.

Tears ran down Angela's face as she stood there watching the two couples expressing their relief and love.

Vic called room service for two bottles of *Dom Perignon* and a pot of hot tea with organic honey and lemon.

"Sorry, Deegan, tea for you and champagne for the rest of us. Now let's tell these lovely ladies what they are dying to know," Vic said.

"It was nothing, really. We just saved a bunch of guys in red dresses from croaking. Now they can go about their business and we can go about ours."

"I, for one, need a shower and shave and to spend some quality time with my favorite gal," Vic said.

"And we have to get you back on your treatment. I'm calling Dr. Bauer and telling him we will be back at the *Klinik* tomorrow afternoon," Gjuliana said.

"Hold on everyone. Watch what I'm about to do," Angela said. The Sicilian beauty picked up her cell phone, scrolled down to a number and touched the call button.

"Hello, Preston? About that date you were asking for…"

JUSTIFIED

CPSIA information can be obtained
at www.ICGtesting.com
Printed in the USA
BVOW04*1916200317
478976BV00004B/8/P